Are We
Living in the
LAST
DAYS?

*The Apocalypse
Debate in the
21st Century*

S. Douglas Woodward

Are We Living in the

Last Days?

The Apocalypse Debate in the 21ˢᵗ Century

A Study in Protestant Christian Eschatology for Believers and Unbelievers Alike

S. Douglas Woodward

Eschatology: From the Greek *eschatos* meaning 'last' and 'logy' combined with "the study of." Hence, Eschatology is the study of 'last things' or oftentimes simply "the end times."

Eschatology links to the Greek word, *aeon*, which means 'century' with a connotation of age as in *epoch*, *eon*, or the end of a historical time-period.

Sometimes the word **'eschaton'** signifies the entire period in which all of the events associated with the Second Coming take place.

On the page opposite: Icon of Second Coming. Greek Icon reprinted from Wikipedia, en.wikipedia.org/wiki /File: Icon_second_coming.jpg – (public domain). Christ is enthroned in the center surrounded by the angels and saints. Paradise is at the bottom, with the Bosom of Abraham (left) and the Good Thief (right) holding his cross. Artist is anonymous, Greece, circa 1700.

Are We Living in the Last Days?

The Apocalypse Debate in the 21st Century

To purchase single copies: www.createspace.com/3390674

To purchase multiple copies: Email > order@faith-happens.com

Faith-Happens LLC. www.faith-happens.com.

EAN-13   9781448636846

ISBN 1-44863-6841

Religion / Christian Theology / Eschatology

viii

Contents

Chapter 3: Advent and Second Advent..... 35

Chapter 4: Amillennialism and Millennialism 55

Table of Figures

Acknowledgements

This book is the final product of much effort and many participants. When I began, I sought out my family and friends to provide input, review, critical commentary, and opinion. They didn't let me down.

To my brother Phil, perhaps the strongest voice of support, my sincere thanks. Your time and good words were a steady source of encouragement. It has been lots of fun to interact over the ideas expressed in this book. We share a common vision for this effort. I heard God speak through you many times!

To my father, William C. Woodward Sr., heartfelt thanks for all the encouragement, love and support, not only on this project, but also for the full extent of my 55 years. Happy 90th birthday again! Your giving spirit and self-sacrifice for all the members of our expanded family is an inspiration and a pattern that I will never be able to fully emulate, but do fully appreciate!

To my cousin Vaughn (Woody) Woodward: Thanks for your willingness to be my 'straw man' Covenantalist! Your challenges, counterpoints, and prayers were enormously helpful in making this book whatever it turns out to be. Thanks also to your pastor, Tony Felich (M.Div., Covenant Theological Seminary, Pastor, Redeemer Presbyterian, Overland Park), for his willingness to point out flaws in my arguments, key points I missed, and his time to try to set me straight!

To my cousin Jim Woodward Jr.: Your thoughtfulness and insights into Jewish philosophy and Catholicism provided helpful perspectives to keep in mind as I worked through the many days of writing and editing. I especially enjoyed our 'back and forth' emails. This is the second of two books on which we've collaborated. Let's do another soon!

To my business partner and 'executive editor' par excellence, Elton Welke: Your experience in publishing and writing was particularly important. I doubt I have produced a book of sufficient quality to make you proud. But hopefully, I have avoided being a source of embarrassment to us both! Thanks for your continued support in this and our other efforts together. I promise on some occasion very soon, we won't just work together, but we will celebrate another big success.

To one of my best friends, Kevin Hoffberg: I know that reading the manuscript in various stages was for you, at best, a labor borne of friendship. Your willingness to tackle a subject matter that is for you personally unpleasant and still to make thoughtful and insightful suggestions was indispensible to the outcome. The dialogue during the past few months has been one of those unpredictable pleasures one has when writing a book. If the book has achieved the intended neutral tone (through its first 270 pages), and encourages those who have their doubts about the Bible to pick up this book and stay engaged, you will have had a big hand in achieving this. Those readers and I thank you very much. Additionally, I look forward to further debate and dialogue. It does me much good.

To other friends that read and commented, thank you. A special thanks to Jay Powers and Lowell Tuttman—your input was welcomed and very helpful and encouraging.

To my kids, Corinne and Nicholas, and to their 'significant others' Andy Lefeuvre and Jessica Briley: You all are the great joy of my life! Your willingness to comment and put up with this obsession for the past many years is essential to this book and my positive attitude! God bless you!

To the love of my life (and my wife!) for 34 years, Donna, who is also the source of my strength and encouragement to persevere in times of great distress, all my love and gratitude! May this book contribute to new opportunities for us to grow closer and thrive in unexpected ways in our future together!

Finally, thanks to 'Nonna,' Mrs. Roy Marie Wilson, for helping Donna and I survive during these difficult times. You are an angel!

Despite all of the good thinking, quality input and editing of others, the factual mistakes, theological misstatements, doctrinal and grammatical errors found in this book are solely my responsibility.

S. Douglas (Doug) Woodward
Woodinville, Washington
August, 2009

*This book is dedicated to
my brother, Chris Woodward:
Great husband, father, and grandfather,
wonderful uncle to my kids,
funny guy and fellow sojourner
along life's difficult highway.*

.

Preface

The obsession with the future – it's as old as humanity. If one looks into the history of the *crystal ball,* you go back over 5,000 years to the Druids in England and the megalithic culture[i] that constructed Stone Henge. *Seer Stones,* which is a more generic name for all transparent or translucent objects used in fortune telling, have been a part of religion and spirituality in every culture since. Even the fairy tale, *Snow White,* relies upon the *magic mirror* – another derivation of using clear or reflective objects – to provide fateful information to the evil Queen. Did you know that early in the 20th century, an old 'wives tale' continued to be popularly believed that if a young maiden placed herself in a darkened room and looked into a mirror she could see a glimpse of her future husband? "On Halloween look in the glass, your future husband's face will pass."[ii] That is, unless it foresaw your death before marriage – in which case you'd see the face of the Grim Reaper instead!

Even in ancient Hebrew Scripture, we read of the *'Urim and Thummin'*, apparently two stones kept in the breastplate of the High Priest and used for 'casting lots.' The stones were made of onyx and had the names of the 12 tribes of Israel inscribed, six on one stone and six on the other (Exodus 28:9-11). These stones appeared to have restricted uses to determine the will of God, but their possession by the Levite priests was one means of validating their priestly rights (inferred from the book of Ezra and Nehemiah). Some scholars believe that these stones were popular during the first few hundred years of Hebrew religion but faded away when the prophets began to 'run the show.' By the deportation to Babylon in 606 BC, they had already vanished or were lost in the commotion of that crisis.

Mormonism's founding was tightly wound with the use *of seer stones* that Joseph Smith called the Urim and Thummin as well, no doubt asserting that what the Hebrews had lost on their way to Babylon, he found in upper state New York. Smith had been a user

---

[i] Megalith is a building method using stones fitted without mortar.

[ii] See 'Modern uses' at http://en.wikipedia.org/wiki/Seer_stone.

of seer stones, well before finding the golden plates – which he supposedly translated with these stones – attempting to make a living by using the seer stones to find lost objects for his fellow townspeople. He wasn't very successful with this activity, but found them much more effective in creating a religion that many would soon affirm as the Latter Day Saints. Even today, the Mormon Church considers their leader, 'a seer.'

Evangelical Christians are certainly no strangers to the desire to see into the future. Unlike the Mormons who believe in many avenues for God to reveal His will, such as seer stones and modern day prophets, for evangelicals the Bible is their only source book. Following Protestant tradition, only *scripture is authoritative* (as the reformers Luther and Calvin asserted, *sola scriptura*!) No other means exists today, including priests or popes, to tell us what God wills and what soon may happen. The Bible has cornered this truth!

For the past forty years, evangelicals have flooded the market with scores of books on the subject of the *Apocalypse* and the *Second Advent* (or Coming) of Jesus Christ. Using only the Bible as their means to discern the future, many authors have contributed to prophetic 'scenarios' that have now become 'standardized.' This reality has matured to the point where we take certain standard scenarios for granted. Perhaps we've even come to the point where books about prophecy have become too predictable!

So you ask, "Why bother publishing another book on prophecy and the Bible? Haven't authors saturated the market today? Haven't writers and scholars already explored and communicated all the key predictions of the Bible? Is there anything else left to say? Hasn't the public heard it all by now? Is there any reason to suppose that the populace can change their minds about what they believe? Are the 'convinced' beyond doubt and the 'unbelieving' unmoved by arguments demonstrating how the Bible is true?"

These are all pertinent questions. It would be easy to agree with the affirmative implication of "each and every one." However, after considerable research and study, both current and cumulative, I've concluded that the answer to all of these questions is "No – there is still more work to be done." Here's why I say that.

- Despite the many titles on the market today, none addresses several very important issues that led me to spend the better part of the last six months gathering my thoughts and preparing this book.

- My research identified many fascinating new insights into what some consider the 'tired' subjects associated with Bible prophecy. I even came up with a few new vistas of my own. These ideas deserve an audience!

- Moreover, 'minds aren't made up.' Both staunch believers and those 'with little faith' retain many questions about Bible prophecy and worry a lot about the future too. We see lots of evidence that this is true in our world today.

So call me a stubborn contrarian. Nevertheless, it feels right to challenge conventional wisdom with yet another book on the subject of Bible prophecy. So why am I enthusiastic about it?

First, I became motivated to create an overview of *eschatology* (the formal term for Bible prophecy), because I could not find any work completed in the past decade or two that brought all the subjects together in a way that the reader could quickly gain perspective on the *various positions that Protestant Christians profess.* The best-known views aren't necessarily the best articulated theologically or the most widely regarded by serious scholars. There are, in fact, several responsible positions—well researched—with historical substance and theological support. Unfortunately, most of the public doesn't know this (not yet at least!)

Secondly, most books today address a very narrow set of issues and include a great deal of speculation *without letting the Scripture speak for itself.* They assume too much about the biblical background of the reader. They don't cite extensive Scripture passages to provide more context and project the panorama that extended sections of Scripture promote. In contrast, my vantage point is that we need *less proof texting and more perspective!* Therefore, as a stylistic approach, I quote extended sections of the Bible to enhance the reader's appreciation of what the biblical writer is trying to teach. I wish to expose 'newcomers' to the Bible directly. Furthermore, in this book *we cover most of the 'cornerstone' biblical passages on prophecy.*

That is intentional. A good overview of biblical prophecy should count this foremost among its goals.

Thirdly, another motivation for penning this book is the many educated people today that have interest in biblical subjects, particularly in the *Apocalypse*, but who are bothered by dogmatic assertions tied to very narrow perspectives on how we must interpret prophecy. Without question, s*ometimes the views expressed by prophecy pundits are 'over the top.'* Virtually every book on the subject is quick to predict, "The e*nd is now*," "This is the generation that will see the return of Jesus Christ," or worse, provide an exact date when the Second Coming will occur. Additionally, as an exercise for this work, I reviewed the web sites of many sources on the topic. My foremost 'take away' from my review is that most commentators aren't just highly opinionated – they can be downright spiteful toward contrasting positions. Oftentimes, they espouse views that simply don't square with what the Bible teaches: Conjecture runs rampant confusing what the Bible says with what *they want it to say.* Generally, too much is made of too little. Indeed, sometimes the claims for what they regard as the biblical point of view are actually *quite obscure if not arcane.*

Let me clarify: Some interpreters of prophecy are overly reliant upon 'hidden messages and meanings' making Christian truth *kabalistic* or esoteric.[i] While it may be true that 'Bible codes' exist in the Torah (the first five books of the Bible, also known as 'the books of Moses'), responsible Bible scholars don't look to such 'mysterious knowledge' as source material to develop biblical doctrine. The explicit teaching of the Bible, 'public information' if you will, is the foundation for what Protestants believe. Of course, a responsible perspective (even if it is the truth), doesn't always make the most interesting story!

Finally, creators who produce material today for videos, newsletters, and books, direct most of it to those who fall in the category

---

[i] The Kabala is defined as "a body of mystical Jewish teachings based on an interpretation of the Hebrew Scriptures as containing hidden meanings," while esoteric means "intended for or understood by only an initiated few" (from the dictionary in Microsoft Word).

of the 'already convinced'—not enough is produced targeting those with serious doubts and little to no background on the subject. To address this audience, the originator must take a more neutral and instructive (but not patronizing!) tone. This I will attempt to do.[i] My efforts will seek to address this audience and fill the void in today's literature and media. In essence, I hope to 'have a word' (well, really several thousand) with the skeptics about Bible prophecy. If that group includes you, outstanding! I hope you stay with me throughout our expedition.

Now to address one of the more common objections: Haven't the prophetic exaggerations of evangelicals proven just how crazy this preoccupation with predicting the future is?

Despite the large and loud amount of criticism to this effect, I actually don't think so. First off, not all evangelicals are inclined to don doomsday placards. Secondly, remember, conservative Christians aren't alone in the quest to forecast the future. Many esoteric teachers are also guilty of speculating when the end will come. There is a tremendous amount of literature today about the projected coming apocalypse in *2012*. Certainly, 2012 is becoming a commercial phenomenon with scores of books already published and Hollywood films that have come to market. The authors of these books are generally not Christian and base their prediction on the termination of the *Mayan Calendar* or the *I Ching* (on December 21, 2012), on interpretations of Nostradamus' *quatrains*, or speculation about pending catastrophes due to solar flares or climate change. Most of these sources have a 'spiritualist' or 'occult' orientation. These writers and 'experts' are influenced by Mayan 'eschatology,' alternate history buffs (especially in Egyptian alternate history), believers in the importance of UFOs as an explanation for human evolution, and the ancient continent of Atlantis as the source for humankind's 'ancient knowledge.'

---

[i] Although I readily admit several key presuppositions: God is real and a distinct entity from nature and humankind, the Bible is uniquely God's revelation to us, Jesus Christ is the promised Messiah of the Jews, and the biblical prophets could see into the future.

Talk about 'over the top!' Despite the unusual nature of these viewpoints, the amount of literature on these topics is stunning. Unbelievably, it dwarfs the number of books written on biblical prophecy! Apparently, there are other ways to create controversy than just predicting the end of the world. It seems if you combine 'alternate history' with the apocalypse, you have twice the chance to assemble a rabid following.

Yet, I might be the first to admit that it's uncanny how many potentially catastrophic issues coalesce around this time in which we live. It is worrisome! Horrible things seem to be happening every-where. But, in the broader context, the only thing that is certain about predicting specific calamities on precise dates (like 2012), is that the time will come and go without the cataclysm coming to pass, once again proving the prediction in question, *dead wrong!* Conse-quently, the book (or books!) offering such a gloomy future is tossed into a pile and the author discredited.

Take it from me: I have read scores of books in every decade, but the only consequential ones *are those that avoid setting dates or the ones that have more to say than just relaying behind-the-scenes information on personalities or pending events in the Holy Land.* That is why we take books written on Bible prophecy serious-ly, *until the prophecy fails.* The record shows prophets and prophecy books that set dates have an extremely short 'half-life!' [i]

In summary, *'Are We Living in the Last Days? The Apocalypse Debate in the 21st Century'* seeks to accomplish several things:

1. Update and recap the essential concepts surrounding the Apo-calypse and the Second Coming of Jesus Christ from the pers-pective of Protestant Christians;

2. Communicate to believer and unbeliever alike what these Christians profess about the *Apocalypse and Bible prophecy generally* – not offering just a single interpretation of what ought to be believed, but presenting today's serious *principal* viewpoints – the perspectives that matter the most; and

---

[i] Prophecies from 'spiritualist' sources, like an Edgar Cayce (1877-1945), *the 'Sleeping Prophet,'* have proven themselves to have more falsehoods than truths.

3. Highlight insights that I have come across from others or those which I have developed (through my own analysis of biblical sources), that break new ground.

4. Lastly, take the reader through a careful examination of the various methods to interpret the Bible (with a focus on how to determine what the Bible really says about the Apocalypse).

This last objective is the most difficult one, because it is the most technically challenging. We will attempt this climb at the end of our expedition. My hope is by the time we get to it, the summit won't be too difficult for most readers to reach. If I've properly bequeathed to you current and accurate information on apocalyptic subjects and adequately explained why Protestant Christians take the various stances that they do on Bible prophecy, we should be in fine shape to scale this last mountain together.

At the outset, let me say that among all Protestant Christians, no matter how liberal or conservative, *there is a consensus about the primary message of prophecy.* This 'least common denominator' for all Christians (and for our conservative Jewish brethren too), is that *Bible prophecy is the story of how God intercedes in history to promote His purposes and protect His people.* The *Apocalypse* is, at the very least, a promise that God will make sure that 'we wind up in the right place.' History is going somewhere! Indeed, the abiding promise is that *Good* conquers *Evil* and the *Kingdom of God will ultimately come in* a way that radically transforms the world and validates the testimony of the Bible's prophets. However, I reiterate my commitment to do my best to maintain a neutral tone and refrain from extolling my personal convictions about the main topic until we arrive at the end of our study. This book is much more about me helping you the reader choose what you *would* believe rather than me telling you what you *should* believe. It's not that I fail to have an opinion on this matter. That will become "crystal clear" as we near the end of the book. Furthermore, I do reserve the right to preach— but I will spare the reader my personal passion about what I believe for the better part of this book. I promise.

Introduction

Why Authors Write Books about Prophecy

Being controversial is a good way to get attention. But it isn't always a good thing. Anyone who has seen TV in the last year could cite many examples of politicians, preachers, and Hollywood celebrities that have become controversial. Usually, the controversy has more to do with their life choices (what they do), than with what they say. While their lifestyle 'flame out' has not helped their careers, 'falling from grace' has certainly inflated their celebrity. However, for better or for worse, by words or by deeds, we would all agree *you have to hit the water hard to make a splash.* Moreover, controversies surrounding public figures sell plenty of ads on cable television!

Authors frequently craft non-fiction books relying on some form of controversy too. A new conspiracy theory is a frequent topic. Uncovering scandal is another. From presidential assassinations to Wall Street debacles, controversy not only catches our eye, it puts books on the bestseller list.

Likewise, controversy is certainly an ingredient of many books written on the subject of Bible prophecy. Authors might upset the apple cart just by laying claim to some new insight or interpretation. Once they've documented enough evidence to support their view, writers may convince their readership how important their discovery is. The promotion might be something like this: "Revolutionary new insights previously hidden in the biblical text." However, for the most part such books won't start a revolution. After all, these books appeal only to those already convinced that Bible prophecy is important. The size of the splash isn't all *that* impressive. In addition, there aren't that many readers in this market. Granted, I might be one of them—but I am hardly the norm.[i] More often than not, to garner attention from the masses, books on prophetic subjects must pander to sensational and somewhat less-than-conscious impulses we all share.

---

[i] Funny how my kids are always the first to remind me of that.

One of those desires is *our curiosity about the future.* We want to know *what will happen next.* This is especially true in desperate times like today where we struggle with only a modicum of optimism.

Could times be grimmer? As I write this in the summer of 2009, during the past nine months we have witnessed the collapse of the financial system that has stood fast for the past 80 years. Many investment banks have folded, major accounting firms have failed, and most commercial and retail banks are teetering on the edge. The backbone of American industry, automobile manufacturing, has had two of its three major firms declare bankruptcy. Government has taken on the largest amount of debt ever in such a short period. The real estate market is suffering enormous price deterioration. This has fueled the number of personal foreclosures to reach new highs. Bankruptcies are becoming common. Energy prices are soaring driving up the cost of nearly everything. What is to become of us?

If a guru can offer some solution, even if it is 'out-of-the-box thinking' like the *'new age'* pundit predicting a transformation of consciousness or a *'pop'* investment advisor promoting a new and painless scheme to get rich quick, we are all ears. In light of these phenomena, it's interesting to note that critics oftentimes accuse authors of books on Bible prophecy playing up the bad times and making things seem worse than they are. This has proven to be very unfair. After all, isn't it astounding how many 'apocalyptic predictions' of the past 40 years are coming true right in front of our eyes? Maybe these 'doomsday' fanatics weren't so nuts after all!

Secondly, many authors can rouse their readers *by playing on the thrill we enjoy when frightened.* Without this sensation, horror movies wouldn't be popular. For some less-than-healthy reason, we do seem fascinated by all the bad things that can happen to us. Authors can write books on prophecy to heighten these fears. The intentions may be for our good—indeed, they may want literally to scare the heck out of us! However, not everyone finds this tactic particularly appealing.

True enough: As we near the end of the first decade of the New Millennium, many would argue that seldom have there been as many things to worry about as there are today. Global warming, galactic perils (enormous solar flares, energetic and dangerous proton clouds in the galaxy, changes in the magnetic fields of the sun and earth), population explosions, exotic and deadly viruses, earthquakes and volcanoes—there seems to be no end to the calamities that may soon befall us. Indeed, natural disasters that could end civilization abound. We hardly need anyone calling attention to this. Still, there is no shortage of books at this very moment on the many ways to calculate the 'end of days.'

Finally, *not everyone is enthralled by the end of the world.* Some avoid this topic like the plague (did I mention a reemergence of the *'Plague?'*). However, to understand why some are fascinated while others are some simply frustrated, we must begin by understanding the history of Protestants and their views on prophecy.

How the Modern Protestant Prophecy Perspective Came to Be

Often fueled by 'parochial and pending catastrophes,' Protestant theologians have penned many biblical prophetic works over the past four hundred years. For example, many books were written in England around 1666, when the pious believed Christ would return (that triple six was a dead giveaway!) The plague had just broken out once again, there was a horrendous fire in London, and a number of remarkable comets appeared at the same time triggering this 'millenarian' speculation. The tumult captured the interest of no less a scientist than Isaac Newton who produced many books on the subject.[i]

Then, a bit less than two hundred years ago, books began to appear proposing a very different view of the Second Advent. J.N. Darby (about whom we will have much to say), formed the Plymouth Brethren around 1840 and put forth the position now known as *Dispensationalism*, which champions *the Rapture* as we commonly know it today and also a very controversial view that *Israel was still*

---

[i] Although only one was published, and even it wasn't distributed—Cambridge didn't want him to appear fanatical!

God's chosen people! With few exceptions, this proclamation was something that Christian orthodoxy hadn't professed for almost 1,700 years. As we will see later, this was a very radical idea.

Forty years ago, Hal Lindsey published the landmark title, *The Late, Great Planet Earth.* Leveraging the dispensational approach, Lindsey sold 35 million copies (to date). Seldom has any single popular book had such a significant effect upon the Church as this one did. Speaking for myself (at that time, a wise old man of 14), I certainly found it tremendously helpful – it caused me to understand that the Bible might actually be relevant.

In the past twenty years, the 'Left Behind' series of Tim La-Haye and Jerry Jenkins has demonstrated just how lively the interest is in the 'end times.' This series, all books counted together, is one of the best selling of all time moving over 65,000,000 units. LaHaye and Jenkins, in contrast to very recent books addressing Mayan prophecies (which are also selling like hotcakes), build their postulated (fictional) stories upon the apocalyptic vision expressed by Jewish and Christian prophets.

As to new non-fiction books on the subject, one can go to Amazon.com and do a search using a phrase like 'the end of days' or 'the apocalypse.' The return results will show a dozen or more titles on just about any prophetic subject written in the last five to seven years. The topic of the apocalypse doesn't lack support from scores of authors—many of course that eagerly share their controversial ideas to get their point across!

However, while there are countless 'single topic' titles on the subject of Bible prophecy, most of them don't sell many copies. So, we can certainly conclude that what most people in America today know about 'the end times' is not from studying the Bible or reading lots of different 'religious' authors on the subject. Their knowledge comes from what they've read *from Tim LaHaye's fictional account of the Apocalypse* or, if they attend an evangelical church, *what their preacher has recently sermonized.* If they are in a liberal church, there is a good chance that their pastors have shared *no insights into the apocalypse whatsoever*—other than to dismiss its relevance to the days in which we live (this will also be a big part of our story).

4

However, much of the population may not be aware that not all Christians subscribe to the LaHaye/Jenkins point-of-view. While this perspective has become the majority position of most evangelicals in America, historically, the *energetic profession of these concepts* is only about 90 years in the making. In fact, the emphasis on the Rapture, the sensational scenario of the Antichrist and the 'Mark of the Beast,' the earthly future reign of the Messiah and the Kingdom of God—all of these beliefs are still contested by serious Christian theologians. Now, *that doesn't mean that these views are wrong.* However, it would surprise some 'unbelievers' that many Christians haven't closed rank around the most popular prophetic positions. It should be obvious that the *'Left Behind Series'* is based on only one particular interpretation of the Bible. Nevertheless, I'm afraid this point isn't widely recognized. Hence, it's a key reason why I wrote this book!

Who Should Read this Book

Therefore, it struck me that perhaps there was a need for a book taking up the subject of Christian prophecy, which highlighted *that there is in fact more than one considered point of view.* Furthermore, the author should structure the book such that the readers could decide for themselves what they believed. Rather than selling the reader on only one perspective like Lindsey and LaHaye do, what if the author surveyed the different (but still *dominant*) opinions and highlighted their respective strengths and weaknesses? Would readers be interested in a book that for the most part, presents these perspectives neutrally and lets the reader decide?

Obviously, I've decided the answer is 'yes.' Clearly, it's my conviction that what is happening in the world perplexes many people today. They wonder if we are living *'in the last days'* as the Bible labels it. They would like to know what other Bible prophecy pundits besides LaHaye and Lindsey teach and appreciate a genuine opportunity to decide for themselves what they think. This doesn't suggest that my targeted readership should be Christian or even religious. It certainly doesn't mean that they must know a lot about the Bible. Nevertheless, it does assume that their curiosity is strong enough that they would pick up a book if they perceive it might help them sort out the matter.

To help keep you – the reader – engaged in this book, one tactic is for me to take a *neutral tone for the better part this book.* Additionally, I will go the second mile and give you a 'customized' reason for you to read on. How can I do this? I have created a *Reader Classification Grid.* My idea is for you to conduct a 'self-assessment' to identify why you should care. If you agree to participate actively in this process, please read on. Your instructions are to first, identify which type of reader you are by reviewing the descriptions below, then secondly, consider the rationale I provide for why you should read this book. It's that simple.

Group One: Open to New Ideas and Willing to Learn. In a many cases, readers will fit into *Group Number One, which* means that you may not know a lot about the Bible. You know it's an important book. However, you may not have a strong sentiment about whether or not its truth is reliable when it comes to its religious assertions. You may also have your suspicions regarding whether the Bible records history accurately. However, these questions won't cause you to dismiss the Bible out of hand. You would like to know what I, the author, think. If the Bible can be made interesting and lively, your verdict is most likely, "I'll read your book, knock yourself out."

I expect many of my readers will fall into this group. Young folks especially should be found in this first group for 'kids' in their 20's and 30's are very open to learn new things and will take an author seriously if he (in my case, *he*) can prove his point. If you fall into this group, I'd very glad to have your attention.

Group Two: Thoughtfully Skeptical. As an author, I know that many of my readers have encountered serious arguments against the validity of the Bible. As a scholar of some depth (however modest!), I am familiar that over the past two hundred years, the Bible's veracity has been the subject of many assaults. And while I may have studied the subjects thoroughly and still believe in the infallibility of the Bible, I certainly know that many of my readers *are persuaded that the Bible has serious problems.* So, if you fall into this group, I suspect that you are unlikely to critically consider what the Bible says about much of anything. I'm not suggesting you are irrationally biased. You have probably given much thought to the issue of the reliability of the Bible and you have already decided that it is suspect. To change your mind, the normal course for me would be to first prove to you the Bible has something to say that's worth hearing despite the fact that you believe it is generally unreliable. If you fall into this group (*Group Number Two*), I submit that you still can find something valuable in the pages that follow. *However, you will have to suspend your disbelief in the Bible's reliability for the time being (that's right, I said, suspend your **disbelief** in its reliability).* I won't mount a direct argument here to prove to you the Bible is worthy of your respect. That is a different book. Nevertheless, I can give you many things to consider—especially by pointing out events that I predict will take place just as the Bible says they will. If you start seeing these things come true, you just might reconsider your opinion on the Bible. If you do, that is outstanding. The fulfillment of prophecy is supposed to 'turn heads' (or *change minds* to be more specific!)

Fulfilled prophecy is in fact the source of faith for many Christians and Jews. The prophets of the Bible proved themselves prophets just for this reason: They could only called a prophet if what they said would happen, in fact did. Thus, we may legitimately determine our verdict on the Bible in this way. The God of the Bible is just fine with this process. Despite rumors to the contrary, God can be reasonable too. He even invites us to reason with Him![i]

Group Three: Willfully Ignorant and Happy. There are those that profess disbelief for little to no reason. If this is you, a solid argument no matter how well articulated likely won't persuade you. You are surprised you picked up this book on Bible prophecy. You normally avoid all such books for a variety of reasons, but mostly because you are predisposed to reject anything, any book says about the Bible (unless it has a negative opinion). You are of this mindset because fundamentally you don't want to deal with the consequences of changing your mind. New beliefs lead to new lifestyles (and giving up old habits!) As a reader, you might ask yourself, "Do I want to

---

[i] Isaiah 1:18, "Come now, let us reason together."

make big changes in my lifestyle—with whom I associate, what I do in my spare time? Perish the thought."

Now, to be clear, I wish you would read this book—but I am not counting on it. You are in *Group Number Three. Woe unto Group Number Three!* (I'm being serious here.) Still, if you have the courage to reconsider your view of the world, you might be making an important decision. I encourage you to take the time. You just might be the better for it!

Group Number Four: Faithfully Committed, Intellectually Indifferent. In many cases, skeptical contentions fail to distract readers. Such readers have reasons to believe in the Bible since it affected their lives so positively. If there are questions or problems in the Bible, they are content to let some intellectual somewhere work out the responses to those problems. They trust challengers have attacked the Bible before and it withstood the test. They trust it will come through criticism today as well. If you fall into this group, you will find yourself right at home. You don't have to be an intellectual to enjoy this book. Regardless, you should learn something intelligent along the way. I'm counting on it. Share it and impress your friends!

Group Number Five: Believe the Bible, Believe in God, just Because. Moreover, God bless those in yet another group that believe for reasons they themselves hold dear and keep 'under their hat.' If this is you, you aren't persuaded very much by arguments for the faith either, but for a very different reason. As the mathematician and philosopher Paschal said, "The heart hath its reason whereof the reason knoweth not." You won't make a fuss if I cite the Bible as an authority. In fact, unless I can quote the Bible to support my point of view on prophecy, you won't be inclined to agree with me. If you are this reader, you will not be disappointed. This book is all about what the Bible teaches about 'things to come.' Unlike some authors, I will do my best to *let the Bible speak for itself without getting in the way.*

Group Number Six: I Believe, Help My Unbelief. However, not all believers in spiritual things are inclined toward faith 'at all costs.' Just like 'Doubting Thomas,' *unless they see the*

8

nail prints in the hands of Jesus, this group of the 'faithful' isn't going to be convinced. Their disposition toward 'faith' and 'fact' is one of extreme sensitivity. Many want 'reasons to believe.' When someone casts doubts their way, they absorb them. They seek the truth. Faith without a basis in fact isn't comfortable. They appreciate faith bolstered by reasoned arguments and evidence. I readily admit *that I am in this group.* Those of us in this group enjoy learning new facts which increase our confidence in our faith be such findings archeological, historical, or even scientific. We say, "The more facts the better. Thank you very much."

If you fall into this camp, I especially like you because you and I are in the same group (*Group Number Six*). I hope that I provide enough points that reinforce your faith, such that by reading what I've written, you will really benefit.

Group Number Seven: Prophecy Pundits and Eschatology Experts. Lastly, I have particular interest in one special group. They are those readers who read just about anything *if the subject is biblical prophecy.* A special promotional argument directed just for folks like you: I expect your reaction to a 'survey' of biblical prophecy to be, "Gee, I already know all about these things." Okay, but a few ideas on why you should read on:

1.   The material here is fresh. I have attempted to study a slew of new sources that contribute to the pursuit of prophetic knowledge and to identify new insights into old topics. I've even come up with a number of new analytic perspectives on my own. I assure you – you will read novel things – even if they are just my many unprecedented speculations for which I am solely responsible.

2.   There is always a value in learning *to see the forest instead of just the trees.* I think you will especially enjoy this aspect of *Are We Living in the Last Days?* I have assimilated a considerable amount of material over the years and will do my best to point out what is paramount and what isn't.

3.   References to history and philosophy don't frequent books on prophecy. I think you will find my inclusion of them especially helpful in gaining new perspectives on the 'standard topics.' I expect to hear from you if you don't.

4.   I present the differing views of Protestant Christians on the standard topics of eschatology. I am not aware of any book that tries to assemble these various viewpoints in a way to let the reader assess the viability of the differing perspectives. For instance, if you believe in the Millennial Kingdom of Christ on this earth and wonder why some Christians don't, what I write should help you understand. If you've read Tim LaHaye's books and question why your preacher doesn't talk about such topics, you will appreciate the reason after reading this book.

A special word to those readers who are committed Christians: I suppose that most of us have shaped our opinion on biblical topics without considering why those who disagree with us choose to be so stubborn. However, this isn't good for us!

First, I believe "a faith never challenged becomes an unstable faith." We must occasionally confront adversarial points of view to sharpen our own thinking. Secondly, since we are usually too quick to criticize those that disagree with us, I hope to sensitize the reader to 'the other side of the argument' so you don't see those who profess the alternative view to be 'random,' truculent, dishonest, or foolish. I hope you will agree that *when forming their opinions 'the other camp' may have had good rationales too.*

Why bother with this? For one very important reason: If we can understand each other better, we might just fulfill our 'prime directive' from the Master—*"Love one another as I have loved you"* (John 13:34). Note also: Jesus didn't tell us to "agree with one another." Somehow, He assumed that despite the fact that we might not agree, we could still treat one another with respect. Winning the argument takes a back seat to 'winning as a team' with our fellow sojourners!

This is Not Just another Book Predicting Doom and Gloom

In concluding my opening remarks, let me offer one other assurance about what this book *isn't.* As we discussed at the outset, many books on prophecy *highlight pending disasters.* They eagerly seek to create the impression that the end is 'any moment now.' Let me assure you, such is not my intent. I am not predicting that the world will end this year, this decade, or this century. Nevertheless, *neither* can I promise that *the apocalypse won't happen for many more years to come.* I confess that I have lived for 40 years now with the understanding that what the Bible teaches about prophecy will influence my life. Yes, I have felt at times that the end was near. Yes, I see many events that I believe point to a possible apocalypse within my lifetime. However, I'm not at the place just yet where I'm ready to sell the farm and move to a bomb shelter in the mountains!

So if you are looking for 'proofs' that the apocalypse will happen in the next decade or less, *you need to look elsewhere.* I happen to believe that as good citizens of the world we should not be eager to see it ruined even if its devastation somehow hastens the coming of the Kingdom of God.[i] It is God's creation and we are its caretakers. Don't expect commendations from the King when someone harms the world He created, while we actively or passively participated in this regrettable course of action.

In addition, I operate on the assumption that God is longsuffering and 'is not willing that any should perish' (see Matthew 8:14). When it's time to close the curtain, I don't want to be the one pulling the cords. That is God's decision and His alone. I anxiously look for Christ to come, but not at the expense of harming the world in which we live or eliminating the opportunity for others to decide they want to join in the celebration when He appears!

On the other hand, if you need assurance that life will go on just as it has in America for the past 60 years or so – I can't offer much comfort to you either. Bob Dylan sang, *"The times, they are a' changin'."* This was true in the 'Sixties.' It's much more the case today. I'm afraid dire circumstances could be our lot throughout the 21st century. We should be concerned about many things. However, the one conviction with which I can assuage your worry is from the words of another old song: *"He's Got the Whole World In His Hands."* I have faith that no catastrophe or destructive event will trump what

---

[i] This is the position taken by Mahmud Ahmadinejad, President of Iran during most of the first decade of the 21st century. He wishes to hasten the coming of the *Mahdi,* somewhat akin to an Islamic Messiah, by unleashing a nuclear bomb! Not a prophetic position we Christians should emulate.

the providence of God *wills or allows.* 55 years of "life experience" has validated my faith in more instances than I can count. And trust me, it hasn't always been easy!

Will comets strike the earth and destroy all of life? Will a genetically engineered virus extinguish the human race? Will extraterrestrials conquer the earth and carry us all away in their flying saucers? I don't think so. My confidence stems from believing in what the Bible teaches about the future. Since such drama *is not in the Bible*, I'm quite certain that *it's not in the cards.* Instead, the Bible's essential message is that despite the countless sordid problems, God is still in charge. Even more than with those insurance people, *we are "in good hands" with Him*!

Stylistic Conventions Used in This Book

A word on FONT CONVENTIONS: I distinguish *Scripture passages* with *italics*, whether set apart or 'in line,' to make sure the reader notes the information provided directly from the Bible. I do *not* italicize Scriptures that I paraphrase. Where I **bold a word**, that word or term will typically be one of the topics covered in more depth—the reader can jump to that topic if you wish. I abstain from using bolding as a means of emphasis. Instead, I use *italics*. In those cases where the font is italicized for another reason (such as a Scripture reference), I resort to **bolding *the selected phrase.***

A word on *Technical Notes* and *Footnotes*: I've placed *Technical Notes* at the end of each chapter that I've intended to provide further 'proof points' or technical information, that while not essential, should help document that the perspective I'm offering isn't just pulled out of thin air. *Technical Notes* will also serve their traditional purpose as a place for citations of authorities or to call attention to relevant information that is available to the reader (referencing a book I've outlined in **For Further Reading,** on page 305). Nevertheless, note that this information *is technical in nature and is optional! Feel free to skip past these notes if you are a casual reader.*

In contrast, *footnotes* will be brief comments that connect to the discussion but are slightly askew from the main flow of the dialogue.

Usually, they add a bit of color but don't amount to a critical point of import. If they seem a bit sassy, forgive my self-indulgence!

At the conclusion of each chapter, I have provided a highlighted area entitled, *"Recapping the Key Points Covered in This Chapter,"* to help reinforce the primary points to remember. I seek not just to inform but also to educate! This review should help call to your attention what is important in each section and "cement" it in your memory. There won't be a test at the end. Well, at least not one I will administer.

PLEASE NOTE: I've also created *technical subject matter sidebars* 'with a gray caption' that I call '**Deep Dives**' to flesh out topics about which I anticipate some *studious* readers will want to know more. *If you find the material there 'too deep', please feel free to skip these too.* I don't want my vocabulary or obscure ideas to stymie your progress with the primary material. I use the *Deep Dive* in most cases as a means to provide additional historical, theological, or philosophical detail on the subject we intersect in the course of the main study. I recognize that some readers want more evidence or at least more explanation. I hope to be responsive to this anticipated request. Nevertheless, if it seems "over your head," don't bother with it.

With these introductory remarks concluded, let me freely admit that there is no subject more controversial than predicting the future, unless one is attempting to explain *what the Bible says about the future.* Therefore, whether you find this information prescient or merely provocative, I do hope you will find it particularly valuable.

Chapter 1: Identifying the Different Protestant Perspectives on Prophecy

Why Prophecy Is So Essential to the Bible

Bible prophecy is a subject that intrigues almost everyone. There may be more books published on the matter of prophecy than any other biblical topic. While it is true that Scripture primarily consists of chronicled history, parables, dramatic stories, psalms, proverbs, poems, and hymns, a surprisingly large portion of the Bible deals with prophecy—including specific predictions about the future.

Allow me to illustrate. Experts separate the Old Testament into three sections: History ('The Law'); prophetic writings ('The Prophets'); and wisdom literature ('The Writings'). *The Law* constitutes about 50% of the Old Testament material, *the Writings* about 20%, and *the Prophets*, 30%. To gauge the importance of prophecy, one only need take note of the fact the *Hebrew prophets wrote almost one-third of the Old Testament.*

The Prophets are classified into two primary groups: There were the 'Major Prophets' consisting of Isaiah, Ezekiel, Daniel and Jeremiah that wrote large sections of the Bible. A dozen 'minor prophets' included Amos, Hosea, Zechariah, Zephaniah, Joel, Jonah, and Malachi. In addition, a third group didn't directly author any books. This group is composed of significant prophets who are the principal characters (if not protagonists) in the historical books, I and II Samuel, I and II Kings, and I and II Chronicles. Noteworthy prophets appearing there included Nathan, Samuel, Elijah, and Elisha. Given the large portion of the Scripture contributed by these prophets, it would seem very safe to say that to understand the Bible well, *one must understand the role of the Bible's prophets and their essential predictions.*

The Prophets spent a great deal of their time challenging their contemporaries (the kings and the people), to change their ways and to return to the true religion of Moses. A considerable amount of their writings was directed to the future of Israel—sometimes 'near term' (within 100 years or less) when they were calling for immediate action to avoid catastrophe—but many times *their writings were addressed to future generations that would witness an individual that would surpass all other prophets in wisdom and power.* This future spokesperson for the LORD would be like Moses in many respects (Moses, 'a part-time Prophet' himself, predicted this), and have a similar impact upon their religion and their lives.

Although sometimes couched in mysterious poetry, the universal message throughout the prophetic writings is that God will send a special emissary to the Jews. His coming will bring salvation to the people and promote Israel to the 'head of the nations.' The Jewish religion knew this envoy as, the 'Messiah'. The Greek world, called the Messiah, 'Christ.' When one boils down the essence of *eschatology*, which is *the study of things to come* (based substantially on the prophets of the Old Testament)—it quickly becomes apparent that the dominant theme of almost all prophetic sections of Scripture is *the coming of the Messiah.* Scripture records two contrasting pictures of what the Messiah will be like and what He will do. First, we see an image of a conquering hero in battle (Zechariah 9; Joel 3, Isaiah 11, among many others), that brings peace to the world and rules over it after destroying the enemies of Israel. Secondly, we read of a suffering servant whose

> **THE KEY POINT TO PONDER:**
>
> *The essential message of Christianity is, from one perspective, the solution to the paradox of the two messiahs in Jewish sacred literature.*

death redeems the people of Israel from their sin (Isaiah 53, Psalm 22, and Psalm 118). From one perspective, the essential message of Christianity is, concisely put, the *solution to this paradox in Hebrew sacred literature.* The Christian position is that *Jesus Christ is destined to fulfill both of these portraits.*

To the dismay of the Jews of the first century AD, the fulfillment of Messiah comes in two stages. Stage One: The Messiah must suffer. Stage Two: The Messiah will reign. As most readers already know, because the Jews wanted what comes second to happen first, they rejected the one for whom they had been waiting (and for whom many still anxiously await). As a result, by repudiating the Chris-

16

tian viewpoint, Judaism forced the split with Christianity. By the close of the first century, Christianity had been orphaned by its Hebrew parent.

After 2,000 years, Christianity remains steadfast that this apparent inconsistency in the Messiah's role will disappear when Jesus Christ returns. It is the view of all Christians that in some real way, Jesus Christ will fulfill 'stage two.' However, to learn exactly how His return will accomplish this, we must understand the meaning of the Bible's 'predictive prophecy.' This is to say that before we foresee the outcome of the play, we have to appreciate what *is yet to come* in the 'second act.' To be sure, there are still many events predicted by the Scripture that have not happened. To comprehend rightly the full meaning of the Messiah, we must come to appreciate what has yet to happen that the Bible declares will soon take place. Unfortunately, there is a major predicament in conducting this undertaking: *Christians don't all agree on what the Bible says about the future!* But then, we knew it wouldn't be easy, didn't we?

Protestants Have Three Principal Contrasting Viewpoints

Certainly, there are many conflicting interpretations of Scripture on every important biblical subject. When the subject is *predictive prophecy*, the interpretations become even more varied and contested. However, looking only at 'macro' interpretations of what is often termed *the Second Coming of Christ (or sometimes simply 'the Apocalypse'),* we ultimately can 'boil it down' and arrive at just three very distinct and rival points of view in Protestantism. (Note: As you read the next few pages, please refer to **Figure 1** on page 22).

The first viewpoint is *Christian Liberalism*, which has dominated the mainline denominations in America for at least the past one hundred years. Liberalism usually construes the 'Second Coming' as a *metaphor*—its fulfillment is some manner of religious encounter with God. For instance, some theologians of the liberal persuasion might see the *Second Coming* referring simply to the gift of the Holy Spirit which came rushing into the Apostles' Jerusalem headquarters at Pentecost (circa 32 AD). Alternatively, as some liberals suppose, it is merely meeting Christ upon one's death. Liberal-

17

ism dismisses many biblical accounts because it *questions that miracles happen in 'space-time'* [i] —and without the supernatural aspect of scripture, the Bible's value and purpose in forming Christian beliefs must be downgraded and, in many cases, cast aside altogether.

On the subject of the 'millennium,' *Liberalism* interprets the 1,000-year reign of Christ *symbolically.* To clarify, when the Bible talks of the *Millennium*, the period of the rule of Christ on this earth, we shouldn't interpret this to mean that Jesus literally reigns for 1,000 years. According to Liberalism, Christ's Kingdom is *forever* and has already begun through the Church that reigns as His agent today and for the past 2,000 years. In this position, the Church influences and gradually transforms the world into the Kingdom over a very long period—synonymous with 'the Church age.'[ii] In this view, Liberalism does not anticipate an actual 'return' of Christ. Rather, the Church counts for the 'return' of Christ. Scholars label this optimistic view, *'post-millennialism.'*

Because of these views, Liberalism chooses not to debate most issues in eschatology. The differences that Evangelicals dispute (e.g., when the Rapture happens, the nature of the Tribulation, the meaning of 'Mystery Babylon'), are for the most part irrelevant questions to Liberal theologians. Liberalism simply does not have an opinion on many of these subjects. Consequently, the liberal's vote on the Apocalypse debate will generally be no more than "Present!"

Therefore, the controversies over most prophetic topics are 'between the family members' of orthodoxy or Evangelicalism, the protestant 'camps' that follow Martin Luther (1483-1546) or John Calvin (1509-1564) in the 'reformed tradition.'[1]

---

[i] I will use this phrase 'space-time' in many more instances. Since Einstein proved that time is a dimension just like length, width and depth, when we talk about *what reality means* (the physical world and how we experience it through our five senses), it has become commonplace today to use this phrase. Hence, I use it throughout this book as a synonym for *the physical or empirical world.*

[ii] The historical period after the resurrection of Christ and before His Second **Advent**—a time in which God through Christ is calling out a 'people for His name,' see Ephesians Chapter 2.

However, while there may be more than two positions *evangelicals* espouse on many prophetic subjects, once we analyze these perspectives carefully, we see that the most significant positions typically coalesce around *two and only two major schools of thought.* Further analysis separates these two most important evangelical perspectives based upon only *two primary issues*: (1) *How we interpret the Bible* and (2) whether *Israel still has an essential place in God's plan of salvation.*

The first of these two groups in Evangelicalism believes that most of what the Bible predicts has already happened—a position labeled *preterist* because it connotes 'past tense' (most romantic languages, like Spanish, call one form of past tense, *preterit* tense). This group, in the same manner as Liberalism, interprets the apocalyptic images and concepts of Revelation *symbolically*—whose fulfillment is not literal, but figurative. Theologians label this prominent evangelical viewpoint '*Covenantalist*' (a view where covenants between God and humankind are crucial to understand the meaning of the Bible – see Figure 1). Covenantalists are normally counted as '*Amillennialists*' because they do not believe in a literal 1,000 'millennial reign' of Jesus Christ upon the earth. However, the important distinction with Liberalism and post-millennialism is their view that *there will be a physical return of Jesus Christ* at the end of history (at the conclusion of 'space-time'). Therefore, we see an interesting contrast with the Liberal viewpoint: Covenantalism interprets the millennium *symbolically*, but the Second Coming of Christ (or Second Advent) *literally*.

Finally, the second evangelical position (which is the third of the three Protestant perspectives), takes most future predictions 'at face value.' They often refer to themselves as *literalists*. In using this term, this group seeks to convey the empirical nature of future prophecies as events that will happen in the space-time world. If the Bible says that Christ will reign for 1,000 years, the Bible means what it says: Christ will be literally on this earth in physical form as King and His rule will last exactly 1,000 years. If the 'lion lays down with the lamb' in the Kingdom to come, while these words might have originally been meant as an *image of peace*—don't be surprised to see *lions becoming vegetarians* and *lambs playing with lion cubs!*

Authors identify this group with a theological label known as *Dispensationalism* (a view that 'dispensations'—or the rules governing 'how God and humankind relate'—is key to interpreting the Bible). These evangelicals are also associated with the term *Millennialist* because they believe in a literal reign of Jesus Christ upon the earth for 1,000 years.[i]

Which of these views represents the historical position of Christianity? That too is a source of argument with the two evangelical positions citing authorities to prove that their perspective has substantial historical precedent. Nevertheless, as we will see, the issue isn't really about who can claim the most backing from church history, but the logical consistency (or lack *thereof*) *of how we interpret the Bible. Biblical interpretive methodology is crucial and indeed determinative on who should win the argument.* Because it is so vital to our understanding, *interpretive methodology* (hermeneutics) will be the *concluding* topic we study together.

We Must Understand the Apocalypse to Understand the Meaning of Christianity

As one drills into the many subtopics, all the variations of belief can overwhelm us. For instance, is the *Rapture* (the resurrection of the Christian living and dead to meet the Lord *"in the air"*), a literal event that Christians will one day experience? If this is so, does it happen before the time of God's wrath upon the earth known as *'the Great Tribulation?'* On the other hand, does it happen in the middle of this time? Then again, could it transpire concurrently with the actual physical 'space-time' return of Christ just before the *Battle of Armageddon* at his *"glorious appearing"* (Titus 2:13)? (See **Figure 3** page 64, for a 'timeline' and sequence of events). There are so many special terms and differing viewpoints that it is easy to get lost in the rhetoric and miss the essential meanings of biblical prophecy. This is unfortunate since true Christianity, a Christianity that is in line with the core teachings of Jesus Christ, must deal with the issues

---

[i] In the last 25 to 30 years, this group has grown rapidly and now constitutes the majority in Protestant Christianity (but I'm sure I didn't need to point this out to any politicians reading this book!)

tied to the *'Apocalypse.'* Without these issues included, purveyors of Christianity compromise its *authenticity*. Jesus preached, *"The Kingdom of God is at hand!"* This theme was essential to His message and it is most certainly vital to what biblical prophecy means. Ultimately, we must settle *the meaning of the Kingdom of God in order to interpret correctly virtually all other matters of eschatology.*

Recapping the Key Points Covered in This Chapter

- Prophecy comprises a significant portion of the Bible – it is a requirement, not an elective for those that want to know what the Bible conveys.
- The primary subject of prophecy is the Messiah.
- There are two contrasting views of Messiah in the Old Testament; Christians believe Jesus Christ fulfills both views.
- Protestant Christians divide into three rival camps regarding the meaning of the Apocalypse and the Second Advent.
- These three camps: Liberalism, Covenantalism, and Dispensationalism.
- Unless we understand the Apocalypse and Second Advent, we will misunderstand the true meaning of Christianity.
- It is ultimately the meaning of the Kingdom of God that must be settled before we can correctly interpret all other crucial matters of eschatology.

Technical Endnotes

---

[1] *This is not to ignore the Baptist and Wesleyan traditions.* Historically these important movements follow orthodox teaching stemming from the Reformed perspective. In only a few major doctrines do they differ with other evangelicals in any meaningful way. We see these differences in regard to the doctrine of 'election' as well as how faith and 'good works' relate to one another – known in classic theology as the debate between *Calvinism and Arminianism.* But on the matter of 'things to come', John Wesley would likely agree with the historic Protestant views we've described. Modern day Wesleyan's (primarily the Methodists) will articulate their position in the Liberal camp. As to Baptist viewpoints, like the Wesleyans, historically they fall into one of the two evangelical 'camps' we describe. In today's world, although generally more traditional or conservative, some Baptist groups like the Methodists, will place themselves instead into the Liberal consortium.

Protestant Christianity	Evangelical or Fundamentalist	**Amillennialist** Post-Tribulation Rapture **Key Doctrine** Hermeneutic **Covenants** Adamic Covenant Noahic Covenant Abrahamic Covenant Mosaic Covenant Davidic Covenant New Covenant *Preterist*—Except for the Physical Return of Christ	**Covenantal Theologians** B.B. Warfield (1851-1921) Charles Hodge (1797-1878) J. Gresham Machen (1881-1937) Cornelius Van Til (1895-1997) J.I. Packer (1926-) R.C. Sproul (1939-) **Seminaries** Westminster Theological. (PA) Covenant Theological Sm. (MO) Greenville Presbyterian (SC) Knox Theological Seminary (FL) Reformed Theological Sm. (MS)
		Millennialist Pre-Tribulation Rapture **Plain Meaning** Hermeneutic **Dispensations** Innocence (pre-Adamic Fall) Conscience (Adam to Noah) Government (Noah to Abraham) Patriarchal (Abraham to Moses) Mosaic Law (Moses to Christ) Grace (Christ to Today) Millennial (Future, 1,000 Yrs.) *Futurist*—For all eschatological events	**Dispensational Theologians** C. I. Schofield (1843-1921) Lewis Sperry Chafer (1871-1952) Dwight L. Moody (1837-1899) John F. Walvoord (1910-2002) Charles C. Ryrie (1925-) J. Dwight Pentecost (1915-) **Dispensational Schools** Dallas Theological Seminary (TX) Moody Bible Institute (IL) Biola University (CA) Baptist Bible Seminary (PA) Philadelphia Biblical Univ. (PA)
	Modernist	**Post-Millennialist** No Tribulation or Rapture **Liberal** Hermeneutic **Theologies** "Social Gospel " (A. V. Harnack) "Synthesis with Existentialism" (P. Tillich) "Process Theology" (A.N. Whitehead) "Neo-orthodoxy" (Barth, Bultmann) "Liberation Theology" (R. M. Brown plus) "Theology of Hope" (Multmann) *'Historicist' or Preterist*	**Liberal Theologians** F. Schleiermacher (1768-1834) Harry E. Fosdick (1878-1969) Alfred Whitehead (1861-1947) Paul Tillich (1886-1965) Karl Barth (1886-1968) Rudolf Bultmann (1884-1976) **Seminaries** Princeton Theological Sm. (NJ) Chicago Theological Sm. (IL) Perkins School of Theology (TX) Harvard Divinity School (MA) Trinity Lutheran Seminary (OH) Berkeley Divinity (Yale) (CN)

FIGURE 1 - PROTESTANT ESCHATOLOGY OVERVIEW

Chapter 2: Apocalypse – It's Meaning to Protestants in the 21st Century

Apocalyptic Literature is One Portion of Bible Prophecy

'A picture is worth a thousand words' and certainly apocalyptic literature has given rise to tens of thousands of words to interpret the meaning of the pictures its authors have painted.

The word *apocalypse* comes from the Greek, a*pokalypsis*, meaning the lifting of the veil or 'revelation' as in *revealing the truth.* Hence, we know the Book of Revelation in the New Testament also as 'the Apocalypse of John.'[i] Several books in the Bible and other non-canonical books (religious books not included in the 66 books of the Bible's canon), are considered *apocalyptic literature.* Apocalyptic literature is considered highly figurative, addressing the battle of *Good versus Evil,* and makes use of dramatic pictures portraying the end of the world. These sources are the primary, but not the exclusive sources, for the Bible's teachings on the Apocalypse. The Bible weaves prophecy like a golden thread, throughout the Scripture, including the Psalms!

Modern scholarship also describes Jesus as 'an apocalyptic rabbi' because he used these images in His teaching, quoting Daniel and other Hebrew prophets who penned their prophetic passages with such vivid pictures.

The Vision: A Means of Revelation or Just a Mental Disorder?

Unfortunately, apocalyptic literature oftentimes is minimized or derided by using the term *apocalyptic* 'dismissively'—as if 'to be apocalyptic' is to be at best, imaginative, and at worst, delusional.

No doubt about it: Visions are non-rational human experiences. In today's scientific world, conventional wisdom dictates that we regard visions as the product of psychotic breaks or other

---

[i] Although many commentators are quick to point out that the book of Revelation itself states that it is the *Revelation of Jesus Christ.*

mental disorders. If someone admits to having had a vision, we would sarcastically assume that he or she was drunk, still asleep, or mentally incapacitated.

I'm not meaning to convey that this view is purely a modern attitude. You may recall in the second chapter of Acts, when the Apostles of Christ 'take it to the streets,' (May or June, AD 32), Peter has to inform the populace that what they are seeing is what the prophet Joel predicted about the coming of God's Holy Spirit. "These men are not drunk as you might suppose. It is only 9:00 AM in the morning. No, what you are seeing is what the prophet Joel predicted—that *in the last days,* that God will pour out His Spirit, not just on the Jews, but all mankind. Old men will dream dreams and young men will see visions." (Joel 2:28, m*y paraphrase*). However, if we are to take apocalyptic material seriously, we must first discard this bias and recognize that visions and dreams, although 'non-rational' are not necessary figments of our imagination— in certain cases they may bear more fruit pointing out truth than rational analysis and discourse. The Bible teaches that God "customizes" His encounter with each of us – *He doesn't intend our experience to be "standard!"*

Certainly, C.G. Jung through his approach, *Analytical Psychology*, lent credibility to this notion.[1] An Episcopal Priest and author, Morton Kelsey, wrote many books in the 1980's on the integration of Jung's psychology and Christian spirituality. (See *Encounter with God: A Theology of Christian Experience)* Dr. Scott Peck, bestselling author of *The Road Less Traveled*, is another fine example of a modern scholar seeking to integrate spirituality and psychology without dismissing the supernatural. These authors are far from orthodox in certain aspects of their theology— but their 'integrated' approach provides many valuable insights. At the very least, their

THE KEY POINT TO PONDER:

True Christianity is supported by reasoned arguments, sincere emotions and passionate convictions. To favor one against the other is to harm our relationship with God that should at the end of the day be profoundly personal.

empirical exploration and scientific documentation of the subconscious mind (and the 'collective unconscious'), has provided an 'apologetic' (i.e., bringing to bear hard evidence), for the fact that there is more to reality than the material world! That's right: Science has proven that a spiritual realm of a definite sort exists![i]

When it comes to truth about God (and 'knowing God'), we should feel safe about asserting that our visions, dreams, emotions and reason all can be brought to bear to personally encounter God in a true and meaningful way. Reasoned arguments, sincere emotions, and passionate convictions support true Christianity. To favor one against the other is to harm our relationship with God that at the end of the day should be profoundly personal. *All Protestant Christians, including liberal ones, would agree with this principle!* Reformed Christians would emphasize however, that only Scripture is authoritative and must be the final arbiter of whether or not an experience is of spiritual value and offers truth we can rely on.

So we may conclude that there is a distinction to be drawn between an (1) *image and (2) its meaning or fulfillment:* One is provided as a *picture* oftentimes not to be taken literally—but at some time in the future its *meaning* should be clearly discerned and may be experienced firsthand. In other words, humans might not just 'see through' the image to visualize what the Prophet saw; we may also encounter *existentially* what he envisioned; in which case, the 'picture' will become our very own personal truth! Finally, language can meaningfully communicate the experience. Visions don't have to be truths that 'we can't find the words to express.'

Finally, there are images that we cannot be sure as to whether or not there will be a *literal interpretation* (or more precisely, a space-time experience that will 'mirror' the vision). We might interpret the Sun turning dark as a solar eclipse and a 'blood red moon' as meaning a lunar eclipse because the 'phenomenological'[ii] language finds a fulfillment in these literal and empirical events. However, what are

---

[i] This does not confirm that 'heaven,' 'angels,' or even God is real, but it does show why atheistic materialism is a very incomplete view of reality. At the very least, a 'mind' or spirit realm transcends our individual brain waves! The evidence for this reality is especially compelling.

[ii] *Phenomenology* is the philosophy of consciousness; it argues that our consciousness serves as a basis to understand the nature of human knowledge.

we to make of *"everyone hid in caves and the rocks of the mountains,"* and whether king or commoner, free man or slave, they were all calling out *"fall on us to hide us from the face of the One who sits on the throne and the wrath of the Lamb"* (verses 15 and 16)? There are many similar statements in Revelation that we could be *interpret figuratively*—and we should. However, there may also be *future fulfillment*, which may transpire in space-time, a fulfillment that ultimately has *a literal meaning as well*. Here is where restraint is appropriate, since we can't verify the manner in which these images will be fulfilled—perhaps for ages to come! To understand what the Scripture says we must be careful that we *read from* and not *into* the Bible with restraint when clarity is not clear-cut.[2]

In this instance, if we interpret the authors' prediction that all humankind will be frightened, suppressing their awareness of God in order to flee the terrors of judgment – *bulls eye* – we hit the target. For the same reason, we might go too far and predict that *to seek safety everyone will regress and become cave dwellers*! It is true that we would be interpreting the statement *literally*—but we would be very wrong to do so. Literal truth and 'the plain meaning' don't always mean the same thing.

The Language of Apocalypse

The most famous usage of the term *apocalypse* is the oft-repeated phrase 'the Four Horsemen of the Apocalypse' (Revelation 6:2-8), who bring war, famine, disease, and economic disaster upon the earth apparently as a prelude to the Second Coming of Christ. The most provocative use of imagery in apocalyptic literature deals with judgment, the wrath of God, and the torment of those who are enemies to the gospel of Christ.

The language of Revelation, Chapter 6, records the ride of these *Four Horsemen*, identifying the judgments they perform, promising retribution to those who murder "believers" because of their witness to Christ and God, and portending horrible natural disasters.

We read:

FIGURE 2 - ALBRECHT DURER, THE FOUR HORSEMEN
OF THE APOCALYPSE

¹ I watched as the Lamb opened the first of the seven seals. Then I heard one of the four living creatures say in a voice like thunder, "Come!"

² I looked, and there before me was a white horse! Its rider held a bow, and he was given a crown, and he rode out as a conqueror bent on conquest.

³ When the Lamb opened the second seal, I heard the second living creature say, "Come!"

⁴ Then another horse came out, a fiery red one. Its rider was given power to take peace from the earth and to make men slay each other. To him was given a large sword.

⁵ When the Lamb opened the third seal, I heard the third living creature say, "Come!" I looked, and there before me was a black horse! Its rider was holding a pair of scales in his hand.

⁶ Then I heard what sounded like a voice among the four living creatures, saying, "A quart of wheat for a day's wages, and three quarts of barley for a day's wages, and do not damage the oil and the wine!"

⁷ When the Lamb opened the fourth seal, I heard the voice of the fourth living creature say, "Come!"

⁸ I looked, and there before me was a pale horse! Its rider was named Death, and Hades was following close behind him. They were given power over a fourth of the earth to kill by sword, famine and plague, and by the wild beasts of the earth.

⁹ When he opened the fifth seal, I saw under the altar the souls of those who had been slain because of the word of God and the testimony they had maintained.

¹⁰ They called out in a loud voice, "How long, Sovereign Lord, holy and true, until you judge the inhabitants of the earth and avenge our blood?"

¹¹ Then each of them was given a white robe, and they were told to wait a little longer, until the number of their fellow servants and brothers who were to be killed as they had been was completed.

¹² I watched as he opened the sixth seal. There was a great earthquake. The sun turned black like sackcloth made of goat hair, the whole moon turned blood red,

¹³and the stars in the sky fell to earth, as late figs drop from a fig tree when shaken by a strong wind.

> *14The sky receded like a scroll, rolling up, and every mountain and island was removed from its place.*
>
> *15 Then the kings of the earth, the princes, the generals, the rich, the mighty, and every slave and every free man hid in caves and among the rocks of the mountains.*
>
> *16They called to the mountains and the rocks, "Fall on us and hide us from the face of him who sits on the throne and from the wrath of the Lamb!*
>
> *17For the great day of their wrath has come, and who can stand?"*

When we encounter words highlighting such frightening images, we are naturally inclined to argue that we shouldn't take such language literally. Primarily our reticence stems from our fear that *life as we know it couldn't continue.*[3] Furthermore, if such judgments happen, we certainly wouldn't want to be present when they did! No doubt, this is the reason why so many cannot delve into prophetic topics. Indeed, we should rate some portions of the Bible like a movie: *'For Mature Audiences Only. This Bible passage contains portrayals of graphic destruction and death.'*

Nevertheless, stepping away from the fearful consequences of possible literal fulfillment,[4] the interpretive question is, *"Should we just understand all of this language to be figurative? Should we try to understand the images just as a writer's attempt to frighten us into repentance? Could the sun really turn black like 'sackcloth and ashes?' (i.e., "black clothes"). Could the moon really 'turn to blood?'"* Let's look at the various types of images in order to see if there aren't some logical and scriptural guidelines we can follow.

Imagery and Literalism in Apocalyptic Literature

We read of the *Lamb.* We read of *white robes.* Some images are very traditional and their interpretation is without debate. The Lamb is certainly 'the lamb of God that takes away the Sin of the World.' White robes signify how the blood of the Lamb makes us pure. Other parts of the Book of Revelation explain these images too. Revelation 3:4, 5, we read *"But you have a few people in Sardis who have kept their clothes clean. They will walk with me, dressed in white, because they are worthy. Those who overcome will also be dressed in white. I will never erase their names from the Book of Life. I will speak of them by name to my Father and his angels."* Likewise, we can understand who the Lamb in Chapter 6 is, because He is discussed again in Revelation 7:15, *"And he said, 'These are they who have come out of the great tribulation; they have washed their robes and made them white in the blood of the Lamb.'"* One Bible verse helps explain another.

Other images are distinct to this passage. We could correctly interpret their meaning as *figurative images*—for instance, the red horse and the rider that takes away peace from the world. We read that this rider is given a large sword and he causes people to kill one another. Did the author see a red horse and a rider that brings war? No doubt he did. However, prophets always understood that the images they saw had meanings that extended beyond the literal. For instance, when we read about Daniel, we will constantly see him seeking to understand what the meaning of the vision or dream is—"what practical applicability should he take from the vision?" "How could the vision be realized in his 'space-time' experience?" Daniel is insistent that he understand this—and in most cases, God gives him the understanding he seeks.[5]

> **THE KEY POINT TO PONDER:**
>
> *Being a literalist has its dangers. Biblical truth isn't always presented in a literal manner. Even if we count ourselves a fundamentalist, we must be more sophisticated in our language when we describe our belief system. Interpreting the Bible literally can miss the point the Bible is making.*

That is why talking about *'taking the Bible literally' can be a troublesome way to explain how one understands what the Bible teaches.* A red horse and red rider could mean many things, but at least in this instance the author conveniently conveys his intended meaning. Here, the author communicates with this metaphor that humankind will experience war worldwide!

> ## Recapping the Key Points Covered in This Chapter
>
> - Bible prophecy is often equated with apocalyptic literature in the Bible – but prophecy is actually woven throughout its pages.
> - The *vision* is the primary means the Bible's prophets gained insights into God's plans for the future.
> - Today, we often assume visions are delusions.
> - But some modern psychology supports *the vision* as one means to uncover deep spiritual truths.
> - We must appreciate that prophetic revelations use both imagery and literal statements – to get it right, we must determine what the author was trying to communicate.
> - Taking everything literally can be as harmful as taking everything symbolically.
> - Symbolism is a powerful language that all timeless human literature uses; it isn't exclusive property of the Bible!

Technical Notes

[1] "Jung did not feel that experimenting using natural science was the best means to understand the human psyche. For him, an empirical investigation of the world of dream, myth, and folklore represented the most promising road to its deeper understanding." (See *en.wikipedia.org/wiki/Analytical_Psychology*).

[2] Scholars would explain that reading *from* the Scripture is known as 'exegesis;' reading *into* the Scripture is known as 'eisogesis.' The former is good, the latter not. Eisogesis is akin to making the Bible say what you want it to say, rather than letting the Bible speak for itself.

[3] As we will discuss later, there is a compelling argument the first six seals, including the Four Horsemen of the Apocalypse, actually occur during the church age (the two thousand years since the ascension of Christ up to today).

[4] The judgments of Revelation are fearful indeed. No commentator should downplay the fulfillment of these judgments in a real and frightening fashion. The Book of Revelation has a blessing for those who read it and look anxiously for Jesus' coming. However, it also holds a curse for anyone who adds to or takes away from the words of its prophecy (Revelation 22:18, 19).

[5] However, this isn't so with Daniel's final vision. Instead of explaining the vision, God soothes Daniel's consternation and assures Daniel that His (God's) words will become clear as the last days approach. *"He said, 'Go your way, Daniel, for these words are concealed and sealed up until the end time. But as for you, go your way to the end; then you will enter into rest and rise again for your allotted portion at the end of the age'"* (Daniel 12:9, 13, NASV).

DD#1 *When Literalism Can Harm Biblical Interpretation*

A red moon isn't literally red—it may appear to us on Earth that it is red. Language about consciousness and the structures of consciousness comprise a philosophy known as *Phenomenology*, founded by Edmund Husserl (1859-1938). Thinking in terms of how we perceive something may make a statement more or less literal depending upon how precisely we wish to define 'literal.' There is, as Immanuel Kant rightly said, a "thing in itself" and there is a "thing as we perceive it." Kant believed the human mind is locked into the latter. He built his philosophy upon this point.

The Christian philosopher Francis Schaeffer suggests that isn't the last word. God created our minds to be able to know and understand the world in which we live. He made the world and our knowledge of it 'coherent.' With faith in God, we break down the 'knowledge dilemma' posed by the skeptic David Hume (1711-1776) and Immanuel Kant. (See Schaeffer's book, *He is There and He is Not Silent*). In essence, our reason may be limited, but through faith our limitations can be overcome. In this way, faith and reason can work together.

However, evangelicals must be careful when classifying themselves as 'literalist.' For instance, if one reads the Gospel of John carefully, it is clear that one of the biggest challenges that Jesus faced in communicating with the religious leaders (and the common people) of His day was their blindness to the truth motivated by their 'literal' ways of thinking. Consider Jesus' statement to Nicodemus: *"'You must be born again.' Nicodemus couldn't help but ask, 'How can a man be born when he is old? Surely he cannot enter a second time into his mother's womb to be born!'"* (See John 3:1-12). Jesus was incredulous. Paraphrasing, Jesus says, "And you are a teacher of Israel? How can you be stumped by such simple Bible lessons? You don't understand earthly matters. How will you then understand heavenly things?" Assuredly, Jesus confounds 'the Jews' in the Gospel of John time and time again by His use of metaphors to describe Himself— *"I am the Light of the Word," "I* am *the Good Shepherd," "I am the Door,"* and especially, *"I am the Bread (manna) from Heaven."* We should recognize that there is much more in these metaphors than mere 'figures of speech.' There is 'reality' in these metaphors—indeed, there is 'ultimate reality!' And yet, taking them literally would be missing the point. It could even lead to spiritual death. We see this explicitly when many of his disciples 'just didn't get it.' *"'These are hard sayings' and from that day forward many of His disciples walked away"* (See John 6:66). Additionally, we should not overlook that Jesus taught in parables intentionally hiding His truth to those 'that did not have hears to hear.' The fact that his principal means to teach his followers was to utilize images and stories which he spoke in 'riddles,' should give us pause when we insist that Christian truth is fundamentally propositional. There is a measure of 'cloaking' the truth for a very specific reason. Proverbs 25:2 sets forth a strategic principle in biblical interpretation: *"It is the glory of God to conceal a matter, but the glory of kings is to search out a matter."* From this statement, we can conclude that it is the nature of God not to 'spell it out' for those that do not want to believe. For those that will take the time to search out a matter, they will be rewarded with understanding.

One of the weaknesses of the Reformed tradition is an overreliance upon stating beliefs propositionally. As we will argue later, Christian truths certainly must be stated propositionally. That is important. However, if that is the only way we experience the truth of our faith, we become overly cerebral, typically legalistic, and somewhat stiff and boring. Yes, the truth can be 'black and white,' but color is usually a more pleasing presentation! Reflecting upon C.S. Lewis' (1898-1963) *Chronicles of Narnia* and J.R.R. Tolkien's (1892-1973) trilogy, *The Lord of the Rings*, who among us believes that such fantastic tales and morality lessons, presented in these wonderful formulations, reduce our ability to understand the Bible's principles and its principal characters? Fantasy doesn't pretend to uncover intricate details and facts. Nevertheless, it does intend to disclose the value of ethics, morality, and faith. Pictures can be worth a thousand words!

DEEP DIVE NUMBER 1

DD#2 What It Means to 'Spiritualize' Scripture

To spiritualize a passage is to interpret its meaning in a manner different from what the author's 'plain meaning' may be. Conservative evangelicals treat a passage's interpretation this way when taking the author's words, 'at face value,' creates an inconsistency with their core doctrines. If this happens, they have only three choices: (1) Admit their understanding of doctrine is wrong; (2) accuse the writer of error, or (3) reinterpret his words as a metaphor, a figure of speech, or illustrative image.

For Covenantal theologians, options one and two are not acceptable. That leaves them with the third option. The questionable passage must be 'spiritualized' to be less than literal and considered subordinate to other scripture. The other position, 'literalness' would state that if the 'plain reading' of the grammar used indicates that the author was using a simile or metaphor, then we should understand his words analogically not literally. However, if the author was trying to convey details about an event he testifies occurred just as he said, we should regard the passage as historically accurate—or at least consistent with what the author says he witnessed. Likewise, if the author is conveying that he is *seeing the future* but is making an assertion *without* using a figure of speech, an image, or simile, we should also take his meaning to be 'taken literally.' That is to say, at some time in the future, we should trust that the events described must take place—that is to say, in the 'space-time' world in which we live.

DEEP DIVE NUMBER 2

DD#3 Universal Images Woven Throughout Scripture

Using elaborate images is hardly unique to Scripture. Symbols are used in all kinds of literature to convey truth and meaning. Symbols are a 'universal' language that Freud and Jung spent their remarkable careers documenting. Joseph Campbell (1904-1987), a follower of Jung, lent great credibility in his many works to the importance of myth, symbols, and images to communicate essential truths about spiritual things. His best known work, *The Power of Myth*, a book and PBS special in 1988 with Bill Moyers, explored many of these topics.

As stated previously, spiritual truth is meant to be more than just 'literal' statements or assertions about what we believe. Indeed, to awaken our 'inner spirits,' images can illumine truth in ways that propositional truths don't faze. The essence of the issue is that it is good to cast truth in both mediums.

What is intriguing about Scripture and its symbols or images, is the consistency in their use between so many authors. Scripture has its own 'universal symbology.'

A good example of this is the use of the term 'stone' and how it is a consistent metaphor for Jesus Christ in both the Old and New Testaments.

- Daniel's "stone cut without hands" (Daniel 2:45) crushes the other kingdoms of this world and becomes the Kingdom of God that never ends.
- The "stone which the builders rejected (Psalm 118:22) has become the chief cornerstone."
- In Isaiah 8:14, He is "a stone of stumbling for both houses of Israel" (they will fail to accept Him).
- In Isaiah 28:16, we see the prophet use the image to proclaim: "Therefore thus says the Lord GOD, "Behold, I am laying in Zion a stone, a tested stone, A costly cornerstone for the foundation, firmly placed. He who believes in it will not be disturbed."

These are only a few examples for this particular image as it is used throughout Scripture. In our study we will see this repetition of common images between Old Testament prophets and New Testament writers—common pictures that have consistent meanings. We will come across images like, 'the little horn,' beasts, time-periods, references to evil, symbols of new beginnings, etc.

DEEP DIVE NUMBER 3

Chapter 3: Advent and Second Advent

The Significance of the Parousia

Advent comes from the Latin word *adventus*, which means 'coming.' We refer to Christ's first coming to this earth as His first advent and His return to the earth a second time as His Second Advent. That there are two 'comings' is foundational to the Christian faith. Consider how important it must be since angels proclaim this fact at the very beginning of the Church. *"Men of Galilee,' they (the angels) said, 'why do you stand here looking at the sky? Jesus has been taken away from you into heaven. But he will come back in the same way you saw him go'"* (Acts 1:11).

The common word used for his Second Advent or 'Coming' is the Greek word, *Parousia* whose primary meaning is 'His coming' but which New Testament authors often use to relate events associated with the 'end times.' *Parousia* is hardly a seldom-used term. According to *Strong's Concordance,* the New Testament employs the term 24 times. The doctrine of the Second Coming (Parousia) is a foundation stone of the New Testament and thus Christian orthodoxy. To sidestep the Parousia, is *to disregard the foundation of our faith and to disrespect its founder!*

Christians have for centuries celebrated the season just before Christmas as 'Advent.' Many of us have lit the 'Advent Candles.' We know this celebration is due to the *first coming* of the Christ child. Without the 'first coming,' there would be no Christianity.

However, throughout the whole of the New Testament, Jesus' Second Coming is the most essential theme. It would be hard to maintain an authentically biblically Christian faith if we overlook or minimize the *Parousia* (or Second Advent). Indeed, the issue of whether there is only *one* Advent (the Jewish position) or *two* Advents (the Christian position), is of such primary importance that *we must examine it carefully the outset of this study.*

Why is this so important? As stated in the introduction, the primary subject matter of biblical prophecy is the *Messiah*. The Messiah, or *'anointed one,'* was an exclusively Jewish concept not like any other concept in the ancient world.

Yes, it is true that there were some notions of a 'go-between' in the divine-human relationship. There was the *'demiurge'* of Greek philosophy; the *logos* in one particular Jewish teacher's philosophy (Philo of Alexandria, a contemporary of Jesus), and the idea of a dying and rising God included in many Greek mystery religions that predate Christ (what C.S. Lewis called, ancient humankind's 'good dreams'). Still the precise nature of what the Jews meant by Messiah was unique, as we shall soon see.

It is also noteworthy to recall that the idea of Messiah was an expectation that virtually all Jews shared in the first century AD. Some scholars suggest there was a 'messianic' buzz in the air. Apocalyptic literature (as we just discussed) was commonplace. The people of Jesus' day were looking for Messiah.

It is at this very moment, when Jesus of Nazareth comes to the River Jordan and commences His ministry. The pop star of his day, John the Baptist, is even willing to step aside to proclaim this man Jesus, the *one* of whom the prophets spoke. From this point forward, all accounts assert He carries out the Mosaic Law flawlessly. His disciples testify that He can work miracles with a slight touch or a single word – He accomplished far more impressive works than any previous prophet of the Jewish nation did. Thousands, even in remote places, attend his religious lessons. His knowledge of the Scripture outstrips even the experts in the Temple. Perhaps *the anointed one*, predicted for over 1,000 years, *has* finally visited His people.

History is clear that despite all of these factors, the officials of Judaism label Him a religious imposter and a political enemy, threatening the security of the nation. What is their verdict? Jesus of Nazareth should be crucified with common criminals on the most fiendish device of torture humankind has ever produced. What's worse, they rush to judgment and carry out the death sentence as quickly as they can to avoid spoiling their sacred holiday feast.

How could this be? How could a nation that waited so earnestly for Messiah, find it easy to put to death the one who many regarded then (and millions more through the ages) as the fulfillment of messianic prophecies? It is one of history's greatest conundrums. Nevertheless, it is this conundrum, this puzzle, where Christianity finds its beginning.

This historical enigma yields a *truism* that by definition almost goes without saying. Nevertheless, to say it aloud and consider the implication is startling: *If the Jewish nation had accepted Jesus Christ as Messiah, there would be no Christianity.* History would be vastly different in more ways than we can possibly imagine. As one current-day comic expresses, "The mind reels!"

Obviously, if Judaism had embraced the Messiah in the first century, there would be no discussion about a 'second advent' today. *The Jewish decision to reject Jesus as Messiah fixes the origination point of Christian eschatology.* That's why it is important to understand how the Jewish concept of Messiah was distinct from what Jesus offered to the Jewish nation. When those of us who are Christian discern the truth about why the Jews rejected Jesus, we may be more than a little surprised. Furthermore, when we come to understand the implications and consequences of the Jewish nations' rejection of Jesus, *we then acquire a keen insight into the meaning and unfolding of the Kingdom of God in our day.*

Judaism and Its View of Messiah

There is a great chasm separating Judaism from Christianity. Distinguishing the meaning of the *Messiah* to Judaism from the Christian concept (developed from the teaching of Jesus and His apostles), is how we best can measure the *divide between these two great religions.*

Therefore, what does Judaism believe about the nature of its Messiah and his mission? The traditional portrait of the Jewish Messiah is a redeemer from the lineage of King David who saves the Jewish people and establishes *His Kingdom* upon the earth—or more precisely, reestablishes *David's Kingdom.* Moses Maimonides (1135-1204), one of the greatest Jewish sages living in the Middle Ages and whose teaching is considered a cornerstone of Jewish theology, stated this about the Messiah:

> The anointed King is destined to stand up and restore the Davidic Kingdom to its antiquity, to the first sovereignty. He will build the Temple in Jerusalem and gather the strayed ones of Israel together. All laws will return in his days as they were before: Sacrificial offerings are offered and the Sabbatical years and Jubilees are kept, according to all its precepts that are mentioned in the Torah. Whoever does not believe in him, or whoever does not wait for his coming, not only does he defy the other prophets, but also the Torah and Moses our teacher. For the Torah testifies about him, thus: *"And the Lord Your God will return your returned ones and will show you mercy and will return and gather you... If your strayed one shall be at the edge of Heaven... And He shall bring you"* (Deuteronomy 30:3-5).

So according to Maimonides, we can identify the Messiah because of five essential accomplishments, unique to His coming:

1. The Davidic Kingdom will be restored to sovereignty;
2. He will rebuild the Temple in Jerusalem;
3. He will gather the dispersed believers from all over the world (even if they are at the edge of Heaven!);
4. He will restore the sacrificial offerings; and lastly,
5. He will ensure that the Sabbatical years and Jubilees are kept.[1]

Maimonides does not appear to connect the so-called 'suffering servant' portrait of the Messiah, such as we see in Isaiah 53 or Psalm 22,[2] to the Messiah who brings political salvation to Israel. Likewise, the concept of redemption through the personal sacrifice of the Messiah for the individual is not considered. *Messiah is not the Lamb of God* – what the Messiah is to accomplish adds no meaning to the Jewish sacrificial system. Neither is there fulfillment in Messiah of what the Passover Lamb signifies. *Messiah is a redeemer of the nation—not the individual sinner.*

So does Maimonides consider Christ as a possible candidate for Messiah? Quite to the contrary—Maimonides believes the evidence clearly indicates Jesus *was not a messianic figure!* Not only should Jews reject Jesus because he failed to save the nation, Maimonides claims *Jesus contributed to its destruction.* Maimonides stated this specifically about Jesus:

> As for Jesus of Nazareth, who claimed to be the Anointed One and was condemned by the Sanhedrin. Daniel had already prophesied about him, thus: 'And the children of your people's rebels shall raise themselves to set up prophecy and will stumble.' Can there be a bigger stumbling block than this? All the Prophets said that the Anointed One saves Israel and rescues them, gathers their strayed ones and strengthens their *mitzvoth*[i] whereas this one caused the loss of Israel by sword, and to scatter their remnant and humiliate them, and to change the Torah and to cause most of the world to erroneously worship a god besides the Lord... [3]

Maimonides rejects Jesus (reason one), because he holds Him to blame for Judaism's devastation at the hands of Rome and because (reason two), *he has led the world to worship another God other than Yahweh*[4] (namely, Himself), something that his Jewish monotheism could not accommodate. Jesus' claim to be a divine figure, to be the Son of God, was *not* something that the Jewish scholars expected the Messiah to do *in either Jesus' time or today.* Indeed, as a modern commentator says "...the Talmud nowhere indicates a belief in a superhuman Deliverer as the Messiah."[5]

To reiterate: There are two Messianic assumptions Christians make that the Jewish faith denies: *First, the Messiah is not the fulfillment of the Passover—he is not the Lamb of God. Secondly, Messiah is not a divine figure. He is special, but He is not God!*

These presuppositions about Messiah (notwithstanding the travesty surrounding the death of Jesus Christ), are simply the criteria by which Judaism would judge whether any candidate fulfills the messianic profile. *The Jewish Messiah is profoundly distinct from what Christians believe the Messiah should be and do.*[ii]

---

[i] *Mitzvoth*, spelled *mitzvah* today, means "a Jewish religious duty or obligation, especially one of the commandments of Jewish religious law" (from the dictionary in Microsoft Word). In this context, it would mean one's ability to 'keep the law.'

[ii] Having said that, that doesn't mean Christians have to agree with their opinion!

Messiah—the Prophet Like Unto Moses

The Jewish concept of the Messiah is a 'prophet like unto Moses' (Deuteronomy 18:15-19), who will come after the Jews have been restored in their homeland following the great dispersion (Isaiah 11:11, 12 and in many other Scriptures). The Jewish people clearly understood this 'second Moses' to be a unique figure, most likely the very Messiah himself. This idea of a 'prophet like unto me' (i.e., Moses) was a traditionally held view among even the common people of Judea. We see this in the New Testament record. John in his gospel relates this story in the opening chapter regarding John the Baptist:

> *19 This is the testimony of John, when the Jews sent to him priests and Levites from Jerusalem to ask him, "Who are you?"*
>
> *20 And he confessed and did not deny, but confessed, "I am not the Christ."*
>
> *21 They asked him, "What then? Are you Elijah?" And he said, "I am not." **"Are you the Prophet?"** And he answered, "No."*
>
> *22 Then they said to him, "Who are you, so that we may give an answer to those who sent us? What do you say about yourself?"*
>
> *23 He said, "I am A VOICE OF ONE CRYING IN THE WILDERNESS, 'MAKE STRAIGHT THE WAY OF THE LORD,' as Isaiah the prophet said."*
>
> *24 Now they had been sent from the Pharisees.*
>
> *25 They asked him, and said to him, "Why then are you baptizing, if you are not the Christ, nor Elijah, nor the Prophet?"*
>
> *26 John answered them saying, "I baptize in water, but among you stands One whom you do not know.*
>
> *27 "It is He who comes after me, the thong of whose sandal I am not worthy to untie"* (John 1:10-27, NASV, emphasis mine).

Jesus confirms John the Baptist's testimony about himself later. Jesus indicates that *John was in fact Elijah* who was to come before the Messiah to prepare his way. *"He is the one written about in Scripture. It says, 'I will send my messenger ahead of you. He will prepare your way for you.'"* — (Jesus, quoting *Malachi 3:1*, in Luke 7:24-28). Likewise, Jesus in Mark 9:12 confirms John's ministry to be that of *Elijah*. Therefore, we see even in Jesus' affirmation of John the Baptist's *identity, a strong assertion of His own*. Jesus states clearly that He is the promised Messiah. John's ministry was preparing His (Jesus') way just as the prophets had foretold.

Why is it that the Jews do not relate the Messiah to redemption? Clearly, they believe the sacrificial system instituted by Moses to be adequate and complete. They see no 'typology' in the Temple sacrifices that foreshadow a future figure that would 'die for our sins.' To Judaism, this is simply unnecessary. The Messiah is to save the nation politically—Moses has provided the means to salvation through the Law and the Levitical Priesthood. The Messiah is to become King and reign on the Throne of David. The law says, *"Cursed is everyone who hangs on a tree."* (King James Version, Deuteronomy 21:23, Galatians, 3:13). From the Jewish vantage point, Jesus was accursed, not exalted!

However, what are we to make of the fact that the Jews were also unwilling to accept the claims of Jesus to be divine? Was the claim of divinity truly in the New Testament? *Wasn't the divinity of Jesus a later invention of the Christian Church?* This is a claim of many scholars in our day (and for the last century)—but it is actually quite far-fetched.[6] Even the earliest gospel written, the *Gospel of Mark*[7] contains many passages illustrating Jesus' own assertions of divinity. In addition to the implicit claim to be Messiah (from Jesus' reference to John the Baptist's mission that we just mentioned), I will point out but two more examples where Jesus stresses that the Messiah should be understood *as a divine being*.

Is the Messiah Divine?

Mark cites one of the most interesting when Jesus teaches the people in the Temple just before His death. Jesus poses a Scripture from a Psalm of King David that intimates that there was more to the Messiah that just being of the line of David:

> [35] *While Jesus was teaching in the temple courts, he asked, "How is it that the teachers of the law say that the Christ is the son of David?*

36 David himself, speaking by the Holy Spirit, declared:
" 'THE LORD SAID TO MY LORD:
"SIT AT MY RIGHT HAND
UNTIL I PUT YOUR ENEMIES
UNDER YOUR FEET." '

37 David himself calls him 'Lord.' How then can he be his son?"
(Jesus quotes Psalm 110:1 in Mark 12:35-37).

Jesus points out that David calls Messiah Lord, so clearly the Messiah has higher rank than David himself does. Additionally, the passage infers that the Messiah existed before David, which would make Him, at the very least, the Son of God or some manner of immortal being. It seems Jesus played a word game: He jibes the 'teachers' who denied the divine aspects of the Messiah. Why bother to do this unless you have a bone to pick with them? However, it was more than simply confounding his enemies. We know that Jesus selected this tactic because his adversaries took the Bible very seriously. If so, he points out to them how explicit the Scripture is regarding the fact that David has a Lord other than God. "The LORD said to 'My Lord'." Since this is so, they should understand the clear implications about the nature of the Godhead.

Another story related to Jesus' divine nature appears in Mark Chapter 9. We know it as the *'Transfiguration.'* On a high mountain in northern Israel, Jesus takes Peter, James, and John with Him separate from all the other disciples. We read:

2 Six days later, Jesus took with Him Peter and James and John, and brought them up on a high mountain by themselves. And He was transfigured before them;

3 and His garments became radiant and exceedingly white, as no launderer on Earth can whiten them.

4 Elijah appeared to them along with Moses; and they were talking with Jesus.

5 Peter said to Jesus, "Rabbi, it is good for us to be here; let us make three tabernacles, one for You, and one for Moses, and one for Elijah."

6 For he did not know what to answer; for they became terrified.

⁷ Then a cloud formed, overshadowing them and a voice came out of the cloud, "This is My beloved Son, listen to Him!"

⁸ All at once they looked around and saw no one with them anymore, except Jesus alone.

⁹ As they were coming down from the mountain, He gave them orders not to relate to anyone what they had seen, until the Son of Man rose from the dead (NASV).

Peter corroborated this witness of such a remarkable event again in the second of his own epistles[i]—confirming that the disciples didn't understand what they experienced on the mountain until after Jesus had risen from the dead. Once he did rise from the dead, this act solidified their belief, and the object of their faith was (perhaps for the first time), properly understood. Jesus was much more than a man—He was also God.

¹⁶ We did not follow cleverly invented stories when we told you about the power and coming of our Lord Jesus Christ, but we were eyewitnesses of his majesty.

¹⁷ For he received honor and glory from God the Father when the voice came to him from the Majestic Glory, saying, "This is my Son, whom I love; with him I am well pleased."

¹⁸ We ourselves heard this voice that came from heaven when we were with him on the sacred mountain." (II Peter 1:16-18, compare also with Mark 9:7 and Luke 9:35).

According to Peter (and to Mark, his secretary who created this gospel account), God's very own voice declares that *Jesus is the Son of God.* If Peter did not see it this way, why would Mark bother to include the story? Remember, Mark was writing within two decades of Jesus' death. If he got the facts wrong, many living witnesses could challenge his account.

In the final analysis, we can clarify the meaning of the theological matter by articulating a series of steps in a logical syllogism:

---

[i] Of course, Liberalism denies that Peter wrote this epistle. They prefer to assign it to a writer who believed he spoke in the 'spirit of Peter' so he could use his name to claim greater authority for what he wrote.

- One, if we were to concede that Jesus is the Messiah, He should be the most reliable source to explain His own identity and purpose;

- Two, He stated unequivocally in many places and ways that He is uniquely divine—indeed, He was crucified for blasphemy because He claimed to be God. Of course, Jesus even predicted His crucifixion on many occasions![i]

- Three, He also confirmed the greatest commandment of Moses: *There is only one God who must be worshipped* ("Hear O Israel, the Lord our God is One God and you shall worship Him only"—the *'Shema Yisrael'—the most important prayer of a Hebrew*);

- Therefore, if Jesus is in fact the Messiah, the nature of the Jewish God must be much different from what the Rabbis taught both then and now.

If this logic seems solid, it would appear that we must update monotheism to include *multiple persons within the Godhead.*

Although an admitted paradox, for Christians Jesus was both divine and human. This of course led Christianity to define the doctrine of the Trinity, which the Nicaean Creed formally articulated, it being the product of the Council of Nicaea in AD 325. There, by a vast majority, (not by a close vote as asserted in the movie, *The Da-Vinci Code* (2006)), virtually all agreed *Jesus was both fully divine and fully human.* The two natures were both present within Jesus. There was no "comingling"; nor did one nature diminish the other (see *"Deep Dive #5"* on page 52).

The Gap between the First and Second Advent

That being so, it still does not fully explain why passages dealing with the Messiah don't separate the two Advents and do obscure the long expanse of time between them. There is no easy way to 'decode' this looking only at the Old Testament. Once again, we must

---

[i] Indeed, the sacrament of the Lord's Supper was Jesus strongest statement that the 'old covenant' of Law had concluded, a 'new' covenant—through His blood—was now in effect. Happening at Passover, which was not coincidental, Jesus became the fulfillment of the Passover.

rely upon the Messiah Himself to divulge this and assure us that this paradox is part of God's plan.

We can see just how aware Jesus was of this issue. We read in Luke Chapter 4, when early in his ministry He comes back to his hometown, Nazareth in Galilee, and the presiding Rabbi asks Him to read the Sabbath Scripture "passage of the day:"[i]

14 Jesus returned to Galilee in the power of the Spirit, and news about him spread through the whole countryside.

15 He taught in their synagogues, and everyone praised him.

16 He went to Nazareth, where he had been brought up, and on the Sabbath day he went into the synagogue, as was his custom. And he stood up to read.

17 The scroll of the prophet Isaiah was handed to him. Unrolling it, he found the place where it is written:

18 "THE SPIRIT OF THE LORD IS ON ME,
BECAUSE HE HAS ANOINTED ME
TO PREACH GOOD NEWS TO THE POOR.
HE HAS SENT ME TO PROCLAIM FREEDOM FOR THE
PRISONERS AND RECOVERY OF SIGHT FOR THE
BLIND, TO RELEASE THE OPPRESSED,

19 TO PROCLAIM THE YEAR OF THE LORD'S FAVOR."

20 Then he rolled up the scroll, gave it back to the attendant and sat down. The eyes of everyone in the synagogue were fastened on him,

21 and he began by saying to them, "Today this scripture is fulfilled in your hearing."

Jesus stopped reading the passage abruptly without finishing the entirety of the second verse of Isaiah 61; for the remainder of that verse and the rest of this Chapter in Isaiah continue to discuss in detail what will happen when the Messiah sets up His kingdom upon the Earth. The crowd in the Synagogue erupted because of such an outrageous claim that He, Jesus, someone who they knew from the time of His childhood forward, could be their Messiah. We can safely assume that once again, Jesus knew exactly what he was saying. He was claiming to be the Messiah. However, because he stopped pre-

---

[i] An interesting coincidence if you believe it wasn't providential.

cisely halfway through the second verse, He was clearly intimating that He was fulfilling *only that particular portion of the Scripture in their hearing.*[8] Whether He would fulfill the remaining portion soon or much later depended upon the response He received from the Jewish nation.

To expand on this point: Evangelicals believe that Jesus was proclaiming that the Kingdom of God was at hand—but for it to come in full power, *the people who heard His teaching must repent and accept Him.* Without their acceptance, God through Christ could withdraw the offer to bring in the Kingdom.

The Kingdom: Contingent upon Israel's Acceptance?

Indeed, one of the great issues of interpreting the timing of the two Advents is whether what was called, *the last days and the events associated with it,* could have happened in the first Century if the Jewish nation repented, choosing to accept Jesus as Messiah. Is it possible that by repenting and accepting Jesus as Messiah, the Jews could avert the devastation of the Roman armies in 67-70 AD? Might Jesus have returned at that moment to rescue the Jewish nation and save the Temple? Might the Kingdom have come in 70 AD?

There is no question—the Apostles believed the Messiah would return in their lifetimes. There are many references by the authors of the New Testament to the fact that they were already living and writing *'in the last days'* (Hebrews 1:2, James 5:3, I Peter 1:20). *Perhaps the duration of 'the gap' between the two advents was contingent upon whether or not the Jewish nation repented.* If this is true, and many scholars believe it is, then this hypothesis addresses many questions about the apparent contradictions inherent in the Apostles using the term 'last days' when the last days so far have proven to be almost 2,000 X 365 days long! The Apostles may have been operating under the assumption that Jesus might return within a decade or two, IF the Jewish nation would repent and change its mind about Jesus, accepting Him as Messiah! *Therefore, we might rightly conclude that the Apostle's offense wasn't in missing the timing of Christ's return, but in being optimistic their Jewish brethren would repent!*

There seems to be a point where Jesus no longer assumes the Kingdom of God *will soon come upon the earth*. He accepts that the nation of Israel has rejected His offer to consummate the Kingdom. Jesus stated, *"O Jerusalem, Jerusalem, the city that kills the prophets and stones those sent to her! How often I wanted to gather your children together, just as a hen gathers her brood under her wings, and you would not have it! Behold, your house is left to you desolate; and I say to you, you will not see Me until the time comes when you say, "BLESSED IS HE WHO COMES IN THE NAME OF THE LORD!"'* (Luke 13:34, 35, NASV) Having accepted the fate of the nation of Israel, Jesus now predicts the complete destruction of the Jewish Temple and the dispersion of all of Judah! (See Matthew 24 and Luke 21) At the very end, in front of Pontius Pilot, He now indicates that *His Kingdom is not of this world*; if it were, His followers would fight! However, during His early ministry Jesus' message had been firmly 'the Kingdom of God is at hand.' It seems obvious that 'the message had changed.' What happened that caused this change? Simply this: *The nation of Israel had rejected their Messiah!*

Likewise, there seems to be a point where the Church stopped taking the message 'first to the Jews' and then to the Gentiles. One could argue that it was just before the destruction of Jerusalem. We know Nero beheaded Paul around 65 AD; he also crucified Peter not long afterwards. Prior to the destruction of Jerusalem, the Romans allowed the Christians to leave the city, heeding the warning of Jesus to flee to the mountains when armies surrounded the city. Certainly, by the time of the destruction of the Temple in 70 AD, the verdict was in. Israel had rejected the Messiah!

For the *preterist*, the Kingdom of God becomes the *Kingdom of Heaven*. The Kingdom is fulfilled in Heaven, where Christ reigns, and in the future *when the earth is recreated into the New Heavens and Earth*. Therefore, the emphasis has become 'the Kingdom of Heaven' – not the Kingdom on earth. To the *Covenantalist*, the Kingdom promise is *binary* – either it belongs to Israel 'corporately' or the Church, *but not both*. Israel rejected the Messiah, so God *turned away from Israel and to the Church* to fulfill His plan for the redemption of humankind. Therefore, all the prophecies concerning the earthly Kingdom are now 'history' metaphorically speaking. The

Kingdom of God has become the Kingdom of Heaven! While Israel's kingdom was to be 'an *earthly* reign,' the Church's kingdom, to be inherited at Jesus' future return, is to be 'heavenly' or 'beyond space-time – ushering us into eternity.'

In contrast, for the *Dispensationalist*, the Kingdom of Heaven is only an 'interim' state. Someday, the emphasis will switch back to earth and the literal meaning of the request from the Lord's Prayer will come to pass: *"Thy Kingdom come, they will be done, on earth, as it is in Heaven."* For Dispensationalism this contingency, the choice Israel made, can be seen as 'opening the door' to the possibility that the gentiles would now be brought into the fold. Indeed, the 'choice' was exactly the point: *The rejection of Israel has become the opportunity to save the gentiles!* From the Dispensationalist perspective, the Apostle Paul constructed his ministry around this very issue, which they regard as the thrust of book of Romans: *Israel's rejection opened the door to the gentiles.* Nevertheless, because the Dispensationalist doesn't believe it's 'either Israel or the Church', there is no reason why the plan of God can't shift back to the future earthly Kingdom centered on the nation of Israel. Thus, Paul's view, according to Dispensationalism, teaches that Israel will repent; then 'all Israel shall be saved.'

To recap: The nature of what the Jews believed about their Messiah was in conflict with the view of Jesus (and thus, Christianity). According to evangelicals, Jesus knew that there were two stages in fulfilling the Messiah's work – there would be two Advents of the Messiah. Admittedly, God hid this truth. The Prophets did not plainly disclose it in their writings. It took the Messiah himself to make this distinction clear and to reveal the 'gap' between the two Advents. Jesus was fully aware that He would not complete His mission all at one time. He must die and then be resurrected. His first Advent was to save the individual. His 'political' mission would be finished *sometime* in the future, 'in the Last Days.'

Therefore, what does the Second Advent mean? Depending upon your stance, the coming of the Messiah (again) would mean one of the following: The salvation of (1) the church (only) – the *Covenantalist* view; or (2) the nation of Israel – *Judaism's* view; or (3) both –

the position of *Dispensationalism*; or (4) *nothing newsworthy*, it is a figure or symbol representing *historical* events to Liberalism.

So to conclude, we must recognize that to appreciate the meaning of Christian eschatology, we first must realize that there is a dramatic difference between Judaism and Christianity in regard to *who the Messiah is* and His role *in securing the salvation of His people*. Judaism still awaits the 'first coming' of the Messiah; Dispensationalism believes that this 'blindness' will be removed as we draw closer to the Second Advent; the Covenantalist sees the blindness of the nation of Israel continuing – 'corporately' Israel will never be saved. Nevertheless, Covenantalists hope that individual Jews will awaken to the good news of Jesus Christ and accept Him *as Messiah despite their limited 'Jewish view' of what the Messiah is and what He is to do*. For Liberalism, it means nothing special. It is only a promise: We will ultimately succeed in our quest to Christianize the world.

Recapping the Key Points Covered in This Chapter

- The church begins with the promise of the return of Jesus Christ.
- Christians believe there are two 'comings' or Advents – first, Jesus' birth; second, Jesus' defeat of His enemies and establishment of His Kingdom.
- The Greek word, *Parousia*, used over two dozen times in the New Testament, means 'His coming.'
- The origin of Christianity is a conundrum – the rejection of Messiah Jesus by the Jewish nation is one of history's greatest enigmas.
- The Second Advent or *Parousia* could not be more foundational to Christianity's most essential meaning.
- Judaism has a very different understanding of what the Messiah is (his nature) and what he is to do (his role). The Messiah is not meant to be divine and isn't the 'lamb of God' – Judaism denies the 'typology' to which Christianity testifies.
- There is a 'gap' between the two Advents – but perhaps it didn't have to be the 2,000-year epoch (which it has been so far).
- The Kingdom promised by Jesus Christ may have been *contingent* – whether or not the first century Jews accepted Him may have established the ultimate timing for the 'return' of the Messiah and the inauguration of the Kingdom of God.
- The issue of 'contingency' regarding the Kingdom is a crucial distinction between Covenantalists and Dispensationalists.

Technical Notes

---

[1] The concept of the Sabbatical year was from the Law of Moses. It commanded that the land should lie fallow every seventh year to allow the soil to be restored. The Jews never honored this law. Likewise, the law of the Jubilee specified that every 50th year those who had enslaved themselves should be freed and the original owners of land that mortgaged their land to another (to pay debts), should be given the land back. In this way, land, the greatest of treasure in an agrarian economy, could be redistributed, keeping poor families from slipping into generational poverty. This law, likewise, was not honored. We will learn later of the 70 years of captivity in Babylon, a captivity the Jews experienced so that the land could finally enjoy its Sabbaths (490 years' worth) and enforce a Jubilee-like redistribution of the land.

[2] Psalm 22 reads like a newspaper account of the crucifixion of Christ. Isaiah 53 explains the meanings behind the sufferings of the Messiah.

[3] From Maimonides's *Treatise on Resurrection,* Trans. Fred Rosner – *See wikipedia.org/wiki/Jewish_messianism).* It is interesting that Maimonides blames Jesus as the reason for the destruction of the Jews in the first century, something that Flavius Josephus (AD 37-100), the noted Jewish historian of the first century, who was very close to the facts, did not do. To the contrary, it was the influence of Jewish nationalism as espoused by the Zealots and the Essenes that led to the Jewish War of 66-72 AD—a violent nationalism that Jesus repudiated. As Jesus told Pontius Pilate at his inquisition: *"My kingdom is not part of this world. If it were, those who serve me would fight. They would try to keep the Jews from arresting me. My kingdom is from another place"* (John 18:36).

[4] The contracted pronunciation of YHWH generally is pronounced Yahweh or sometimes Jehovah. Both relate to the four consonants that connote who God is as conveyed by God in the burning bush to Moses (Exodus 3:14). YHWH is generally translated LORD by most versions of the Protestant Bible.

[5] Cohen, *The Hereafter,* Chapter XI, The Messiah, p. 247. 1949. This is amazing for there are many Scriptures in the Old Testament that testify that the Messiah is divine and at minimum 'closely associated' as a begotten son is of his father. We can hear the words of Isaiah 9:6 from Handel's Messiah ringing in our ears: *"For unto us a Child is born, unto us a Son is given. And His name shall be Wonderful, Counselor, the Mighty God, the Everlasting Father, and the Prince of Peace."* The next verse indicates that He will reign on David's throne. It's a compelling portrait of the Messiah that calls Him, the *mighty God* and *Everlasting Father.* Clearly, these are the highest of divine appellations and certainly appear attributed to the Messiah.

[6] Bart D. Ehrman has authored over 20 books, most on the subject of 'alternative' or lost Christianities. Recently, with his book entitled, *Jesus, Interrupted* (he likes appropriating pop culture into his titles!), Ehrman is emphatic that New Testament claims' to Jesus divinity were not authentic to 'what Jesus said.' It takes a bona fide skeptic (or a biased scholar) to make such bold assertions! Ehrman is in fact a self-professed agnostic who is uncharacteristically certain about this element of the New Testament (that Jesus' claims are simply

an invention of the early church). Maybe he should be equally agnostic in making this claim! A fair reading of the four gospels by itself may not refute his assertion, but it creates a great deal of doubt regarding whether Ehrman as a scholar is fair-minded or simply disingenuous in order to be controversial. Skepticism cuts both ways!

[7] All scholars, both liberal and conservative, consider Mark to be the first complete gospel. Mark most likely wrote his gospel within 25 years of the death of Christ in 32 AD and was contemporary with thousands of still-living witnesses who could confirm or challenge his contentions.

[8] Jesus could have picked many other examples from the Old Testament for virtually every major prophecy about the Messiah would require the same clarification. Jesus would have to distinguish between what He would do at that time and what He would do after He had died on the cross for the sins of the world (including the Jewish people). His suffering and death would save Israel and all those before and after Him who would profess faith in Him, thus becoming the spiritual children of Abraham. Knowing this fate, the gospel says that He 'set his face like a flint' toward Jerusalem! A flint, as you may know, is a very hard rock that can make sparks fly and, from which, we can make other tools. Therefore, we see that Jesus was stubbornly steadfast to face His death – the threat of dying did not deter Him.

DD#4 *Why Judaism and Christianity Went Their Separate Ways*

Does God have distinct plans for Israel and for the Church? This matter historically is one of the most important questions in Christian theology. The story begins in the first century in the controversy among the Apostles regarding the relationship between 'Law and Grace.' Certainly, almost all of the first Christians were Jews and saw 'Christianity' as simply a fulfillment of Judaism, not as a separate religion. For this reason, there was little impetus to depart from the Mosaic Law, as well as Jewish tradition and custom, to guide daily living. Early Christians, being racially Jews, were not eager to cut themselves off from their families and communities.

However, over time, the emphasis changed to salvation through 'Grace' and not through 'Law.' Furthermore, as Christians were persecuted by the Jewish authorities (and since the Jewish religion had Roman sanction during this time), Christians were ultimately 'kicked out' of the synagogues. This dispute became even more pronounced with the ministry of Paul 'to the gentiles' and the rampant growth of gentile believers in the new faith. Finally, when Polycarp was put to the stake, Irenaeous indicates that 'the Jews' helped gather kindling for the fire 'as was their custom.' Hatred grew between Jews and Christians. So it became inevitable that Christians saw themselves separate. No longer were religion and race connected.

Thus, it became the orthodox position of the Catholic Church (and the early reformers like Luther and Calvin) that the Church did in fact replace Israel.

After almost 1,700 years, some Christian theologians expressed the view that God continued to have a special purpose for Israel (that He had not forsaken His chosen people). We begin to see this contemplated in the 17th and 18th centuries (notably with Jonathan Edwards in America). Early Christian support for the Jewish people began with the teachings of Darby (c. 1820's) and was reinforced as the Zionist movement began to 'get legs' in the last two decades of the 19th century. With the Balfour Declaration and the retaking of Jerusalem by the English (from the Ottoman Turks) in 1917, it became a reasonable possibility that the Jews could once again become a nation.

Finally, On May 14, 1948, by the vote to partition Palestine at the U.N., that possibility became a reality.

DEEP DIVE NUMBER 4

DD#5 What the Council of Nicaea Was Actually Charged to Do

Ironically, Church Bishops convened the Council of Nicaea to define how *Jesus was Man*, much more than how He was God. In the fourth century AD, this debate created a great schism in the Church and the Emperor Constantine wanted the matter resolved.

The Gnostics, like the orthodox Christians, believed Christ was fully divine. They tried to solve the logical dilemma of a being that was both human and divine by stating that *His humanity was illusory or that His human and divine natures were distinct and separate.* The Gnostic gospels of Thomas, Peter, Mary Magdalene, and Judas, all promote this spirit-matter dichotomy.

The so-called 'New School' wisdom in the 21st century (notably, (1) Bart Ehrman, Professor of Religious Studies at North Carolina University and (2) Elaine Pagels, Professor of Religion at Princeton), appear eager to give Gnosticism a new and sympathetic hearing—a second chance on the mistaken basis that orthodoxy emphasized Jesus' divinity while Gnosticism asserted his humanity. This is only partially true. Indeed, for the most part, the reality is exactly the opposite! Gnosticism either expressly *denies Jesus' humanity* or *distances it from His divinity.* This separation is important to the Gnostic because the body, being material, is *contemptible.* The Gnostic imperative was spiritual; thus, the Gnostics radically *differentiated Jesus' divine being from his human being.*

We see this in the assertion that Jesus didn't suffer on the cross. Because Gnostics contend there was a separation between the man Jesus and the spirit being, Christ, the spirit being could, as stated in one of the Gnostic gospels, sit on top of the cross observing Jesus and his enemies, laughing at those who thought he suffered! In contrast to orthodox history (and in contradiction to the 'spiritual emphasis' of the Gnostic gospels), is the inflated relationship between Jesus and Mary Magdalene. The Gnostic gospels infer a romantic affection between the two. However, did Jesus and Mary really have a sexual relationship? From this supposition stems the fantastic plot line of *The Da-Vinci Code* (Dan Brown)—that Jesus and Mary had a daughter who began a 'royal blood line' of Jesus. Based upon this historically unsupportable conclusion, the modern advocates for Gnosticism (Pagels and Ehrman) suppose that an authentic assertion of Jesus' humanity is thereby vouchsafed. But given other human qualities emphasized in the gospels (Mark's gospel in particular, e.g., Jesus gets tired, gets angry, 'feels compassion' for the 'rich young ruler,' and 'sleeps on a pillow' in the back of the boat during a storm), one wonders why this 'reach' seems necessary.

It is curious that this proposed sexual relationship is emphasized at all given the inherent conflict with the 'metaphysical' assertions supposedly uttered by Jesus. These 'Gnostic sayings' reinforce the negative aspects of material existence! We are wont to ask: "Which is most important to the Gnostic position? Is it the mystical state-ments (purported to be Jesus' words) which emphasize the value of 'knowledge' enabling us to transcend our physical existence? Or is it the 'carnal knowledge' the Gnostic infers (that Jesus and Mary shared) which proves He was human?" At best, it seems that these different assertions contradict one another. At worst, it appears cer-tain that the Gnostic Jesus didn't practice what he preached!

Putting it in modern conversational terms, the real question at Nicaea was, "We all agree that Jesus Christ is in some manner 'equal to' God, but how could He then still be human?" The Nicaean Creed affirms both natures, without contradiction, without separation and without comingling.

Related to this topic is the issue of the *Virgin Birth*. Ironically, once again, the virgin birth of Christ was a creedal assertion of the early church emphasizing that the divine Christ was born of a human woman. Thus, he was *fully human* as well as fully divine. This point is made clearer when we couple it with the Gnostic contention that matter was corrupted and incapable of hosting the spirit or divine nature of the Christ. Furthermore, given the second-place status of women at that time, why would the Gnostic Christ originate from any *woman*? Wouldn't it be more in keeping with the Gnostic 'Christ' and his assertions about the nature of reality if he wasn't born of a human woman at all? For the Gnostic to be consistent, he should answer, "Yes!" That is why early Christians asserted the virgin birth so strongly. Ironically, in the 20th century, the virgin birth had the opposite meaning – it sought *to underscore the divinity of Jesus*. It was one of the 'fundamentals' proclaimed by J. Gresham Machen and other conservative theologians early in the 20th century. Conse-quently, if one understands the historical context, it throws a very different light on the subject! The Virgin birth means that Jesus was both human and divine!

DEEP DIVE NUMBER 5

Chapter 4: Amillennialism and Millennialism

In Eschatology, the Millennium is the Watershed Issue

In the Book of Revelation, Chapter 20, we find the single location in Scripture where the Kingdom of God is associated with the *Millennium*. Interestingly, the author doesn't actually utilize this term. John, the 'Revelator,' does state however, no less than *five* times, that this period endures for exactly 1,000 years; and it is here that we read that the Christian Messiah, Jesus Christ is the ruler of this earth for this thousand-year time period:

> *¹ And I saw an angel coming down out of heaven, having the key to the Abyss and holding in his hand a great chain.*
>
> *² He seized the dragon, that ancient serpent, who is the devil, or Satan, and bound him for a thousand years.*
>
> *³ He threw him into the Abyss, and locked and sealed it over him, to keep him from deceiving the nations anymore until the thousand years were ended. After that, he must be set free for a short time.*
>
> *⁴ I saw thrones on which were seated those who had been given authority to judge. And I saw the souls of those who had been beheaded because of their testimony for Jesus and because of the word of God. They had not worshiped the beast or his image and had not received his mark on their foreheads or their hands. They came to life and reigned with Christ a thousand years.*
>
> *⁵ (The rest of the dead did not come to life until the thousand years were ended.) This is the first resurrection.*
>
> *⁶ Blessed and holy are those who have part in the first resurrection. The second death has no power over them, but they will be priests of God and of Christ and will reign with him for a thousand years.*

Despite the fact that the Bible never describes the Kingdom of God as a 1,000-year period anywhere else in Scripture, the notion of the 'Millennium' is at the center of the debate between Protestants concerning the exact nature and extent of the Messianic Kingdom.

For Protestant *Liberalism*, the Millennium and the New Jeru-salem are both pictures of a utopian society, achieved someday through the efforts of the Church of Jesus Christ, once it can apply the principles that Jesus Christ taught his followers, and after it can successfully evangelize the masses around the world. The key to world peace and prosperity, for the Liberal, is that we must have re-gard for one another the way that Jesus asserted in His ministry. There is no reason today to believe that God will intervene in some dramatic and supernatural way to alter radically the course of histo-ry. Resorting to a belief in a literal and historical return of Jesus Christ (and any sort of theocracy achieved through His physical presence upon the earth), is an old-fashioned and ultimately mislead-ing way of thinking. Liberalism associates symbology with the Apo-calypse in most every detail. The Millennium is no different. It too is a symbol. As such, scholars know this position as 'post-millennial.' Jesus Christ reigns today through His church. The millennium is now.

Evangelicals interpret this passage quite differently. Some see this passage conveying clearly that there will be believers resur-rected who will rule with Christ for 1,000 years (verse 4). The rest of the dead (those who died and didn't believe in Jesus Christ), will not be resurrected until *after* the 1,000 years have ended. Only *those who believe* are resurrected 'in the first resurrection'[i] to serve in the role of 'priests and kings' ruling alongside Jesus Christ. This role of 'priests and kings' will include believers from 'the church age' (from Pentecost to the Rapture) and those who were martyred during the *Great Tribulation*. These 'saints' will establish a true theocratic gov-ernment with Christ ruling over all the peoples of the world.[1]

This Millennium doctrine is a core position of *Dispensational Theology,* one of the two principal schools of thought in Evangelical-ism today (and for the past 170 years).[2] Most authors who follow this school of thought point out that the future Millennium is assurance that humankind will not destroy the world by during *the Great Tri-*

---

[i] The second resurrection is only for those who will be judged and whose names will not be found in the Book of Life. This occurs at the end of the Millennium according to Revelation. It coincides with the 'Great White Throne Judgment.'

bulation period or at the *Battle of Armageddon*. Likewise, Dispensationalists are quick to point out that the return of Christ is NOT the end of the world, but in fact, the beginning of a world filled with peace and fulfillment. Additionally, those who believe in a literal Millennium see humans surviving the Great Tribulation and re-populating the earth (overcoming the decimation of the population during the Tribulation period).

In contrast, the other principal school of Evangelicalism, *Covenantal theology* teaches that *this* Scripture, unlike most, cannot be taken literally—it must be understood in a symbolic way. There will be a future rule of Jesus Christ, but this reign will not transpire in history; *history must end (space-time) before eternity begins*. Therefore, to make it especially clear for evangelical Christians, whether Dispensational or Covenantal, the issue isn't if there will be a Kingdom, but (a) *whether or not that Kingdom occurs in history (space-time) or (b) whether it commences when the earth is recreated afresh and space-time is concluded.*[3]

Many theologians describe Covenantal believers as '*a-millennialist*' (no millennium). This is not because they don't believe in the Kingdom, but *because they do not believe it will be a literal 1,000-year reign of Christ on this earth*. Those, whose names God has written in, what the Bible calls, the 'Book of Life,' will reside with Christ and one another in the New Jerusalem (see Revelation 21). We could consider this position consistent with many reformed thinkers including John Calvin and Martin Luther. It also may be the position of many Catholics. (See **Figure 3** on page 64, for a graphical overview of the three essential protestant perspectives on the Millennium).

As we can see, the three different Protestant camps have extremely different interpretations of the idea of the Millennium. This subject constitutes the dividing line or *watershed* between their respective viewpoints. Not only that, but because the concept of Millennium is synonymous with how the Kingdom of God is 'implemented' in heaven or on earth, we see the most telling expression of what each believes the Kingdom of God means. *That's why most scholars have historically classified or categorized different perspectives on eschatology principally based upon how they interpret the meaning of the Millennium.*

The Millennium Is Equivalent to the Jewish Concept of Kingdom

The promise of such a Kingdom is at the core of the Old Testament prophecies regarding the Messiah. One of the classic prophecies about the future Kingdom is from the Prophet Isaiah.

> *² In the last days*
> *the mountain of the LORD's temple will be established*
> *as chief among the mountains;*
> *it will be raised above the hills,*
> *and all nations will stream to it.*
>
> *³ Many peoples will come and say,*
> *"Come, let us go up to the mountain of the LORD,*
> *to the house of the God of Jacob.*
> *He will teach us his ways,*
> *so that we may walk in his paths."*
> *The law will go out from Zion,*
> *the word of the LORD from Jerusalem.*
>
> *⁴ He will judge between the nations*
> *and will settle disputes for many peoples.*
> *They will beat their swords into plowshares*
> *and their spears into pruning hooks.*
> *Nation will not take up sword against nation,*
> *nor will they train for war anymore. (Isaiah 2:2-4)*

Likewise, in the latter chapters of Ezekiel (40-48), is an account of what appears to be a very detailed description of the establishment of the Kingdom in Israel. We read about:

- How the promises made to Israel will be fulfilled,

- What the far reaching boundaries of its lands are and how they will be partitioned among the 12 tribes of Israel;

- How its Temple worship and its religious ceremonies will be reinstated.

The details are explicit and the descriptions are amazing. The Dispensationalist would affirm that these sections of Scripture are awaiting fulfillment. The Covenantalist would consider them obsolete since the Jews rejected Jesus Christ in the first century AD.

Tabernacles: Convocation of the Millennium?

Some Jewish *Christians* believe that the beginning of the Millennium may coincide with a particular Jewish Holiday, *The Feast of the Tabernacles*. The beginning of the Millennium will follow within a matter of weeks from Christ's Second Advent (also conjectured to occur on another Jewish holiday, a future *Yom Kippur)*. To understand why, we need to understand what the word 'tabernacle' actually means. In essence, tabernacle means, 'to dwell with.' The Gospel of John states that when the Logos (Jesus) came to earth that He literally *"tabernacled"* with us (John 1:14). Likewise, in the Millennium, *God will dwell with His people.* These are the exciting final words in the Book of Ezekiel. In fact, Ezekiel says that the Lord renames the city of Jerusalem, "The LORD dwells there!" Thus, we may regard the Millennium as the fulfillment of the Feast of Tabernacles.[4] (See **Figure 8** on page 176 for a discussion on all the Jewish Holidays and their possible fulfillment in Christianity).

Prophecy as a Cornerstone of Biblical Inspiration

As we mentioned, the Liberal interpretation of the Kingdom of God is often called *'post-millennial'* and its adherents believe that the 'Church Age' (the time in which *we live now*), is in fact the Millennium. The Church, acting as Christ's agent upon this earth, brings the world to salvation without a physical return of Christ. The 'social gospel' movement in America during the 1920's and 30's, was inspired by this optimistic conviction. Most groups today, who consider themselves Christian 'social activists,' fall into this category.

The post-millennial position calls for a 'spiritual' or figurative interpretation of Scripture. We should remember that Christian Liberalism grew out of the 19th century *Enlightenment* where human *reason* was exalted, and is therefore *skeptical regarding any and all supernatural occurrences.* Since predictive prophecy denotes an ability to 'see the future' (a *supernatural* ability), Liberalism generally dismisses *predictive prophecy* out of hand.

So then, is *prophecy* without value to the Liberal? No – prophecy has a place but it is valued for a different purpose than predicting the future. To Liberalism, prophecy is *'forth telling'* instead of *foretelling*. *Forth telling* is the role that Prophets played in which they called the King and the people to account. As such, we could understand *forth telling* as 'confrontational preaching.'[i] While there is no debate among Christians that the Prophets of old fulfilled this role, the issue is, can one truly revere the Bible while implying that its predictive parts are either inaccurate or intentionally misleading (reporting history as if it is predicting it)?[ii] Didn't the Prophets indicate that they were predicting the future? Were they that mistaken about their message, their role and their capabilities?

The prophets of the Bible predict very specific events including the rise and fall of nations, future Kings who would rule, and calamitous events that would befall the Jews if they did not repent and turn to God. It is a fundamental assumption of orthodox biblical interpretation that the Prophets *did have the ability to see the future.* However, is this predictive ability true to the facts? Does it make any real difference if it isn't factual? There is no question that to the ancient Hebrews it made all the difference in the world. Throughout the Protestant tradition too, believing in prophecy and its fulfillment was a litmus test of orthodoxy.

We read that the rule for testing a Prophet was whether the thing that the Prophet said *actually happens.* This is how a Prophet authenticated his stature as a Prophet. If what he said failed to happen, he must not be a Prophet! (See Deuteronomy 18:22). The Bible expects its prophets to be 100% accurate, 100% of the time. *Foretelling* was the way the Hebrew people knew they could trust their Prophets to speak the Word of the Lord. Furthermore, we could legitimately go so far as to say, *"If a Prophet failed to predict the future, he couldn't comment on the present!"* Perhaps to its detriment, Liberalism doesn't take this very important aspect of the 'credential-

---

[i] Or as one preacher that I used to work for said, "It's *'meddlin'*."

[ii] Ironically, most prophetic passages are written in past tense because the prophets are so certain that the events they are describing will come to pass; it is as if they have already happened. But this is quite different than reporting history and conveying you are predicting it.

ing' of Prophets seriously. It also connects to its view that religious truth isn't subject to verification in any historical or scientific way.

According to evangelicals, if we dismiss the predictive abilities in the prophets of the Bible, then our method of interpreting Scripture becomes exclusively symbolic or *existential* (see *"Deep Dive #16"* on page 301 for an extensive discussion of this topic). No longer do creeds or statements of what we believe affirm truth the same way they did for early Church. We then have a Bible that is little more than Jewish history, poems, and myths. As some conservative theologians would say, we have denied *the possibility of propositional[i] truth.* When it comes to making statements regarding what is true or false in Christianity, logically the liberal position is very cautious. Not that Liberalism would try to be this consistent with its core principle of 'knowing;' for liberal churches still repeat creeds like 'The Apostles Creed.' Nevertheless, it doesn't appear to be for the same reason as the church has historically practiced.[5]

While Liberalism today isn't rigorously against the possibility of miracles, it denies predictive prophecy nonetheless. Consequently, *I will have little to say about 'Liberalism's viewpoint' on many of the subsequent individual topical subjects—because these topics are simply irrelevant.* So let's be clear: Liberalism asserts apocalyptic authors wrote their literature principally for the early Christians as a means to *bolster their faith.* Its value to us today is only inspirational, symbolic, or allegorical. *Liberals don't sanction predicting the future.* Therefore, Liberalism doesn't see future fulfillment in the predictions of *Daniel* or *Revelation* except in the 'existential' sense of encouraging confidence and reassurance in daily living.

After the Millennium

What comes after the Millennium? According to Revelation, a series of events bring history (more specifically the concept of space-time) to its conclusion.

---

[i] Microsoft Word's dictionary defines the word *propositional* in the context of philosophy as "a declarative sentence that expresses something that can be true or false."

- First, a future battle occurs; God "looses" (releases) Satan from 'the bottomless pit.' The Devil stirs up the nations of the world against Christ and His government one final time. However, this battle is apparently very short-lived. Satan is defeated in 'the final battle' and throne into the Lake of Fire.

- Secondly, the next event is the *great white throne judgment*—a judgment meant only for the resurrected unbelievers. All will stand before the Throne of God and those whose names are not found written in the Book of Life are judged[6] are cast into the Lake of Fire along with the Antichrist, the False Prophet and Satan.

- Finally, God recreates the heavens and earth—He brings forth a New Jerusalem consisting of fantastic dimensions as the final residence for all believers.

John doesn't supply many details about the New Jerusalem. However, what he does say is the stuff that hymns "are made of." The New Jerusalem is composed of precious stones and the streets are paved with gold. We don't need the sun because henceforth, the glory of God provides all the light we need. In its center is the *Tree of Life* and the waters of the *River of Life* (see Revelation 21, 22).

Recapping the Key Points Covered in This Chapter

- Revelation 20 describes a 1,000-year period of peace, the Millennium. The actual term isn't used. Nevertheless...
- The key issue, the 'watershed' to distinguish between the three Protestant points of view, is the matter of the Millennium.
- Covenantalism *is 'a-millennial'* because it rejects a literal 1,000 reign of Jesus upon earth in 'space-time.'
- Dispensationalism is 'millennial;' it believes in the literal 1,000 year reign of Jesus Christ seated on a throne in Jerusalem, ruling the world.
- Liberalism believes the Second Advent may have already come symbolically – the Millennium may refer to the Church carrying out Christ's work in the world today. It is 'post-millennial.'
- Liberalism sees prophecy more as 'preaching' than 'predicting.'
- However, Prophets in the Old Testament had to prove themselves by making "verifiable" predictions– the standard was 'accurate 100% of the time.' Liberalism disregards this point in assessing the value of prophecy. It also challenges the Bible's prophetic approach to validating 'religious truth' ('truth' equates to making a statement that can be proven true or false).

Technical Notes

¹ It merits mention that John states five times in this passage that the period of time is 1,000 years. As an author, if you repeat yourself so many times it is usually significant – you are trying to make your position crystal clear. This is akin to the author of Genesis stating thrice that God created man in a single verse. Genesis 1:27, "So God created man in his own image, in the image of God he created him; male and female he created them." The author was making a point: God created men and women! Likewise, the Kingdom is 1,000 years long.

² This also should be understood to refer to the Kingdom of God or Kingdom of Christ. It is understood to be the same as what the prophets of the Old Testament meant by the Messiah ruling on the earth, establishing His Kingdom and ruling from the Throne of David. John Nelson Darby began teaching this system of biblical interpretation regularly when he moved to Plymouth around 1840 and founded the Plymouth Brethren primarily as a reaction to what he considered a dead Church of England that offered no true spiritual benefit. According to Tim LaHaye in his book, *The Rapture*, Darby had his theology well formulated much earlier, including the Rapture. Documentation shows that it was 'in place' at least by 1827.

³ As stated before, Jews who believe in a future Messiah likewise see references to the Kingdom of the Messiah and its fulfillment associated with some sort of national or political salvation of the nation of Israel in space-time. This is one of the key reasons that Dispensationalists have a strong affinity for the nation of Israel—they share a similar understanding of the Kingdom 'on this earth.' Other key reasons will be discussed later.

⁴ The study of the Hebrew holidays and their possible fulfillment in the Life of Christ provides deep insights into prophetic topics, helping to both clarify and confirm them. We take up this theme in the later section, ***The Voice of God – The Trumpet of God?*** on page 229.

⁵ Which is to say, the church affirmed specific orthodox beliefs to avoid confusing its understanding of its faith with conflicting assertions of the 'heterodox.' Liberals will say creeds to link its congregation with Christian history primarily for inspirational purposes. Technically, a Gnostic affirmation of faith, in the liberal church, might be just as valuable if the congregation is 'encouraged.'

⁶ At this judgment, everyone that stands before the White Throne is a nonbeliever. Readers should note that those who have professed faith in Christ are not to be judged here for Christ, by His death, bore our sins and therefore, we are freed from being judged—our names ARE FOUND in the Book of Life. Therefore, Christians do not appear at the 'Great White Throne Judgment.' However, there is a judgment for believers known as the 'Judgment Seat of Christ,' where our works are judged and rewards given. But our salvation is not in question. *"Each man's work will become evident; for the day will show it because it is to be revealed with fire, and the fire itself will test the quality of each man's work. If any man's work which he has built on it remains, he will receive a reward. If any man's work is burned up, he will suffer loss; but he himself will be saved, yet so as through fire."* (II Corinthians 3:13-15, *NASV*).

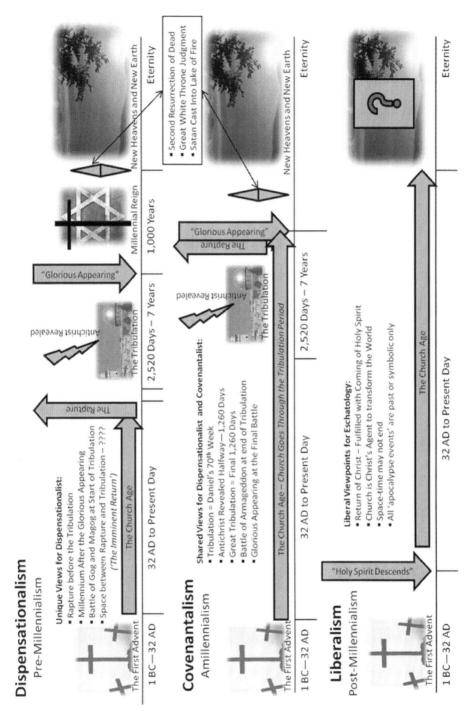

FIGURE 3 - SUMMARY OF MILLENNIUM VIEWPOINTS

Chapter 5: Antichrist

The Many Names of the Antichrist

He is known by many names in the Bible: The *Beast* of Revelation, the *Little Horn* of Daniel 8:9, and the *Man of Sin* in Paul's epistles (II Thessalonians 2:3).[i] Only in the epistles of John is he referred to as *"the Antichrist."* The most explicit characterization of the Antichrist and his reign is the apocalyptic description of him in Revelation Chapter 13:

> *¹ And the dragon stood on the shore of the sea. And I saw a beast coming out of the sea. He had ten horns and seven heads, with ten crowns on his horns, and on each head a blasphemous name.*
>
> *² The beast I saw resembled a leopard, but had feet like those of a bear and a mouth like that of a lion. The dragon gave the beast his power and his throne and great authority.*
>
> *³ One of the heads of the beast seemed to have had a fatal wound, but the fatal wound had been healed. The whole world was astonished and followed the beast.*
>
> *⁴ Men worshiped the dragon because he had given authority to the beast, and they also worshiped the beast and asked, "Who is like the beast? Who can make war against him?"*
>
> *⁵ The beast was given a mouth to utter proud words and blasphemies and to exercise his authority for forty-two months.*
>
> *⁶ He opened his mouth to blaspheme God, and to slander his name and his dwelling place and those who live in heaven.*
>
> *⁷ He was given power to make war against the saints and to conquer them. And he was given authority over every tribe, people, language and nation.*
>
> *⁸ All inhabitants of the earth will worship the beast—all whose names have not been written in the book of life belonging to the Lamb that was slain from the creation of the world.*
>
> *⁹ He who has an ear, let him hear.*

---

[i] Chuck Missler in his video on *The Antichrist: the Alternate Ending*, states that there are 33 names for the Antichrist in the Old Testament and a dozen in the New.

> *10 If anyone is to go into captivity,*
> *into captivity he will go.*
> *If anyone is to be killed with the sword,*
> *with the sword he will be killed.*
>
> *This calls for patient endurance and faithfulness on the part of the saints.*

The Antichrist Revealed

The descriptions from these passages assert that the Antichrist will make verbal war on the God of Heaven and His Saints—thereafter he will reign conspicuously as Antichrist for 42 months. The Antichrist reveals himself when he exalts himself above all others, speaking blasphemies against God. The Antichrist will be seen ruler of the entire world (he is given authority *"over all people, nations and tongues"*)—although his leadership will not be equally regarded in some regions (particularly, the Far East).[1] All of the world will worship him whose names are *not* found in the *Lambs' Book of Life*. Daniel, Chapter 11 confirms and enhances this description is with these words:

> *36 "The king will do as he pleases. **He will exalt and magnify himself above every god and will say unheard-of things against the God of gods.** He will be successful until the time of wrath is completed, for what has been determined must take place.*
>
> *37 He will show no regard for the gods of his fathers or for the one desired by women, nor will he regard any god, but will exalt himself above them all.*
>
> *38 Instead of them, he will honor a god of fortresses; a god unknown to his fathers he will honor with gold and silver, with precious stones and costly gifts.*
>
> *39 He will attack the mightiest fortresses with the help of a foreign god and will greatly honor those who acknowledge him. He will make them rulers over many people and will distribute the land at a price.*
>
> *40 "At the time of the end the king of the South will engage him in battle, and the king of the North will storm out against him with chariots and cavalry and a great fleet of ships. He will invade many countries and sweep through them like a flood.*

⁴¹ He will also invade the Beautiful Land. Many countries will fall, but Edom, Moab and the leaders of Ammon will be delivered from his hand.

⁴² He will extend his power over many countries; Egypt will not escape.

⁴³ He will gain control of the treasures of gold and silver and all the riches of Egypt, with the Libyans and Nubians in submission.

⁴⁴ But reports from the east and the north will alarm him, and he will set out in a great rage to destroy and annihilate many.

⁴⁵ He will pitch his royal tents between the seas at the beautiful holy mountain. Yet he will come to his end, and no one will help him.

Paul confirms the same in II Thessalonians, Chapter 2:

³ Don't let anyone deceive you in any way, for (that day will not come) until the rebellion occurs and the man of lawlessness is revealed, the man doomed to destruction.

⁴ He will oppose and will exalt himself over everything that is called God or is worshiped, so that he sets himself up in God's temple, proclaiming himself to be God.

Paul points out that his crowning moment of contempt will be when he asserts in the very Temple of God that *he is God.* He will cause worship in this *third Temple* in Jerusalem to cease (which assumes the Temple will be rebuilt and the Judaic rites of the Temple will be reinstated prior to this event—a key topic later in our study, see **Chapter 21: The Third Temple** on page 193).² He will cause an *abomination that makes desolate*—dishonoring the 'Holy of Holies' (the innermost portion of the Temple), by setting up an image of himself asserting that he and he alone is to be worshipped.

The Relationship between Antichrist and Satan

Most scholars have suggested that the Antichrist is actually *Satan incarnate* (incarnate: 'in the flesh'), as Christ was God incarnate. Most dispensational commentators (Lindsey, Jeffrey, and others), believe that the key event causing the world to believe in the divine nature of the Antichrist will be an apparent resurrection *from a fatal head wound* (Revelation 13:3). The world will witness this amazing event. It will lend credence to his claim of divinity.

With these descriptions laid out before us, can we attempt to identify who the Antichrist is before he reveals himself?

There is probably no topic of predictive prophecy more popularly debated than the identity of the Antichrist. More discussion on this subject is evident in books, videos, and web sites than any other prophetic topic. *Naming the Antichrist* is indeed something of a sensationalist endeavor to which many commentators fall prey. However, from the 'Church Fathers' forward, Christian scholars have cautioned against focusing too much on this—believing it is ultimately unprofitable and harms the credibility of predictive prophecy. We should be mindful that while there have been hundreds of accusations since the first century AD; it goes without saying, that every single one has been wrong! In addition, we should remember that guessing wrong 100 times doesn't make guess 101 any more likely! See the deep dive below, ***Avoiding Attraction to the Antichrist Issue,*** page 78).

The Apostle John indicates that while there will be a future literal figure known as the Antichrist—the spirit of Antichrist is already in the world—indeed, there are many Antichrists. Certainly, in the 16th through 19th centuries, Protestants saw Catholics so antagonistically that the Pope was regarded as 'the Antichrist' (Martin Luther certainly regarded him as such) and the Catholic Church, 'Mystery Babylon.' The many horrific inquisitions and persecutions exacerbated this view, although a fair reading of history would acknowledge such actions were not completely one-sided.[3]

Nevertheless, the Bible does tell us that when he reveals himself, the Antichrist identity will be obvious to those that are watchful. Paul indicates that there will be no question about this event and triggered by it, the beginning of the period known as the *Great Tribulation (see **Chapter 22: The Tribulation and the Great Tribulation** on page 201).

[1] *Concerning the coming of our Lord Jesus Christ and our being gathered to him, we ask you, brothers,*

> *² not to become easily unsettled or alarmed by some prophecy, report or letter supposed to have come from us, saying that the day of the Lord has already come.*
>
> *³ Don't let anyone deceive you in any way, for (that day will not come) until the rebellion occurs and the man of lawlessness is revealed, the man doomed to destruction.* (II Thessalonians 2:1-3).

Apparently, the church at Thessalonica was worried that they were already in the Tribulation period. Someone had written a letter to the church, purporting to be Paul the Apostle, and indicating that this was so. However, Paul points out that the revealing of the Antichrist will be *the* event that signals the Great Tribulation has begun. In other words, we can't be living in the Great Tribulation unless this revealing has already happened. He says:

> *⁵ Don't you remember that when I was with you I used to tell you these things?*
>
> *⁶ And now you know **what is holding him back**, so that he may be revealed at the proper time.*
>
> *⁷ For the secret power of lawlessness is already at work; but the **one who now holds it back** will continue to do so till he is taken out of the way.*
>
> *⁸ And then the lawless one will be revealed whom the Lord Jesus will overthrow with the breath of his mouth and destroy by the splendor of his coming. (II Thessalonians 2:5-8).*

The Restrainer: Who Is He?

Another matter of great debate is whom this *'restrainer'* is (the one who now holds that power of sin back). Some suggest it is the rule of law—that 'the lawless one' won't appear until the rule of law is totally disregarded. Some have proposed that the Roman Empire was this restraining influence. However, the most common evangelical position (in Dispensationalism), is that the restraining influence is in fact *Jesus Christ through the power of the Holy Spirit who indwells every believer.* This restraining influence must be removed from the earth before the Antichrist can take control. As such, this is another traditional argument for the *pre-tribulation Rapture of the church*—removing the Holy Spirit from the earth by removing all believers at that single moment in time—a removal that will be sudden and dramatic just as was the Holy Spirit's first coming at Pentecost (you can read the full account in Acts Chapter Two).

In the sections ahead, we will offer much more detail about the Antichrist, his program, the characteristics of his rule, and his impact upon the world's political, financial, and religious systems. In this section, we have pointed out that the *revealing of the Antichrist will be unmistakable*: The Antichrist will be known as 'the man of sin' and will be known principally by His claim to be God (Daniel 11:36, 1 Thessalonians 2:3). He will appear in the Temple of Israel, announce that he is divine, and make the sanctuary desolate most likely by placing an image of himself in the 'Holy of Holies.' (We will discuss the **abomination of desolation**, below).

Later, we will learn that he will commence his authoritarian rule from a power base composed of former nations within what was the Roman Empire. In addition to this political control, he will dominate the world's financial systems through a mechanism he implements known as **The Mark of the Beast** (see page 145). Lastly, he will control world religion through the powerful association with yet another 'beast' known as the **False Prophet** (see page 115). There are many other fascinating characteristics to consider – but they are likely to generate even more controversy and speculation.

The Antichrist and Islam

In the 21st century, due to the horrific rise of Islamic terrorism, there is a strong movement afoot today to see Islam as the religion of the Antichrist and the Antichrist Himself, an 'Assyrian' (which was the ancient name for the peoples living in the 'fertile crescent – Lebanon, Syria, and Iraq). Islam's hated for Israel and the United States certainly marks it as a target for 'antichrist consideration.'

Books by Walid Shoebat, who claims to be a former Islamic terrorist (*Why I Left Jihad* and *God's War on Terror*), Joel C. Rosenberg (*Epicenter 2.0* and *Inside the Revolution*, Tyndale House Publishers), and Joel Richardson (*Antichrist: Islam's Awaited Messiah*, Winepress Publishing), have all emphasized the possibility that Islam is the power base for the Antichrist. Therefore, the nations comprising the makers of the covenant with Israel could be 10 nations from the 'eastern leg' of the old Roman Empire – that is, those nations that are in conflict with Israel today. (We will discuss this scenario further in *Chapter 17: Mystery Babylon,* see page 153). Could Iraq recover with the help of the US and become the wealthiest nation in the region? Could it lead the other nations to make a seven-year 'peace treaty' with Israel? Could the Antichrist be a future leader of Iraq or Syria that leads this effort? It does seem like a possible scenario, given enough time for the tempers to cool in the Middle East and for Iraq to get to its legs. Mark this one down for further analysis in the months and years ahead!

Recapping the Key Points Covered in This Chapter

- The Antichrist has many names in the New Testament.
- The revealing of the Antichrist is very clear-cut – in the Jewish Temple in Jerusalem, he will proclaim that he is God and everyone must worship him.
- There is a direct relationship between the Antichrist and Satan – just as Jesus was 'God incarnate,' the Antichrist is to be inwardly 'possessed' by the devil.
- The Antichrist is restrained from appearing today.
- The nature of this 'restrainer' is the subject of debate.
- In the 21st Century, the prospect now looms large that the Antichrist may be closely associated with Islam.
- Could we see Iraq emerge as a central player in the final 'end times' scenario?

Technical Notes

¹ This becomes evident when we read that 'the Kings of the East' (Revelation 16) march to Israel, 200 million strong, to war against the Antichrist—a war whose combatants turn to fight a different enemy when Christ and His Saints return in glory at the Battle of Armageddon. *"It was also about these men that Enoch, in the seventh generation from Adam, prophesied, saying, 'Behold, the Lord came with many thousands of His holy ones, to execute judgment upon all'"* (Jude 1:14, 15, *New American Standard Version-NASV*).

² Rebuilding the Temple is not underway or publicly contemplated by Israel at this time. Rumors persist that the Temple will be rebuilt but Moslem holy places (the Dome of the Rock and the al-Aqsa Mosque), continue to occupy the Temple Mount blocking the path for this to occur. This is taken up later under the topic, **The Third Temple**. Covenantal theology tends to discount the probability that a Third Temple is important to the working out of eschatology, as they tend to interpret the Third Temple symbolically as the Temple of the Body of Christ that he rebuilt in three days at His resurrection.

³ John Calvin is sometimes accused however rightly or wrongly of the death of many in Geneva. In 1553, the Geneva governing council burned Michael Servetus at the stake after condemning him. However, we should note that Catholics as well as Protestants considered him a heretic (see Wikipedia.org/wiki/Servetus). In Prophecy studies, we label the Protestant view that Catholicism is the Antichrist as '*Historicism*.' In contrast, we label those who believe most prophecies are yet to be fulfilled as '*Futurists*.'

Chapter 6: Abomination of Desolation

The Meaning of Abomination

The term *abomination* is generally associated with idols. Idols are an 'abomination to the Lord' because they falsely take the place of God who cannot be illustrated, explained, or substituted by any created thing—God demands that no image of Himself be made or worshipped.

Daniel, John, Paul, and Jesus himself all specifically discuss this event. Jesus says, *"So when you see standing in the holy place 'the abomination that causes desolation,' spoken of through the prophet Daniel—let the reader understand"* (Matthew 24:15). Jesus was quoting Daniel 9:27, *"And he shall confirm the covenant with many for one week: and in the midst of the week he shall cause the sacrifice and the oblation to cease, and for the overspreading of abominations he shall make it desolate, even until the consummation, and that determined shall be poured upon the desolate"* (King James Version).

What is the Nature of the Abomination?

The traditional view by students of prophecy is that Satan 'possesses' the *Antichrist* in the spiritual realm the way that demons are thought by many to possess humans. However, the *abomination that makes desolate* may also refer to the fact that Satan incarnates himself, even mingling the DNA of 'angels' and humans, thus creating an 'abomination'—an unnatural hybrid between human and angel (albeit a fallen angel—Lucifer). This is the supposition of movies like *Rosemary's Baby (1968)* and *The Omen (1976)*.

There are a number of commentators today who believe that the 'angel-human' hybrid which is in fact spoken of in Genesis 6 and Numbers 13 should be taken literally (the so-called 'Nephilim' who were created when angels—the Sons of God—'lay with women' begetting a race of giants).

Although supposedly wiped out during the flood of Noah, the Nephilim reappear and apparently live in the land of Canaan when Moses sends Joshua and eleven others to 'spy out the land.' The giants were so frightening that the Hebrews wouldn't go forth to take the land—leading to their wilderness wandering for forty years. *"There also we saw the Nephilim (the sons of Anak are part of the Ne-philim); and we became like grasshoppers in our own sight, and so we were in their sight"* (Numbers 13:33, *NASV*).

When one studies the conquest of the Holy Land, it appears that vir-tually all the tri-

> **THE KEY POINT TO PONDER:**
>
> *Many commentators suppose that virtually all the tribes of Canaan were 'infected' with the genetic re-engineering carried out by the fallen angels. Could this be the reason God ordered the killing of every man, woman, and child?*

bes of Canaan were 'infected' in this way. Could that be the reason that God gave such stringent orders to 'destroy every man, woman, and child'? Many scholars in recent books think so. God was react-ing to the 'genetic reengineering' of the fallen angels![i] For God to keep the promise made to Adam and Eve in the Garden of Eden (a *future child of Eve would redeem humankind* – see Genesis 3:15), humankind could not be tainted with some other form of DNA. Mes-siah must be purely human.[1]

We read of David and Goliath during a turning point in the battle between the Philistines and the Hebrews almost 450 years later. We also gather that Goliath was a descendant of the Nephilim.[ii]

The Bible says that Goliath had six fingers on each hand and six toes on each foot and was six cubits (roughly ten and a half feet tall) linking him to the number 666 and thus making him a type of Antichrist. Therefore, it follows that David's defeat of Goliath is seen as a fore type of Israel's victory over the Antichrist at the Battle of Armageddon (see *Chapter 7: The Battle of Armageddon* on page

---

[i] Which is the same phenomenon Eric Van Däniken (and those who believe in the 'alien astronaut theory') recounts in his books. Of course, in his theory *the 'actors' are aliens instead of angels.*

[ii] Obviously, the Nephilim were relentless—you can throw rocks at them, but they weren't so easy to eradicate!

81 below). *"Make it desolate"* would infer that what was once alive and vibrant became *void without life*. The Holy of Holies once contained the Glory of God (also known as the *Shekinah* presence of God), which resided above the 'mercy seat' between the Cherubim on the Ark of the Covenant. Even after the Ark was no longer present in the Holy of Holies—which seems to be the case prior to the destruction of the Temple by Nebuchadnezzar in 586 BC—many believed that God's presence still resided there. However, once in the presence of the abomination, God could no longer remain and the Temple became *desolate*—devoid of the presence of God.

Desecrations of the Temple in Times Past

This act has already occurred at least two times in the history of the Jewish Temple. The most famous instance was with the destruction of Jerusalem in 70 AD by the Roman general (and soon be to Caesar) Titus, son of Vespasian. With the destruction of the Temple, the daily sacrifice was stopped and the Holy of Holies desecrated.

However, this same thing occurred almost 240 years earlier in 167 BC when Antiochus IV Epiphanes, a descendent of Alexander's general Seleucid, set up a stature of Zeus in the Holy of Holies stopping the daily sacrifice as part of a failed attempt to Hellenize the Jews.

This latter incident is associated with the Jewish Holiday of *Hanukkah*. The 'Holiday of Lights' celebrates the cleansing of the Temple after the Jewish revolt led by Mattathias, a Jewish priest,[i] defeated Antiochus Epiphanes and won freedom for the Hebrews (a freedom which they enjoyed for 102 years until the Roman General Pompey conquered the Holy lands in 63 BC).[2] This story is told in the *Books of the Maccabees* (an apocryphal book not included in the Protestant Bible). Interestingly, Antiochus chose the title *Epiphanes* as an assertion of divinity meaning 'God manifest' (the first Hellenist leader after Alexander to do so). Claiming divinity, Antiochus appears in some respects to fulfill the prophecy of the Antichrist who asserts his equality with God.

---

[i] Judas Maccabeus was also the leader from a military perspective.

One of the key prophetic issues between Christian 'camps' is whether Antiochus is the *one and the only* Antichrist or whether there is yet to be another. Dispensational scholars acknowledge that the *'abomination of desolation'* has already occurred twice (at least twice, see endnote reference), yet they maintain it will occur a third time when the future Antichrist reveals himself.

Were Daniel's Predictions Really Predictions?

In stark contrast, modern liberal scholars believe that the writing of the Book of Daniel was at the time concurrent with the war of the Maccabees and was reporting history as if it was prophecy. One key reason may be because the predictions about the 'king of the east' (the Seleucids) and the 'king of the south (the Ptolemy's) recorded in the latter part of the book of Daniel were so precise in detail after detail that it simply had to be history. No prophet could be that accurate![i] Therefore, from the liberal Christian perspective, Antiochus is the Antichrist of Daniel, with no future fulfillment forthcoming.

However, this appears to overlook some important facts. Although Antiochus appears to be the subject of many of the predictions in Daniel, there are elements of the description that clearly were not fulfilled by him. We should consider the future *seven-year covenant* with Israel (which Antiochus did not make), and the fact that *Messiah Prince must come before the final desecration* (Messiah came after, not before Antiochus).

Furthermore, we may see this view discredited when we note that the Book of Daniel was included in the *Septuagint*, a Greek version of the Hebrew Bible, compiled, and published by 70 Jewish scholars for King Ptolemy II of Egypt around 285 BC (roughly 120 years before the events prophesied by Daniel).[3]

Finally, Daniel's prediction about the appearance and death of the Messiah in 32 AD appears to provide strong support to the evan-

---

[i] Note how this is a "case-in-point," which illustrates that liberal scriptural interpretation invalidates the stated—or traditional—author and his associated 'supernatural' story elements (i.e., *his claim to predict the future*).

gelical view that predictive prophecy is essentially telling us *what will happen in the future.*

Recapping the Key Points Covered in This Chapter

- An abomination is an unnatural creation or blasphemous event – the Bible could mean either or both in this case.
- Genesis 6 speaks of fallen angels fathering offspring that were a mixture of human and angel 'DNA' – the 'Nephilim.'
- There is much more to the story of the Nephilim that traditional teachers don't teach.
- The event of desecrating the temple has already happened at least twice, perhaps three times.
- Liberals debate evangelicals on when the author of the Book of Daniel wrote the book, and whether the author was in fact Daniel himself.
- Liberalism believes that the Book of Daniel wasn't prophecy but history in the guise of prophecy. Why? Perhaps because it is so accurate in describing the Seleucids and the Ptolemy's (successor rulers to Alexander the Great), Daniel's writings obviously couldn't be predictions!
- Even if this portion of the book was history, the prediction of the First Advent still holds, forecasting both the death of the Messiah and the destruction of the Temple by the very same people.

Technical Notes

---

[1] This is why, in the Genesis account, God selected Noah and his children to carry on the human race. The writer indicates that Noah was "pure in all his generations." According to this theory, *his DNA hadn't been tainted!*

[2] In addition, it appears that Pompey may have desecrated the Temple yet another time upon conquering Jerusalem, killing many of the Levitical priests inside the Temple itself.

[3] However, some scholars question the timing of the translation of Daniel. Wikipedia states: "Modern scholarship holds that the LXX was written during the 3rd through 1st centuries BC. But nearly all attempts at dating specific books, with the exception of the Pentateuch (early- to mid-3rd century BC), are tentative and without consensus."

DD# 6 Avoiding Attraction to the Antichrist Issue

When one studies the literature of the apocalypse, the most frequent subject matter to which authors devote themselves is the identity of the Antichrist. In searching for books at Amazon.com with the name *Antichrist* in the title, after reviewing over 800 different titles (more still to review), I stopped counting. Most of these have been penned in the past 20 years. A few were classics but most were 'contemporary' speculation on whether Ronald Reagan, George Bush, the Pope, or some other modern day public figure is Antichrist. *I rest my case!*

We should be cautious, for the study of the Antichrist identity, particularly the attempt to determine exactly who he is before he reveals himself, may be *akin to the fascination that one can stumble into with the occult and Satanism.* C.S. Lewis wrote about this phenomenon and taught us that Satan can trick us in two very different ways, but both are equally effective. First, he can do his best to hide himself and convince us that he does not exist. Alternatively, Satan can cause us to become so fascinated by his activities and awful character that we overlook the fact that he is unworthy of such attention.

Perhaps the other problem with too much focus on who the Antichrist might be, is the eagerness to label a world leader whom we dislike with this moniker. What better disparagement can we ascribe to someone than to suggest that he is the son of the devil? However, whatever the value one perceives in hanging this label on someone, he or she does pay a big price. The 'name caller' experiences a considerable loss of credibility in making such a public statement. It is not wise for anyone, much less a professing Christian, to go down this path.

The Antichrist will be a dominating and powerful figure—but ultimately, his reign will be for a *very short time indeed* (only 42 months), and then he will be defeated and according to the Book of Revelation, *"thrown alive into the lake of fire."* We read:

"And the beast was seized, and with him the false prophet who performed the signs in his presence, by which he deceived those who had received the mark of the beast and those who worshiped his image; these two were thrown alive into the lake of fire which burns with brimstone." (Revelation 19:20, *NASV*).

Accordingly, we do well to avoid too much 'Antichrist speculation' no matter how fascinating it may be.

DEEP DIVE NUMBER 6

Chapter 7:   The Battle of Armageddon

Armageddon Defined

Armageddon is the English transliteration of the Hebrew, *Harmegiddo*, or the *Mountain of Megiddo*. Megiddo is in northern Israel. Megiddo is a valley with a wide and expansive plane that even Napoleon, upon seeing it, declared could indeed contain all the armies of the world at one time.[1] It is destined to be the final battle of the Apocalypse according to Revelation 16:16. We read:

> *12 The sixth angel poured out his bowl on the great river Euphrates and its water was dried up to prepare the way for the kings from the East.*
>
> *13 Then I saw three evil spirits that looked like frogs; they came out of the mouth of the dragon, out of the mouth of the beast and out of the mouth of the false prophet.*
>
> *14 They are spirits of demons performing miraculous signs, and they go out to the kings of the whole world, to gather them for the battle on the great day of God Almighty.*
>
> *15 "Behold, I come like a thief! Blessed is he who stays awake and keeps his clothes with him, so that he may not go naked and be shamefully exposed."*
>
> *16 Then they gathered the kings together to the place that in Hebrew is called **Armageddon** (Revelation 16:12-16).*

Clarifying the Two Battles of the Last Days

The battle will take place at the culmination of the period known as 'The Great Tribulation' (also **Daniel's 70th Week**, see page 97), spoken of by John the author of Revelation, Paul the Apostle, and most of the great prophets of the Hebrews, notably including Daniel, Jeremiah, Joel and Zechariah.

Oftentimes, this enormously important battle is confused with the **Battle of Gog and Magog** (which we will look at next—see page 85). Should these battles be identified as one and the same? Most scholars say 'no' for two principal reasons: (1) The participants in the battle are different and the (2) circumstances immediately after each battle strongly convey that these battles happen at different times.

Ezekiel tells us that after the Magog war, Israel will bury the dead for seven months and burn the weapons used by Gog and Magog for seven years (Chapter 39:9-11). John tells us that after the battle of Armageddon, Christ immediately returns to set up his Kingdom on the earth. The Battle of Gog and Magog involves the hordes of peoples immediately north of Israel, along with Libya, Ethiopia, and Persia (Iran). The Battle of Armageddon is fought between the Antichrist and nations from all over the world (Isaiah 13:4, Zechariah 12:3), 'headlined' by the Kings of the East who bring an army of 200,000,000 through Asia (and across the Euphrates River, the ancient dividing line between the 'east' and the 'west').

One subject debated for several decades has been whether any nation could field an army of 200 million. Back in the 1970's, supposedly China boasted that it could achieve this astronomical number.[i] It was used as a data point to validate interpreting this passage literally. It does seem remarkable that John selected this number given the population of the entire world in the first century was likely less than this number. Could we see this fulfilled in the future?

Armageddon and the Battle for Jerusalem

Oftentimes, we use Armageddon as a descriptive noun to include all the events associated with the Apocalypse. However, we should remember that primarily, Armageddon is a *place*. Specifically, it is a mountain (Megiddo) and a valley (also known as Jezreel) near the Sea of Galilee and Nazareth—Jesus' hometown (in fact, while growing up Jesus could look across the valley from his village every day). Secondly, as we stated above, Armageddon is a specific battle at the very end of the **Great Tribulation** period (see page 201). At its conclusion, Jesus Christ returns to the earth. John states:

13 The sixth angel sounded his trumpet and I heard a voice coming from the horns of the golden altar that is before God.

14 It said to the sixth angel who had the trumpet, "Release the four angels who are bound at the great river Euphrates."

---

[i] If memory serves, Hal Lindsey made this point in *The Late Great Planet Earth.*

15 And the four angels who had been kept ready for this very hour and day and month and year were released to kill a third of mankind.

16 The number of the mounted troops was two hundred million. I heard their number. (Revelation 9:13-16)

There are passages elsewhere that talk of the battle for Jerusalem and seem to imply that *these are part of the same conflict.* We read the words of Zechariah from His book, Chapter 12:

3 On that day, when all the nations of the earth are gathered against her, I will make Jerusalem an immovable rock for all the nations. All who try to move it will injure themselves.

4 On that day I will strike every horse with panic and its rider with madness," declares the LORD. "I will keep a watchful eye over the house of Judah, but I will blind all the horses of the nations.

5 Then the leaders of Judah will say in their hearts, 'The people of Jerusalem are strong, because the LORD Almighty is their God.'

6 "On that day I will make the leaders of Judah like a firepot in a woodpile, like a flaming torch among sheaves. They will consume right and left all the surrounding peoples, but Jerusalem will remain intact in her place.

7 "The LORD will save the dwellings of Judah first, so that the honor of the house of David and of Jerusalem's inhabitants may not be greater than that of Judah.

8 On that day the LORD will shield those who live in Jerusalem, so that the feeblest among them will be like David, and the house of David will be like God, like the Angel of the LORD going before them.
9 On that day I will set out to destroy all the nations that attack Jerusalem.

The prophet indicates that all the nations of the earth, not just the list from Ezekiel 38, are gathered against Israel. He indicates that Jerusalem (i.e., Israel) will be seen as *the* enemy that all the nations agree must be wiped off the map. However, Ezekiel indicates that the issue of Jerusalem will be like an immovable rock.[2] Is this not a clear and unprecedented fulfillment of biblical prophecy in our day?

Next, we read that God confuses the nations and blinds them. Furthermore, we learn that Messiah will first 'secure Jerusalem' (verses 7 and 8), before going north to fight His enemies at Armageddon. This coincides with Zechariah's later prophecy that says that Christ will return first on the Mount of Olives and His 'touch-down' will cause a great earthquake, the mount itself to split, and waters to gush forth forming new rivers, one to the Mediterranean Sea and the other running to the Dead Sea. We read from Chapter 14 of Zechariah:

> *4 In that day His feet will stand on the Mount of Olives, which is in front of Jerusalem on the east; and the Mount of Olives will be split in its middle from east to west by a very large valley, so that half of the mountain will move toward the north and the other half toward the south...*

> *5b Then the LORD, my God, will come, and all the holy ones with Him!*

> *6 In that day there will be no light; the luminaries will dwindle.*

> *7 For it will be a unique day which is known to the LORD, neither day nor night, but it will come about that at evening time there will be light.*

> *8 And in that day living waters will flow out of Jerusalem, half of them toward the eastern sea and the other half toward the western sea. (NASV)*

Zechariah proclaims that this day will be a day of darkness that will remain dark until evening and then light will return.

Isaiah 13:10, confirms the same phenomena:

> *The stars of heaven and their constellations*
> *will not show their light.*
> *The rising sun will be darkened*
> *and the moon will not give its light.*

When the Lord returns, whom Zechariah calls *'my God'* (Note: he identifies the Messiah as God), all of his holy ones will come with him. These holy ones are the previously raptured believers (the 'Saints'). These Saints have been raptured either immediately prior to their return—the *Covenantal* position, or at least seven years earlier—the *Dispensational* position).

Importantly, Zechariah 12 adds that it is at this time that the residents of Israel will no longer reject Jesus as their Messiah. We read,

> *10 "And I will pour out on the house of David and the inhabitants of Jerusalem a spirit of grace and supplication. They will look on me, the one they have pierced, and they will mourn for him as one mourns for an only child, and grieve bitterly for him as one grieves for a firstborn son.*
>
> *11 On that day the weeping in Jerusalem will be great...*

At this time, Israel will understand that their Messiah is in fact Jesus Christ. After 2,000 years of denial, they will embrace the one who previously they rejected!

Recapping the Key Points Covered in This Chapter

- We often equate *Armageddon* with 'the end of the world' but it is actually a *place* – a mountain and valley in northern Israel.
- There are two major battles that occur in the 'latter days' – the Battle of *Gog and Magog* and the Battle of *Armageddon*.
- There is confusion about whether these are different conflicts or are the same.
- The combatants and circumstances appear to be different, so most Bible scholars believe the battles are distinct.
- Zechariah discusses the *Battle for Jerusalem*, which may be synonymous with Armageddon – so there is a second biblical name for the Battle of Armageddon.

Technical Notes

---

¹ Napoleon unsuccessfully tried to conquer Palestine and create a homeland for the Jews in 1799, even going so far as to publish a letter on April 20, 1799, to Jews worldwide to encourage them to return to the Holy Land. After learning from his uncle, a Bishop in Paris, that the return of the Jews to their land was a precursor to "the end of the world," he ceased trying to bring this about! (Cited by David Flynn in his book, *The Temple at the Center of Time*, pg. 173, citing John Holland Rose, *The Personality of Napoleon*, pg. 243).

² Chuck Missler verbally shared in a seminar I attended in June of 2009 that in Hebrew the connotation is that those who try to move it will suffer a hernia! Ouch.

Chapter 8: The Battle of Gog and Magog

Description of the Battle and Its Participants

What's 'next up' on most lists of events that trigger the Apocalypse? Most scholars say it is a battle between Israel and a consortium of Arab nations led by Russia. We know it as the *Battle of Gog and Magog*.

The Book of Ezekiel, chapters 38 and 39, describes the land of Gog and Magog, along with identifying other peoples (e.g., Meshech, Tubal), that refer to tribes settling to the far north of Israel after the flood of Noah. Most conservative scholars believe that Gog and Magog are today's Russian people and the peoples geographically associated with them.[1] There is strong support that the people in ancient times knew Gog and Magog as the *Scythians*. Some Arab cultures knew the Great Wall of China as *the Wall of Gog and Magog* (a wall built to keep Gog and Magog *out* of China!) Others suggest that Gog and Magog refer to tribes that settled in East Germany or Turkey. However, today, this is still the minority view.

The prophet Ezekiel indicates that in the latter days there will be an alliance of nations led by Russia against Israel that includes Persia (modern Iran), Libya, and Ethiopia. For the past two hundred years, even before Russia gained prominence as a world power, Bible scholars proposed that this battle would transpire just before or at the beginning of the Tribulation period. Evangelical scholars typically distinguish this battle from the final battle of Armageddon *as the participants and circumstances are quite different.* The description of the battle in Ezekiel indicates that the God of Israel comes to the aid of Israel. Against all odds, the LORD strikes down the armies of Gog and Magog. This demonstrates to the world that the God of Israel is alive and still protecting His people. We read in Chapter 39:

> [7] *"I will make my holy name known among my people Israel. I will no longer let them treat my name as if it were not holy. Then the nations will know that I am the Holy One in Israel. I am the Lord.*

85

⁸ The day I will judge you is coming. You can be sure of it," announces the Lord and King. "It is the day I have spoken about.

⁹ "At that time those who live in the towns of Israel will go out and light a fire. They will use it to burn up the weapons. That includes small and large shields. It also includes bows and arrows, war clubs and spears. It will take seven years to burn all of them up.

¹⁰ People will not gather wood from the fields. They will not cut the forests down. Instead, they will burn the weapons. And they will rob those who robbed them. They will steal from those who stole from them," announces the Lord and King.

¹¹ "Gog, at that time I will bury you in a grave in Israel. It will be in the valley where people travel east of the Dead Sea. It will block the path of travelers. That is because you and your huge armies will be buried there. So it will be called The Valley of Gog's Armies.

¹² "It will take seven months for the people of Israel to bury the bodies. They will do it to make the land 'clean' again.

¹³ All of the people in the land will bury them. That will bring glory to me. It will be a time to remember," announces the Lord and King.

When Does the Battle Occur?

Protestants professing the 'preterist' point of view suggest that this battle has already taken place. Since the language used is of horses, crossbows and ancient types of warfare, it seems a 'literalist interpretation' could not easily substitute 'atom bombs, tanks, and particle laser beams.' Of course, the counter argument from the Dispensational side points out that the events depicted are not easily associated with any former historical event when such an alignment of nations collectively made war on Israel. In this case, the author may have been employing the names of these archaic weapons metaphorically since he had no other words available for his use. Nevertheless, to be fair to the dispensationalist, let's remember that 'taking the author literally' isn't the point – the goal is to seek understanding concerning what the author *intends* his words to mean. There may be legitimate examples where literal statements aren't historically accurate and weren't meant to be, especially when the 'category of fact' is beyond the scope and capacity of the writers' language.

This passage points out that the battle is in 'the latter days', which is an idiom slightly different from 'the last days' and may suggest that the battle happens just *before* the 'last days.' It does seem evident that the battle is not referring to any event that transpired prior to the first advent of the Messiah in 1 BC. When Peter quotes the prophet Joel to the masses at Passover immediately after the resurrection, he uses the phrase 'the Last Days.' By doing so, Peter asserts that the epoch 'of the Last Days' has therefore arrived. However, soon thereafter, Israel ceases to exist and remains dispersed for almost 1,900 years. Was the 'timing' of, *The Last Days,* **reset** because of the Jewish nation's rejection of Messiah and His message? Was it reset to some point far into the future? Or was Peter simply mistaken about the day in which he lived?

To Dispensational scholars, it appears necessary that this battle happens *after* Israel comes together again and is restored. Since the description of the battle follows the **Valley of Dry Bones** (see page 219) in Ezekiel 37, 'the latter days' must refer to a time near the Second Coming of the Messiah—not prior to His first advent.

Most commentators suggest that the Battle of Gog and Magog is the 'very next event' that will transpire soon leading the world into the Tribulation period. Dispensationalists would predict that if we witness a battle today between Israel and the many nations led by Russia, Israel will miraculously prevail with God's intervention; and secondly, we should recognize that the Tribulation period is beginning or has, in fact, already begun. Because of this widespread perspective, students of prophecy are constantly seeking to know what is happening behind the scenes with Russia and Iran. Are they now traveling down a path to make war on Israel? So many of the television shows addressing prophecy 'in the news,' often update their audiences on what happens in the Middle East and what step Israel must take to fend off attack from Iran, Syria, or the Russian 'bear.' Indeed, we see in the news in 2009, Iran's intention to build a nuclear capability with Russian assistance. This 'smoking gun' keeps those who study prophecy very much 'on the edge of their seats.' Should Israel take military action against Iran, almost all prophecy students would speculate the Battle of "Gog and Magog" is right around the corner.[2] Furthermore, with the destruction of Russia's army and the armies of most of Israel's neighbors, we could safely speculate that the geopolitical changes have been achieved allowing the **Third Temple** to be rebuilt (see page 193).

The Importance of the Battle as a Salvation Event

One final thought: the wording used in this passage suggests that this event is perhaps on the same level as the *Exodus, the most important event in the history of Israel.* This event convinces the nation of Israel that God (a.k.a., Yahweh) does exist, and that He and He alone has brought about their salvation.[3] We should make note that *there is more detail about this battle than there is about the Battle of Armageddon.* Consequently, we should understand that the *Battle of Gog and Magog* is an enormously important event not only because it shakes up the political order of things, *but also because it is the single most significant episode that effectively reconciles Israel to her God.*

Recapping the Key Points Covered in This Chapter

- The battle is described in Ezekiel chapters 38 and 39.
- Gog and Magog appear to be the ancient 'Scythians,' today's Russians and the peoples associated with that area.
- Other allies to Gog and Magog are Arab nations.
- Israel miraculously wins the battle, the entire world is amazed.
- The battle jars Israel into reconfirming its faith in 'YAHWEH.'
- This battle becomes virtually as important to Israel as 'the Exodus.'

Technical Notes

---

[1] See Chuck Missler's Book, *The Magog Invasion*, listed in **For Further Reading,** to provide an elaborate analysis of the historical data to substantiate who 'Gog and Magog' are. His view on this topic is representative of most dispensational scholars of which I am familiar.

[2] There are some who believe that the Battle may actually happen at the mid-point of the Tribulation Period and may be the 'final straw' that allows the Antichrist to accede to power. If so, the 'covenant' between Antichrist and Israel would clearly be associated with this war (perhaps a cause or an effect), and thus be a defining event.

[3] It is important to remember most Israelis today are agnostic or atheist.

Chapter 9: Daniel the Prophet

The Timing of the Book of Daniel

The prophet Daniel is one of the most important figures in the Bible and counted among the four 'major' Hebrew prophets. Chronologically, he followed another major prophet, Jeremiah (circa 635 BC), who predicted that the Kingdom of Judah would be conquered and taken off to captivity for 70 years by the Babylonians. Daniel was also a contemporary with the prophet Ezekiel (whom Ezekiel mentions in his writings—14:14, 20 and 28:3). As to his age, we know only that he was a young man when carried off to Babylon in 606 BC and an old man when he completed his writings in the book that bears his name (around 535 BC).

Daniel was most likely written over a 30-year period from around 565 BC to 535 BC. Interestingly, those parts of the book that deal with gentile kingdoms are written in Aramaic, the language of Babylon at the time, while sections dealing with Israel are written in Hebrew. Nebuchadnezzar, the King of Babylon who plays a major role in the Book of Daniel, writes a section of the book testifying to God's sovereignty over his kingdom of Babylon.

In our study, we will look closely at three of Daniel's visions: *Daniel's Vision of the 70 Weeks* and the *Vision of the Four Great Beasts* in two subsequent sections, and the *Vision of the Colossus* here.

The Identity of Daniel

Who was Daniel? He was one of a number of Hebrew children of noble birth who were taken from Jerusalem to Babylon in 606 BC (the third year of Jehoiakim) by Nebuchadnezzar. The Babylonian king made it his practice to train children of noble birth from the lands that he conquered to become his advisors. We learn of these details from the book of Daniel, Chapter 1:

> *¹ In the third year of the reign of Jehoiakim king of Judah, Nebu-chadnezzar king of Babylon came to Jerusalem and besieged it.*
>
> *² And the Lord delivered Jehoiakim king of Judah into his hand, along with some of the articles from the temple of God. These he carried off to the temple of his god in Babylonia and put in the treasure house of his god*
>
> *.³ Then the king ordered Ashpenaz, chief of his court officials, to bring in some of the Israelites from the royal family and the nobility-*
>
> *⁴ young men without any physical defect, handsome, showing aptitude for every kind of learning, well informed, quick to understand, and qualified to serve in the king's palace. He was to teach them the language and literature of the Babylonians.*
>
> *⁵ The king assigned them a daily amount of food and wine from the king's table. They were to be trained for three years, and after that they were to enter the king's service.*
>
> *⁶ Among these were some from Judah: Daniel, Hananiah, Mishael and Azariah. ⁷ The chief official gave them new names: to Daniel, the name Belteshazzar; to Hananiah, Shadrach; to Mishael, Meshach; and to Azariah, Abednego...*
>
> *¹⁷ To these four young men God gave knowledge and understanding of all kinds of literature and learning. And Daniel could understand visions and dreams of all kinds.*
>
> *¹⁸ At the end of the time set by the king to bring them in, the chief official presented them to Nebuchadnezzar.*
>
> *¹⁹ The king talked with them, and he found none equal to Daniel, Hananiah, Mishael and Azariah; so they entered the king's service.*
>
> *²⁰ In every matter of wisdom and understanding about which the king questioned them, he found them ten times better than all the magicians and enchanters in his whole kingdom.*
>
> *²¹ And Daniel remained there until the first year of King Cyrus.*

Daniel's First Great Vision

Therefore, Daniel became one of the King's most capable servants. Later, he steps up to a governing role in Babylon after he declares to the King what dream he had dreamt and provides its interpretation. Chapter 2 of Daniel tells the story of how the King summons the wise men of Babylon and how, upon failing to tell the King his dream, he orders the execution of them all. Daniel hears of the King's proclamation and comes to the rescue:

24 Then Daniel went to Arioch, whom the king had appointed to execute the wise men of Babylon, and said to him, "Do not execute the wise men of Babylon. Take me to the king, and I will interpret his dream for him."

25 Arioch took Daniel to the king at once and said, "I have found a man among the exiles from Judah who can tell the king what his dream means."

26 The king asked Daniel (also called Belteshazzar), "Are you able to tell me what I saw in my dream and interpret it?"

27 Daniel replied, "No wise man, enchanter, magician or diviner can explain to the king the mystery he has asked about,

28 but there is a God in heaven who reveals mysteries. He has shown King Nebuchadnezzar what will happen in days to come. Your dream and the visions that passed through your mind as you lay on your bed are these:

29 "As you were lying there, O king, your mind turned to things to come, and the revealer of mysteries showed you what is going to happen.

30 As for me, this mystery has been revealed to me, not because I have greater wisdom than other living men, but so that you, O king, may know the interpretation and that you may understand what went through your mind.

Daniel describes to the King his dream of a Colossus:

31 "You looked, O king, and there before you stood a large statue—an enormous, dazzling statue, awesome in appearance.

32 The head of the statue was made of pure gold, its chest and arms of silver, its belly and thighs of bronze,

33 its legs of iron, its feet partly of iron and partly of baked clay.

34 While you were watching, a rock was cut out, but not by human hands. It struck the statue on its feet of iron and clay and smashed them.

35 Then the iron, the clay, the bronze, the silver and the gold were broken to pieces at the same time and became like chaff on a threshing floor in the summer. The wind swept them away without leaving a trace. But the rock that struck the statue became a huge mountain and filled the whole earth.

This is Daniel's first vision which predicts the coming of these kingdoms that would successively subjugate the nation of Israel for the next seven hundred years. As to the interpretation of the vision:

1. The 'head of gold' represented Nebuchadnezzar and the great wealth of Babylon.

2. The 'chest and arms of silver' represented the Medes and Persians who were not a Kingdom of wealth like Babylon but were much stronger militarily dominating Mesopotamia for over two hundred years.

3. The third kingdom was the kingdom of bronze—the 'belly and thighs'—and represented the Greeks led by Alexander the Great. Next, the 'legs of iron and feet of clay' represented the Roman Empire, the most powerful of all kingdoms until the final kingdom comes.

4. The last kingdom is characterized as a rock cut 'without hands,' (meaning it had a divine origin), which would come forth and (1) crush the other kingdoms of the world, then (2) become a mountain, and finally (3) fill the entire earth. The last Kingdom spoken of by Daniel we can safely interpret *to be the Kingdom of God.*

FIGURE 4 – DANIEL'S ANSWER TO THE KING BY BRITON RIVIERE, R.A., 1890 (MANCHESTER CITY ART GALLERY)

The Handwriting on the Wall

Daniel was also the interpreter of 'the handwriting on the wall' that appeared to a subsequent King of Babylon (Belshazzar, not Nebuchadnezzar) when the Jewish Temple vessels were used (and thus desecrated) at a decadent party held by the King. Daniel was called from retirement to read the words on the wall and to interpret their meaning. In Chapter 5 of Daniel we read his interpretation:

> [25] *"This is the inscription that was written:*
> *MENE, MENE, TEKEL, PARSIN*
>
> [26] *"This is what these words mean:*
> *MENE: God has numbered the days of your reign and*
> *brought it to an end.*
>
> [27] *TEKEL: You have been weighed on the scales and found wanting.*
>
> [28] *PARSIN: Your kingdom is divided and given to the Medes and*
> *Persians."*

So it was that that night, the Medes and Persians, by damning up the river Euphrates, were able to sneak under the walls of the City and conquer Babylon – a city that was thought to be impregnable. Belshazzar was slain that night and Darius the Mede became the emperor of the mighty Media-Persian Empire.

Daniel in the Lion's Den

One of the most famous Bible stories is known as *Daniel in the Lion's Den*. As a punishment for praying to his God, Daniel was thrown into a den of lions. Darius the king at the behest of his advisors (who were jealous of Daniel's power and privilege), had established a law against praying to any god other than the King and his image. Daniel, not aware of the law, continued his thrice daily prayers (as was his custom) and was caught in the act. To comply with the law, the King reluctantly decreed that Daniel must be executed. However, this trap backfired on the deceitful advisors who had targeted Daniel. First, God miraculously delivered Daniel and then, in turn, Daniel's enemies were thrown to the lions for their treachery. Daniel Chapter 6, tells the story:

16 So the king gave the order, and they brought Daniel and threw him into the lions' den. The king said to Daniel, "May your God, whom you serve continually, rescue you!"

17 A stone was brought and placed over the mouth of the den, and the king sealed it with his own signet ring and with the rings of his nobles, so that Daniel's situation might not be changed.

18 Then the king returned to his palace and spent the night without eating and without any entertainment being brought to him. And he could not sleep.

19 At the first light of dawn, the king got up and hurried to the lions' den.

20 When he came near the den, he called to Daniel in an anguished voice, "Daniel, servant of the living God, has your God, whom you serve continually, been able to rescue you from the lions?"

21 Daniel answered, "O king, live forever!

22 My God sent his angel, and he shut the mouths of the lions. They have not hurt me, because I was found innocent in his sight. Nor have I ever done any wrong before you, O king."

23 The king was overjoyed and gave orders to lift Daniel out of the den. And when Daniel was lifted from the den, no wound was found on him, because he had trusted in his God.

24 At the king's command, the men who had falsely accused Daniel were brought in and thrown into the lions' den, along with their wives and children. And before they reached the floor of the den, the lions overpowered them and crushed all their bones.

The Prophet Daniel and the Apostle John are the two primary sources of revered apocalyptic literature, besides the teachings of Jesus Himself. As we will see, although written six centuries apart there are many elements common to both prophetic books. Christians often regard Daniel himself as the greatest of all Hebrew prophets. He is one of a very few characters in the Bible in which nothing negative is said.

Recapping the Key Points Covered in This Chapter

- Daniel is one of the most important prophets in the Bible.
- He followed Jeremiah and was a contemporary of Ezekiel.
- Daniel became a great government ruler under the Babylonian and Persian emperors, and became the head of the 'Magi' – the Wise Men.
- There are three famous stories about him: the 'Fiery Furnace,' the 'Handwriting on the Wall,' and 'Daniel in the Lion's Den.'
- His visions are the basis for much of the Bible's teaching about the Apocalypse and Second Advent.
- Three key visions will be discussed: The *Colossus* (here), the *70 Weeks of Years*, and the *Four Great Beasts* (in the next 2 sections).

Chapter 10: Daniel's Vision of the 70 Weeks

Gabriel Explains the Vision

Daniel's writings are filled with several sweeping visions. No vision is as important to predicting both the First and Second Advents of the Messiah as the vision of the 70 Weeks.

We read of Daniel's experience with the angel Gabriel in Chapter 9 of the Book of Daniel (Gabriel is the same angel who announced to Mary how she would become the virgin mother of Jesus Christ):

> *20 While I was speaking and praying, confessing my sin and the sin of my people Israel and making my request to the LORD my God for his holy hill-*
>
> *21 while I was still in prayer, Gabriel, the man I had seen in the earlier vision, came to me in swift flight about the time of the evening sacrifice.*
>
> *22 He instructed me and said to me, "Daniel, I have now come to give you insight and understanding.*
>
> *23 As soon as you began to pray, an answer was given, which I have come to tell you, for you are highly esteemed. Therefore, consider the message and understand the vision:*
>
> *24 "Seventy 'sevens' are decreed for your people and your holy city to finish transgression, to put an end to sin, to atone for wickedness, to bring in everlasting righteousness, to seal up vision and prophecy and to anoint the most holy.*
>
> *25 "Know and understand this: From the issuing of the decree to restore and rebuild Jerusalem until the Anointed One, the ruler, comes, there will be seven 'sevens,' and sixty-two 'sevens.' It will be rebuilt with streets and a trench, but in times of trouble.*
>
> *26 After the sixty-two 'sevens,' the Anointed One will be cut off and will have nothing. The people of the ruler who will come will destroy the city and the sanctuary. The end will come like a flood: War will continue until the end, and desolations have been decreed.*
>
> *27 He will confirm a covenant with many for one 'seven.' In the middle of the 'seven' he will put an end to sacrifice and offering. And on a wing of the temple he will set up an abomination that causes desolation, until the end that is decreed is poured out on him."*

(NASV)

The prophet Daniel predicted very specific events would transpire in the life of Israel over 70 'weeks' of years. Virtually all scholars agree this means 70 sets of 7 years or 490 years. The weeks are divided into three groups: (1) 7 weeks, (2) 62 weeks, and the (3) final or 70th week. The first 69 weeks are contiguous, meaning they run consecutively from the starting point for 483 (prophetic) years. The final seven years are separated by an undisclosed period of time. Dispensational scholars (and some post-tribulationalists) believe the final week is clearly the same period as discussed in the Book of Revelation and known as the *Tribulation*.[1]

The Prophetic Calendar

To understand the dating and to appreciate the prediction, one must understand that the Jewish calendar prophetically is 360 days rather than 365.25. The beginning date is the date that *Artaxerxes*, the King of the Medes and Persians, allowed *Nehemiah* to return to Jerusalem and begin rebuilding the city walls (which was 1 Nissan or March 14, 445 BC (Artaxerxes' 20th year). From this date it is 483 times 360 days (173,880 days) to the date of April 6, 32 A.D., which was Palm Sunday—the date Jesus rode into Jerusalem on the back of a donkey. Daniel clearly indicates that this day is when Messiah will present Himself to the nation; he will then be 'cut off' (killed), to 'make an end to sin' and 'bring in righteousness'. This concludes the 69 weeks. Daniel writes that the Messiah is killed by the *people* (the Romans, through Pontius Pilate), of the *prince who is to come* (the *Antichrist*). These people (the Romans through Titus) will destroy the city and the sanctuary (which Titus did in AD 70). In addition, since it is the prince of these people who makes the seven year covenant, scholars have—since the second century— understood that the Antichrist is a leader of the *'revived Roman empire.'*

Messiah's First Advent Predicted to the Day

According to Grant Jeffrey in his book on Daniel (*Countdown to the Apocalypse*), based on Daniel's 70 weeks, numerous Jewish scholars predicted (circa 50 BC), that the Messiah would be coming to Israel in their lifetime (which coincided with the life and death of

Jesus Christ). Jeffrey states: "Rabbi Nehumiah, who lived fifty years before the birth of Jesus, concluded on the basis of Daniel's prophecy of the seventy weeks that the arrival of the promised Messiah could not be delayed longer than fifty years... (Therefore) Rabbi Nehumiah concluded that the Messiah would be born approximately 1 BC."[2] As it turns out, he was exactly right![3]

Why did the Jews of that time reject Jesus as the Messiah (a rejection that obviously continues for the most part to this day)? There are two primary reasons: First, in the Hebrew view, God cannot become a human being (His nature cannot be 'incarnated' as He is too "other" in substance or essence to become human).[4] Consequently, His claim to be divine and God's unique Son was rejected. He was condemned for blasphemy and crucified as a result. Secondly, Jesus failed as Messiah because he did not redeem Israel politically as Jews maintain their Messiah would (see the discussion under the topic *Advent and Second Advent* for further elaboration).

Of course, the traditional Christian view is that Jesus redeems the world spiritually in His First Advent then physically and politically in His Second Advent answering both this challenge to His credentials and reconciling the two contrasting views proclaimed in the Bible. Daniel's final week (the last seven years), brings us to the Antichrist and the *abomination of desolation* (see page 73) which Jesus confirms in His Olivet discourse of Matthew 24.[i] The week begins with a seven-year covenant or treaty between the Antichrist and Israel then ends with the *Battle of Armageddon* (see page 79). Additionally, it is noteworthy that Christ quotes Daniel. By so doing, he verifies that Daniel was a historical figure and his prophecies were to be believed and fulfilled.[5] This point is significant as it pertains to the infallibility of Scripture and to the divinity of Christ. Evangelicals point out that if we regard Jesus Christ to be the Son of God it would seem probable that He would know about the authenticity of the Book of Daniel. On the other hand, if Liberalism is correct that the real Daniel didn't write the book that bears his name, Jesus appears to be fallible too. *Therefore, not only is the Bible unreliable, but*

---

[i] Olivet refers to the Mount of Olives where he held this discussion with his Apostles.

so is the Son of God! Liberals would counter by saying that in becoming human, God gave up omniscience and was subject to human learning and the capacity to make incorrect statements based upon what he learned from the knowledge of the times. We shouldn't expect Jesus to know everything.

How Do We Explain the Fulfillment of This Prophecy?

Daniel's 'prophecy of the 70 weeks' is considered the most impressive prediction in the entire Bible as it predicts the specific time when the Messiah would come and present Himself to the nation of Israel and 'make an end to sin.'

If you are an agnostic or an atheist, how do you explain this historical fact? Is it purely coincidence? Do you believe that Jesus conspired with His disciples to make Himself out to be the Messiah? Was His bid to be Messiah contrived? If so, you must believe that Jesus was able to manipulate the Priests and the Romans into crucifying Him on the Jewish Passover ('on a

> **THE KEY POINT TO PONDER:**
>
> *Many scholars consider Daniel's prophetic 70 Weeks the most important prophecy in the Bible. It predicts the very moment the Messiah will present Himself to the Jewish nation.*

tree' which fulfilled numerous prophecies and typologies in the Old Testament). If you believe this, do you also believe the disciples were able to fake his resurrection? Do you think they stole His body? Or do you think everyone in Palestine went to the wrong tomb?

Perhaps you might want to consider all the facts of the matter. As He predicted to all of His disciples, Jesus was crucified. It wasn't accidental. The Romans and the Jewish authorities crucified him – and not a manner of death that anyone would willingly choose. He was buried in a rich man's tomb borrowed from Joseph, a member of the Sanhedrin.[i] Three days later, despite a sizeable guard composed of many soldiers who secured the tomb ensuring no one tampered

---

[i] Therefore, the tomb was unlikely to be so obscure it could easily be mistaken for someone else's.

with the grave, Jesus' body disappears. His followers claim to have seen Him alive. They especially reminded their opposition, the 'authorities,' that what had happened wasn't 'done in the dark.' The events of that day were common knowledge. Finally, Paul the Apostle says that Jesus appeared to over 500 followers at one time.[i] In this passage, Paul admits that *if God did not raise Jesus from the dead*, as he and the other Apostles contended, then *Christians were of all people the most miserable*. Instead of believing, we should "eat, drink, and be merry' for tomorrow we die!" (See I Corinthians Chapter 15 for the full account).

Over the years, Jesus' followers die bloody and gruesome deaths. Did the Apostles die for a lie that they concocted? On the other hand, did they willingly die because of their conviction that *death* would now be overcome? Which story is the most plausible? Which version do you believe?

Recapping the Key Points Covered in This Chapter

- The Vision of the 70 Weeks is the most important prophecy in the Bible.
- The angel Gabriel explains the meaning of the 70 'weeks of years', *which* equals 490 years of 360 days.
- The vision predicts the very day the Messiah will appear to present the Kingdom in Jerusalem – but predicts he will be killed by the 'people of the prince who is to come,' a reference to the Antichrist.
- This passage also predicts the Antichrist committing the *abomination of desolation* half way through the 70th Week.

---

[i] This appearance is of such magnitude that it makes the *'hallucination'* theory of the Resurrection of Jesus Christ (proposed by some skeptics), more incredible than believing Jesus rose from the dead.

Technical Notes

[1] The issue of whether there is a distinction between *The Tribulation* and *The Great Tribulation* is somewhat academic. The Bible expressly talks about a period of Great Tribulation that lasts for three and one-half years. Daniel's 70th week is a seven-year period of which the Great Tribulation is the final three and one-half years. It has become commonplace to refer to the entire seven year period as the Tribulation—perhaps to give a 'macro name' to the seven year period. But technically, it is correct that the Bible doesn't formally 'title' the final seven years, the *Tribulation*, although Jesus may be referring to the entire seven year period in Matthew 24 when it talks about a time of tribulation that will come upon the world that has seen no equals.

[2] Jeffrey, Grant R Jeffrey, *Countdown to the Apocalypse,* 2008, Water Brook Press, page 122.

[3] Numerous authorities have evaluated the various historical markers in the various Gospel accounts to ascertain the date of Jesus' birth—most notably, who was 'governor,' when they held office, and when various censuses taken by the Roman leaders took place. The latest study in this subject suggests that Jesus was born in 1 BC. See Jeffrey as cited above for more information on this analysis.

[4] This is of particular importance: Jews understood their Messiah is to be a man, great and powerful, and anointed with God's Spirit. However, He is not divine. Jesus tried numerous times to attack this misunderstanding by asserting His equality with God—an assertion that caused many to pick up rocks to stone Him and ultimately was the principal reason the Romans and Jews crucified Him.

[5] Was Jesus asserting that the *abomination of desolation* would occur when Titus conquered Jerusalem *or* that the Antichrist would commit this act in Daniel's 70th week? Commentators who believe the 70th week is yet to be fulfilled, would say, "Both." Those who doubt the Antichrist is a literal character assert that Jesus' prediction has already been fulfilled in the first century. We should expect No further fulfillment.

Chapter 11: Daniel's Vision of the Four Great Beasts

Consistent Images between Daniel and John

Daniel, Chapter 7, provides another vision of great importance to prophecy. It is a vision predicting the successions of the six empires that will rule over Israel, including: (1) Babylon, (2) Media-Persia, (3) Greece, and (4) Rome, (5) the Antichrist and ultimately, (6) the Son of God. We read of the vision in Chapter 7:

¹ In the first year of Belshazzar king of Babylon Daniel saw a dream and visions in his mind as he lay on his bed; then he wrote the dream down and related the following summary of it.

² Daniel said, "I was looking in my vision by night, and behold, the four winds of heaven were stirring up the great sea.

³ "And four great beasts were coming up from the sea, different from one another.

⁴ "The first was like a lion and had the wings of an eagle. I kept looking until its wings were plucked, and it was lifted up from the ground and made to stand on two feet like a man; a human mind also was given to it.

⁵ "And behold, another beast, a second one, resembling a bear. And it was raised up on one side, and three ribs were in its mouth between its teeth; and thus they said to it, 'Arise, devour much meat!'

⁶ "After this I kept looking, and behold, another one, like a leopard, which had on its back four wings of a bird; the beast also had four heads, and dominion was given to it.

⁷ "After this I kept looking in the night visions, and behold a fourth beast, dreadful and terrifying and extremely strong; and it had large iron teeth. It devoured and crushed and trampled down the remainder with its feet; and it was different from all the beasts that were before it, and it had ten horns.

⁸ "While I was contemplating the horns, behold, another horn, a little one, came up among them, and three of the first horns were pulled out by the roots before it; and behold, this horn possessed eyes like the eyes of a man and a mouth uttering great boasts. (NASV)

We see in this vision a number of consistent images: (1) the sea which gives rise to the Beasts; (2) the succession of four empires, the final empire which seems to have two stages and in the second stage; (3) it is composed of ten nations (or horns), but three of which are overcome by *"the little horn"* who utters great boasts. Not only does this vision of *Daniel* provide many points of confirmation for what we read in the Book of Revelation, it also provides a complete historical spectrum of all the major empires affecting Israel.

- The first beast is a lion with wings, *Babylon,* the most *revered*[i] and *richest* of the empires (also referred to as 'the head of Gold' in Daniels' earlier vision of the Colossus in Daniel, Chapter 2). We can confirm that this beast is Babylon by recalling that Nebuchadnezzar went mad at one point in his reign; then as predicted by Daniel he dwelt in the wild as a beast for seven years. He was not left in this state, but after being humbled, God lifted him up and restored his human mind.

- The second beast is *Media-Persia*, ponderous and strong like a *bear*, whose three ribs C.I. Scofield in his commentary suggests are the three-fold substance of the Kingdom: Babylon, Media, and Persia. In contrast, Grant Jeffrey suggests this image conveys the three kingdoms Media-Persia conquers: Babylon, Lydia and Egypt.[ii]

- The third beast is *Greece,* a *leopard* (a strong but agile and fast cat). Scholars note Alexander for his clever use of cavalry enabling him to defeat armies many times the size of his own. He moved swiftly conquering many lands one after another. Then upon his death, not long after the time he had conquered most of the known world, four kings divided the kingdom among themselves: Lysimachus, Cassander, Seleucid, and Ptolemy. We see the latter two continue to play an important role in history and in the other portions of the Book of Daniel.

- The fourth beast is *Rome*, not identified with a particular animal, but larger, mightier, and more dreadful than all the others are, possessing iron teeth. (John indicates in Revelation 13 that *the Beast from the sea* has characteristics of all of the first three: A lion, a bear, and a leopard). The beast also had ten horns, as does

---

[i] Indeed, we often refer to the Lion as *regal* and the 'king' of all beasts.

[ii] Jeffrey, Grant R., *Countdown to the Apocalypse*, op. cited, page 98.

the Beast in Revelation 13. From this beast comes 'the little horn,' the *Antichrist* who uproots three kings who do not consent to grant it power (likewise, consistent with the Beast of Revelation 13).

The Son of Man—A Title of the Messiah

Daniel continues describing his vision (*NASV*):

> [11] *"Then I kept looking because of the sound of the boastful words which the horn was speaking; I kept looking until the beast was slain, and its body was destroyed and given to the burning fire...*

> [13] *"I kept looking in the night visions,*
> *And behold, with the clouds of heaven*
> *One like a Son of Man was coming,*
> *And He came up to the Ancient of Days*
> *And was presented before Him.*

> [14] *"And to Him was given dominion,*
> *Glory and a kingdom,*
> *That all the peoples,*
> *nations and men of every language*
> *Might serve Him*
> *His dominion is an everlasting dominion*
> *Which will not pass away;*
> *And His kingdom is one*
> *Which will not be destroyed.*

This final conqueror is none other than *"one like the Son of Man,"* a phrase that Jesus quotes at the questioning of Caiaphas the High Priest. We read in Matthew (Matthew 26:64, NASV):

> *But Jesus kept silent. And the high priest said to Him, "I adjure you by the living God, that you tell us whether you are the Christ, the Son of God." Jesus said to him, "You have said it yourself; nevertheless I tell you, hereafter you will see* **THE SON OF MAN** *SITTING AT THE RIGHT HAND OF POWER, and COMING ON THE CLOUDS OF HEAVEN." Then the high priest tore his robes and said, "He has blasphemed! What further need do we have of witnesses? Behold, you have now heard the blasphemy."*

Caiaphas understood the claim to divinity and rejected that Jesus, being a man could also be divine. He declared that Jesus had blasphemed and thus 'rent' or tore his clothing due to Jewish tradition. However, from the perspective of Jewish law, this act was considered 'improper' if not illegal—perhaps because it was akin to cursing!

The Final Victory Belongs to the Stone Cut without Hands

This final kingdom is the *'stone that was cut out of the mountain without hands'* in Daniel's Colossus vision of Daniel 2, that destroys the Colossus and from which all of the world is blessed. *"In the days of those kings the God of heaven will set up a kingdom which will never be destroyed, and that kingdom will not be left for another people; it will crush and put an end to all these kingdoms, but it will itself endure forever"* (Daniel 2:44). An angel provides this additional explanation:

> [23] *Thus he said: "The fourth beast will be a fourth kingdom on the Earth, which will be different from all the other kingdoms and will devour the whole Earth and tread it down and crush it.*
>
> [24] *"As for the ten horns, out of these kingdom ten kings will arise; and another will arise after them, and he will be different from the previous ones and will subdue three kings.*
>
> [25] *"He will speak out against the Most High and wear down the saints of the Highest One, and he will intend to make alterations in times and in law; and they will be given into his hand for a time, times, and half a time. [26] But the court will sit for judgment, and his dominion will be taken away, annihilated and destroyed forever.*
>
> [27] *"Then the sovereignty, the dominion and the greatness of all the kingdoms under the whole heaven will be given to the people of the saints of the Highest One; His kingdom will be an everlasting kingdom, and all the dominions will serve and obey Him"* (Daniel Chapter 7, NASV).

In summary, through this vision of Daniel we see a recap of many predicted eschatological events that culminate in the assurance that the ultimate King of Kings is Jesus Christ, whose rule will be everlasting, overcoming all other dominions. We also see the strong consistency between the visions of Daniel concerning the kingdom of the Antichrist and the visions of **John the Apostle,** author (see page 119) of the Revelation.

Key Points Covered in This Chapter

- Daniel's vision of the Four Great Beasts talks of future empires that will subjugate Israel.
- This vision compares with the Apostle John's vision of the Beast rising from the Sea (the Antichrist – Revelation 13).
- This vision includes the use of the phrase, *Son of Man*, a messianic title that Jesus used to identify Himself to the High Priest, Caiaphas – which led to His crucifixion.
- The vision concludes with the 'stone cut without hands' – a stone that represents the empire of the Son of God, which will crush all the other empires of the earth.

Doctrinal Position	Liberalism	Covenantalism	Dispensationalism
Millennial Position	*Post-Millennial*	*Amillennial*	*Millennial*
Replacement Theology?	Church and Israel have distinct 'access' to God	Church replaces Israel as God's 'elect'	Church and Israel have distinct 'programs' with God
Hermeneutic	Liberal Method	Key Doctrine Method	Plain Meaning Method
Rapture Position	No rapture	Post-Tribulation Rapture	Pre-Tribulation Rapture
Eschatology Position	Mostly historicist	Mostly preterist	Futurist
Naturalism or Supernaturalism	Mostly naturalism	Supernaturalism	Supernaturalism
Religious Truth Position	Religious truth distinct – Knowledge dichotomy	Religious truth part of unified field of knowledge	Religious truth part of unified field of knowledge
God's Means of Revelation	Emphasis on encounter with God – 'inwardness'	Emphasis on objective Word of God, learned, applied.	Emphasis on objective Word of God, learned, applied.
Scripture Position	'Testimonies' and poetry. Human book that can err.	God's Word. Infallible. Truthful if touches history.	God's Word. Infallible. Truthful if touches history.
Christology and Soteriology	Heterodox	Orthodox	Orthodox

FIGURE 5 – OVERVIEW OF THEOLOGICAL POSITIONS

Chapter 12: Dispensationalism and Covenantalism

Dispensationalism, Its Origin and Claims to Fame

Dispensationalism is a form of fundamentalist or evangelical theology that believes in a series of key tenets, foremost among them the view that God relates to humankind *differently at different times in history.* Many regard John Nelson Darby (1801-1882), and C.I. Scofield (1843-1921), as the principals of this school of thought. Hal Lindsey's best-seller, *The Late Great Planet Earth,* published in 1970, first popularized the Dispensationalist theological position (which, as mentioned earlier, sold *35 million* copies worldwide). Lindsey attended Dallas Theological Seminary which is the principal school that taught (then and now) Dispensational theology. In today's literature the *"Left Behind"* series by Tim LaHaye and Jerry Jenkins (a fictional set of stories whose plot relies upon the 'end times'), also is based upon this interpretive method.

The Definition of Dispensation

What is a dispensation? The general definition of the term has to do with a special rule or command proclaimed by an authority to guide behavior (in some cases to relax a law, e.g., "I received a special dispensation from the Church to hold this meeting on a Sunday"). It follows from the concept of 'dispensing of power.' However, in this theological school of thought, dispensations are 'ages' or periods of time characterized by well defined differences in how God relates to humankind. (See **Figure** 1 on page 22).

The Dispensations usually number seven, and may include Innocence, Conscience, Human Government, the period of Law, the 'Church Age' or the Age of Grace, and finally, the Millennium Kingdom. Nevertheless, more recent Dispensational theologians (so-called 'Progressive Dispensationalists'), are inclined to see perhaps no more than five such distinctions in biblical history (See Charles C.

Ryrie's book, *Dispensationalism*, described in **For Further Reading,** page 305). Dispensations begin with a promise from God for what He will do if humans follow His commandments; dispensations conclude with a judgment from God when humankind fails to heed the commandments—and therefore forfeit the promise. Dispensationalism is best known for the literal interpretation of the **70 Weeks of Years of Daniel,** the **Rapture** (see page 169) of the Church, and the 1,000 year physical reign of Christ on the earth (the literal **Millennium,** see page 55). Dispensationalists believe the current time period in which we live is 'the Church Age' and is a parenthetical epoch resulting because the Jewish nation rejected Jesus as their Messiah. This is known in Paul's theology as *"the mystery of godliness,"* (I Corinthians 2:7), a time in which Gentiles and Jews who believe in Jesus Christ are joined together in the *Body of Christ*. Dispensationalists believe this Body begins at the first Pentecost[1] (Acts, Chapter Two) with the coming of the Holy Spirit and concludes when the Body of Christ, the Church, is *raptured* from the earth (I Corinthians 15:51).

Covenantal Theology: A Counterpoint to Dispensationalism

Covenantal Theology, in distinction to Dispensationalism, sees the Covenants of God as the formal delineations in how God interacts with humankind. Covenantal distinctions are built around the *Covenant of Law* that came with Moses, and the *Covenant of Grace* that came with Jesus Christ. The Covenant of Law is often further subdivided into eras that would be distinguished roughly from the time of Adam to Noah, from Noah to Abraham, from Abraham to Moses, from Moses to David, and finally David to Christ. There is no debate that there should be 'distinctions' in the revelation of God to humankind. Both schools of thought draw out these distinctions based upon God's self-revelation, which grows more explicit as history progresses. However, are these schools of thought really different?

We can easily grasp the essence of Covenantal Theology by several key doctrines essential to its position. First, we should understand that *there is no distinction anymore between Jewish and Gentile 'believers.'* Christ's saving work did away with these distinctions (see Galatians 3:28). The Church has inherited the promises God made to Abraham. Romans Chapter 4 goes into great depth to point out that Abraham's true spiritual children are those who have the *faith* of Abraham, not those who are *racially* of the lineage of Abraham. As such, Covenantal Theology would suggest that the Kingdom God promised to Israel, He later transferred to the Church—Christians inherit the unfulfilled promises made to Israel. As mentioned earlier, Covenantal Theologians are typically *amillennialists*, believing that the future Kingdom is a heavenly Kingdom and is not the same as the Messianic Kingdom foretold by the Jewish prophets and for which the believing Jews of this day still wait. (I provide a graphical presentation of the chronology is above; See **Figure 3** on page 64).

Distinction One: Hermeneutics

Therefore, these evangelical schools primarily base their distinctions on two key points. *The first is the method of biblical interpretation.*[i] Dispensationalists argue for interpreting Scripture consistent with grammar and historically understood meanings to words. 'The plain teaching of Scripture' is crucial. Dispensationalists willingly wear the label of 'literalism' even though most would be quick to point out that they respect figures of speech, allegories, metaphors, and 'types.' At issue is 'what did the author intend? What was his plain meaning?' On the other hand, Covenantal theologians interpret many passages symbolically or figuratively. If a passage doesn't appear to mesh with a cherished doctrine, it may be necessary to transpose its meaning into a symbol or *type* to ensure consistency with their theological perspective.[2]

Distinction Two: The Place of Israel

However, it is the second distinction where the sparks really fly. Indeed, at the pinnacle of Dispensational teaching *is the assumption even today that Israel remains God's chosen people.* Dispensa-

---

[i] This is also known as *hermeneutics* as mentioned earlier.

tionalism believes that *God's plan for Israel and for the Church is distinct and is not to be confused.* As Paul states, *"Has God rejected the Jews? God forbid... For the gifts and calling of God are **irrevocable"** (*Romans 11:1, 2, 29, emphasis mine, NASV). On this point Covenantal Theology energetically disagrees with Dispensationalism claiming it holds the historically dominant view – Jews missed the promise of God and the Church replaced Israel as God's chosen or 'elect.' This is known as *replacement theology* (the Church replaces Israel), which indeed most Reformed churches historically believed and which most mainline Christian denominations follow today. The emotion is strong because to suppose otherwise, *appears to question the sufficiency of the sacrificial death of Christ for our sins.*

> **THE KEY POINT TO PONDER:**
>
> *Covenantalism espouses 'replacement theology' – the view that the Church replaces Israel as the center of God's plan. To believe otherwise, to them, is to question the sufficiency of the sacrificial death of Christ for our sins.*

So are the Covenantalists correct in making the assertion that history is on their side? In point of fact, the history of the Church through its first 17 centuries generally supports their position. Still, the evidence isn't completely one-sided. Covenantalists are prone to overlook the fact that there are a number of instances where Israel's election as 'God's chosen people' is professed in the theology of other much smaller 'protesting' groups who were at odds with the Catholic Church (several claims to this effect can be found in the 15th through 18th centuries). Ultimately, at issue is not 'who has history on their side?' The real question becomes 'who has the Bible on their side?' As we will discuss later, since this is right approach there seems to be little reason to debate the historical record.

Dispensationalists: Supporters of Modern Israel

Because Dispensationalism holds a favorable view of Judaism's prospects for future redemption, it is primarily *responsible for Christians in the United States supporting modern Israel.* On the positive side, the popularity of Dispensationalism and its influence has transformed the relationship between Christians and Jews overcoming centuries of hatred. However, this change for the better is not without its downside: Many evangelical Christians seem to affirm that siding with Israel is the same as siding with God.[3] This political position is particularly more problematic when one remembers that the Israeli government today falls far short of a true theocracy, with many of the most influential and powerful governmental leaders' atheist or agnostic. However, Dispensationalists usually look past this Israeli 'shortcoming' by reckoning that as stated in the Book of Romans *"someday all Israel shall be saved"* (Romans 11:26). In contrast, Covenantal theologians are more likely to be critical of Israel arguing that God no longer has any special regard for the nation of Israel—only insomuch as individual Jews chose to turn to Christ Jesus.[4]

How Serious Are These Distinctions?

In summary, one could suggest that these distinctions are in fact, *merely a family argument.* Both sides demonstrate strong biblical support to substantiate their positions. As to God's relationship with us, there is consensus that historical distinctions are valid which define the progression of God's revealing Himself to us. In addition, they agree on virtually every major doctrine that makes them distinctly *evangelical.* Both sides profess:

- *Total depravity of humankind* (that sin has affected every part of man's nature);
- *Substitutionary atonement* (that Christ died as our substitute on the cross to cleanse us from sin);
- *Predestination* (that God has 'elected' those who shall be saved); and
- *Perseverance of the saints* (that once saved, there is no 'fall from grace').

Furthermore, both regard *Scripture* as the only authority in matters of faith and practice as well as the full and unique divinity of Jesus Christ (the position known as *Trinitarian – one God in three persons*). Nevertheless, when it comes to e*schatology*, these two camps are very much at odds.

Recapping the Key Points Covered in This Chapter

- *Dispensationalism* was 'founded' less than two hundred years ago.
- The most impactful books on prophecy have been written by those who ascribe to this method of understanding the Bible.
- *Covenantalism* is the competing approach and enjoys stronger historical precedent, more clearly in line with the 'reformers.'
- The two groups differ on 'hermeneutics' (interpreting the Bible).
- Both agree that to make sense of the unfolding story of the Bible, it is important to draw distinctions in how God interacts with humankind – *these distinctions are either dispensations or covenants.*
- Dispensationalists tend to be strong supporters of modern Israel – believing that the earthly Kingdom will be shared by all believers, both Christian and Jewish; for someday 'all Israel will be saved.'
- Covenantalists reject Israel's hope for the Kingdom – 'that ship has sailed!'

Technical Notes

[1] Gary Stearman writes in a newsletter for *Prophecy in the News* (May, 2009), that all Dispensations appear to begin at Pentecost. His research indicates that this was true when God made a covenant (1) with Noah commencing the "Dispensation of Human Government;" (2) with Moses at Mount Sinai commencing the 'Dispensation of Law;' (3) at the coming of the Holy Spirit, the beginning of the 'Dispensation of Grace;' and correspondingly, he has speculated that the (4) next dispensation, the 'Kingdom,' will also commence at Pentecost with the Rapture of the Church.

[2] Charles Ryrie points out the difficulty that Daniel Fuller, a noted Covenantal Theologian, has with the prophecies of the Old Testament. Fuller admits in one passage, according to Ryrie, that he simply can't decide how far he can take the prophecies of the Old Testament prophets, because to take them literally would be to decide that a physical earthly kingdom seems inevitable. Ryrie is quick to assert that a literal, plain meaning interpretation would say such a view is in fact mandatory to understand rightly God's intention across the whole of Scripture. Therefore, to Dispensationalists, there will be an *earthly* Kingdom.

[3] Believing that 'those that bless Israel, God will bless; those that curse Israel, God will curse.' God's covenant with Abraham includes this promise. John Hagee, a leader in Evangelicalism today, is criticized because he is uncritically supportive of the Israeli Government even if it acts in such a way that may appear inconsistent with what God has taught about justice in the world.

[4] The 'overarching' theme of the Bible is another distinction made by Dispensationalists. Covenantalism sees redemption or salvation as central; Dispensationalism sees the 'glory of God' as the primary theme. See Ryrie, op. cit., page 106-107).

Chapter 13: The False Prophet

The Second Beast and His Role

Revelation 13 doesn't just describe the Antichrist. It portrays a second sinister character too. It depicts another Beast arising from the earth immediately after the emergence of the first 'Beast' or the *Antichrist* from the *sea*.[i] Bible scholars know this second Beast as 'the False Prophet.' Unlike most other characters or events described in Revelation, this notion of the False Prophet is found explicitly *only* in the Book of Revelation.

John describes the False Prophet with an image of two horns like a lamb and a voice of a dragon:

11 Then I saw another beast, coming out of the earth. He had two horns like a lamb, but he spoke like a dragon.

12 He exercised all the authority of the first beast on his behalf, and made the earth and its inhabitants worship the first beast, whose fatal wound had been healed.

13 And he performed great and miraculous signs, even causing fire to come down from heaven to earth in full view of men.

14 Because of the signs he was given power to do on behalf of the first beast, he deceived the inhabitants of the earth. He ordered them to set up an image in honor of the beast who was wounded by the sword and yet lived.

15 He was given power to give breath to the image of the first beast, so that it could speak and cause all who refused to worship the image to be killed. (Revelation 13:11-15).

Most experts identify the False Prophet as a spiritual leader in contrast to the Antichrist who they strictly consider a political ruler.

It is suspicious that John compares the *'False Prophet'* to 'a lamb', which suggests that he may appear as a Christian leader. Yet given that his voice is 'like a dragon,' it confirms his motivations are evil. Furthermore, just as we could compare Antichrist to Christ,

---

[i] Most scholars agree that the *sea*, with waves that toss back and forth, is symbolic of the political tumult of humankind.

many suggest that the False Prophet, the second beast, completes an evil trinity: *Satan, Antichrist,* and the *False Prophet* (Revelation 16:13). In the Christian Trinity, the Holy Spirit's role is to point to Christ and to encourage belief in and adoration of Him. In an analogous way, here we see the False Prophet enforcing worship of the first Beast and working miracles 'in his name.' Specifically, the False Prophet gives *life* to the *image* of the Beast.

There is little consensus among commentators as to what this actually means. There have been many fanciful speculations. Today, we might guess it has something to do with a hologram or three-dimensional picture that can arise 'in space' at various locations concurrently, making it apparent that the Antichrist has the potential or power to be 'anywhere at any time' and many places at once. This attribute would mimic the power of omnipresence. Furthermore, the image isn't stationary or static. The image moves and talks – it is alive![i]

Nevertheless, while the exact nature of the image is unknown, there is consensus that this sign will be extraordinary, enhancing the claims made by both. The message of the False Prophet is straightforward: The Beast is divine and all must worship him – or else!

The Religion of the False Prophet

What can we ascertain from the fact that this beast emerges 'from the Earth' rather than from the sea? We can consider numerous possibilities:

1. The first alternative is the second beast has no true spiritual message—his is purely an *earthly religion*. This could mean nothing more than he embraces Naturalism. However, this seems unlikely.

2. The religion of Babylon is another possibility. Historically, this belief system seeks to join the earth with the sky, (hence, the implied meaning behind the Tower of Babel, the Pyramids, and Obelisks—an attempt to reach up to the sky and join the heavens with the earth—"as above, so below." This system of religion im-

---

[i] I can't help but hear the voice of Gene Wilder screaming this when he sees his creation, his monster come to life in the movie, *Young Frankenstein!* Perhaps this image of the Frankenstein monster isn't so far off the mark!

plies *pantheism* (that God is everywhere and 'imbedded' in everything).

3. Thirdly, the spirit of the False Prophet could emerge from 'beneath the earth.' In the imagery of the Old Testament, spirits of evil angels were locked away until the 'end of days' (usually considered by the Hebrews *Sheol*, or to the Greeks, *Hades or Tartarus*—a place of the dead). This possibility connects the 'fallen angels' and the Nephilim mentioned earlier. Powerful beings could appear which demonstrate the same power and ability as those from the 'days of Noah.'

4. Fourth, the miracles and magic of the false prophet may refer to the same source of power often believed to exist within 'the forces of nature', which are purported to be manipulated by shamans and witches to achieve some earthly or selfish benefit. We could consider this *animism* (magic) or *polytheism* (many gods in the manner of Hinduism, but more precisely in today's new age parlance, '*we are all gods*').

5. Fifth, the most common proposal is that the final 'world religion' will consist of the belief in the evolution of the human species with the aid of extraterrestrials. Several books today talk about UFOs and extraterrestrial contact as the 'great deception' that will come upon the earth in 'the last days.' ET may finally appear for all to see and claim the ability to solve all our problems! If so, no doubt he will become the object of our admiration and worship. See L.A. Marzulli's book, *Politics, Prophecy, and the Supernatural: The Coming Great Deception and the Luciferian Endgame*, in **For Further Reading**, page 305).

6. As mentioned earlier, with the increasing influence of Islam throughout the world and the fact that radical Islam is no lover of Christianity or Judaism, it is easy to suppose that Islam might be the religion of the Antichrist and False Prophet. Biblical scholars who have studied the Koran and the history surrounding the rising of Mohammed in ancient Arabia believe that the religion, while monotheistic, was actually a reworking of the moon God of the Arabs. Allah is not Yahweh!

7. I should also mention that there is no reason that the final world religion can't combine a number of these elements into a 'synthesis.' To be sure, many earthly religions adopt a 'syncretistic' approach. Deceptions usually combine many 'crazy' notions—the more 'way out' the better. It goes without saying: Humans have proven themselves willing to believe almost anything.

Finally, another interesting Jewish tradition refers to the two ancient beasts referred to a number of times in the Old Testament— *Leviathan,* a beast from the sea (see Israel 27:1); and *Behemoth,* a beast of the Land (see Job 40:15). Folklore exists in some extra-biblical Hebrew texts and traditions tying these beasts to the Antichrist and the False Prophet. Furthermore, the 'saints' will feast upon these two beasts at The Marriage Supper of the Lamb! While this culinary experience isn't exactly what I'm looking forward to, the concept of the enemies of the Messiah being food for celebration is an intriguing image emphasizing the defeat of the Antichrist and False Prophet.

No matter the other particulars, Daniel reports that the Antichrist has respect for *"the god of forces"* and is able to understand *"dark sentences"* (see Daniel 8:23, 24). Hence, occultism is certainly a key element of his religion – and perhaps the most important aspect that the False Prophet promotes.

In conclusion, the Book of Revelation states unequivocally that the False Prophet is destined to accompany the Antichrist upon his defeat at the *Battle of Armageddon* and be likewise thrown into the Lake of Fire (Revelation 19:20).

Recapping the Key Points Covered in This Chapter

- John's apocalyptic vision revolves around 'two beasts' – the first is Antichrist, the second is known as the 'False Prophet.'
- This second beast comes up 'from the earth' in contrast to the first beast that arose 'from the sea.'
- The nature of his role is to promote the first beast and cause the entire world to worship him and to accept his 'mark' (666).
- The nature of his religion is not fully known, but most scholars believe it could be akin to animism, occultism, and perhaps 'Satanism' evidenced by 'signs and wonders' deceiving the entire world.
- More recent interpretations of the final 'great deception' involve UFOs and 'God as an alien astronaut.'
- Another less 'out-of-this-world' candidate is Islam, which many evangelicals point out is really a religion of the Moon God, not Yahweh!

Chapter 14: John, Author of Revelation

Background on the Apostle and His Writing

John wrote the Book of Revelation while exiled on the Isle of Patmos in the Aegean Sea. Most orthodox Christians believe that this John was in fact John the Apostle. The Church Fathers and the first church historian Eusebius testify to his authorship. In their writings composed within 60 years of John's death, both Irenaeous and Clement confirm that John the Apostle, their mentor, was the author. True, some believe that the John of Revelation was 'John the Presbyter' who is mentioned in some of the early documents of the church. However, this is not the common or traditional view and the evidence for this position is scant. The internal evidence (the author's use of particular Greek words), provides further strong support for John the Apostle as the author. At the very least, the John who wrote Revelation also wrote the gospel and the letters that bear his name.

Some believe that John may have written Revelation as the first of his New Testament writings around 85 AD (which conflicts with the common view that Revelation was his last writing as it is the last book in the Christian Bible). Others believe that He may have written His gospel earlier (before 64 AD and the destruction of Jerusalem). The debate on timing centers mostly on whether John wrote during the time of the persecution of Nero (around 64 AD) or the persecution of Domitian (around 90-95 AD).

Most authorities today believe that John wrote the Revelation around 90-95 A.D. because references to the churches in Chapter 2 and 3 – that is, specific characteristics of those churches, make much more sense with the later date than the former.[1] The First Epistle of John, which most authorities believe was genuinely from the Apostle, was written perhaps as late as AD 100. This would be likely if the late date of Revelation is accepted.

Liberalism and the Book of Revelation

Liberalism, like evangelicals who are 'preterist,' believes that whoever John was, he was writing to his contemporary audience. At the end of the first century, Christians were suffering great persecution. John reminds his audience that no matter how bad things get, ultimately Christ will have the victory! While true, evangelicals would comment that Liberals haven't said very much in making this statement; they could also say this about the rest of the New Testament!

Liberalism would also contend that to interpret Revelation accurately, the first order of business is to recognize the connection of the symbols of John with those of the Old Testament Prophets such as Daniel, Ezekiel, Zechariah, and several others. Evangelicals would find no problem with this assertion. Likewise, a good liberal study on the Book of Revelation might illustrate the continuity with other Scripture (especially apocalyptic literature) and assert that *good will triumph over evil.* Liberalism will also interpret the Antichrist in the same way as John in his First Epistle when he says 'there are many evil doers—so the spirit of Antichrist is already evident within the world.' However, Liberalism would reject any attempt to connect the symbols and imagery of Revelation to present day events. *In the liberal mindset, Revelation looks backward not forward.* As such, scholars consider Liberalism a 'post-millennial' eschatology.

As you might guess, liberal ministers in mainline denominations avoid the Apocalypse in sermons and few have authored books on the subject. Needless to say, there are no best sellers among this camp on the subject of eschatology. It appears difficult to write a great book on a subject about which you have little enthusiasm!

The First Chapter of Revelation

We should pay careful attention to the first chapter of Revelation for several reasons: One, it is foundational for everything else we discuss in our study. Two, it lays out some ground rules about who is talking and why we need to take the subject matter seriously. Three, it plainly connects the visions of Daniel to those about to be disclosed by John in his book – thus, it underscores Scriptural continuity! What has been said in the Old Testament is about to be given a first century AD facelift! So let's review the entire first chapter:

¹ The revelation of Jesus Christ, which God gave him to show his servants what must soon take place. He made it known by sending his angel to his servant John,

² who testifies to everything he saw—that is, the word of God and the testimony of Jesus Christ.

³ Blessed is the one who reads the words of this prophecy, and blessed are those who hear it and take to heart what is written in it, because the time is near.

⁴ John, to the seven churches in the province of Asia: Grace and peace to you from him who is, and who was, and who is to come, and from the seven spirits before his throne,

⁵ and from Jesus Christ, who is the faithful witness, the firstborn from the dead, and the ruler of the kings of the earth. To him who loves us and has freed us from our sins by his blood,

⁶ and has made us to be a kingdom and priests to serve his God and Father—to him be glory and power forever and ever! Amen.

⁷ Look, he is coming with the clouds,
and every eye will see him,
even those who pierced him;
and all the peoples of the earth will mourn because of him. So shall it be! Amen.

⁸ "I am the Alpha and the Omega," says the Lord God, "who is, and who was, and who is to come, the Almighty."

⁹ I, John, your brother and companion in the suffering and kingdom and patient endurance that are ours in Jesus, was on the island of Patmos because of the word of God and the testimony of Jesus.

¹⁰ On the Lord's Day I was in the Spirit, and I heard behind me a loud voice like a trumpet,

¹¹ which said: "Write on a scroll what you see and send it to the seven churches: to Ephesus, Smyrna, Pergamum, Thyatira, Sardis, Philadelphia and Laodicea."

¹² I turned around to see the voice that was speaking to me. And when I turned I saw seven golden lamp stands,

13 and among the lamp stands was someone "like a son of man," dressed in a robe reaching down to his feet and with a golden sash around his chest.

14 His head and hair were white like wool, as white as snow, and his eyes were like blazing fire.

15 His feet were like bronze glowing in a furnace and his voice was like the sound of rushing waters.

16 In his right hand he held seven stars, and out of his mouth came a sharp double-edged sword. His face was like the sun shining in all its brilliance.

17 When I saw him, I fell at his feet as though dead. Then he placed his right hand on me and said: "Do not be afraid. I am the First and the Last.

18 I am the Living One; I was dead, and behold I am alive forever and ever! And I hold the keys of death and Hades.

19 "Write, therefore, what you have seen, what is now and what will take place later.

20 The mystery of the seven stars that you saw in my right hand and of the seven golden lamp stands is this: The seven stars are the angels of the seven churches, and the seven lamp stands are the seven churches.

As Revelation begins, John encounters the risen Christ as he is *"in the Spirit on the Lord's Day (Sunday)"* and records the words of Christ to seven Churches in the region known as Asia Minor (today's Turkey)—Revelation, Chapter 2 and 3.

John encounters an angel sent to tell him what is to happen soon. This angel,[2] which we should remember could also mean 'a messenger,' is none other than Jesus Christ—but not in a form that John readily recognizes Him. Nevertheless, John's description conveys that His presence is nothing less than awesome!

Comparable Visions of John and Daniel

The description of John is virtually the same with the vision of *Daniel* about which we read in Daniel, Chapter 10. In Daniel, the heavenly being he sees is *"like the Son of Man"* (the same phrase that

John uses in Revelation 1:13). Daniel describes his vision with these words:

> *4 On the twenty-fourth day of the first month, as I was standing on the bank of the great river, the Tigris,*
>
> *5 I looked up and there before me was a man dressed in linen, with a belt of the finest gold around his waist.*
>
> *6 His body was like chrysolite, his face like lightning, his eyes like flaming torches, his arms and legs like the gleam of burnished bronze, and his voice like the sound of a multitude.*
>
> *7 I, Daniel, was the only one who saw the vision; the men with me did not see it, but such terror overwhelmed them that they fled and hid themselves.*
>
> *8 So I was left alone, gazing at this great vision; I had no strength left, my face turned deathly pale and I was helpless...*
>
> *10 A hand touched me and set me trembling on my hands and knees.*
>
> *11 He said, "Daniel, you who are highly esteemed, consider carefully the words I am about to speak to you, and stand up, for I have now been sent to you." And when he said this to me, I stood up trembling.*
>
> *12 Then he continued, "Do not be afraid, Daniel.*

The two accounts differ only slightly in the descriptive similes selected. However, they agree in so many ways that it is clear they are seeing the same person: *His face is brilliant, his voice roars, his legs, arms, and feet seem ablaze, and his eyes were like torches.* It appears that the person that Daniel sees, who was *"a man"* and who John sees initially *"as a son of man"* is more clearly identified by John as the *"first and the last" (verse 17)—which is simply another way of saying the "Alpha and Omega."* It is Jesus Christ, the personage providing the revelation to John, whose titles *clearly equate Jesus with God.* This ascription of deity is not a 'passing comment.' This attribute is crucial to establish the importance of the Revelation and the reason we must listen carefully.

Jesus, like *"the man"* in Daniel, reassures John (verse 17) and begins to explain who He is (verse 17 and 18) and the meaning of the symbols of stars and lamp stands (verse 20). He says, the stars are the angels of the churches and the lamp stands are the churches themselves. Would that John could have explained all of his images quite this simply!

The Messages to the Seven Churches

Then, in the next two chapters, the 'Son of Man' will dictate John specific messages that he wants communicated to the seven churches. We won't delve into these messages as they actually are outside the scope of our study. Nevertheless, please note that most authorities believe each church represents not just the church of the city in question, but is a prediction of *how the Church of Jesus Christ will progress in the two thousand years that follow.* Each church depicts an 'age' or stage of the evolving Church. We know that there were other large churches in Asia Minor besides these seven. Therefore, their specific selection was intentional and had prophetic import.

For the most part, the churches receive praise; but Jesus also rebukes those who have shortcomings. The Church at Laodicea, the last of the seven churches and perhaps the 'figure' of the Church during the time of the tribulation period, receives no praise at all. It is this church that Jesus warns, 'If you remain lukewarm, I will spew you out of my mouth!' (Revelation 3:16). It's no surprise that evangelicals equate this Church to today's church, specifically those 'mainline denominations' and to Liberalism![3]

The Revelation of the Things to Come

After the messages to the seven churches, John's revelation changes perspective. The rest of the vision will pertain to things 'that are to come,' mostly to the time of *Tribulation* (Daniel's 70th week), the Kingdom of Christ—the *Millennium*, and the New Heavens and New Earth to come. At the beginning of Chapter 4, John is *"caught up"* into the Heavens to see visions of what *"is to come."* Note the voice *speaks like a trumpet* and calls to John, *"Come up here."* We will see this same situation at the resurrection of the **Two Witnesses** later in our study (see page 207). We should take note of the usage of the identical phrase with the 'Two Witnesses' in Revelation 11. We will see in that account as we see here that the voice sounds *"like a* *trumpet.*" Thus, we see a pattern emerges. With the shout of the Lord's voice, *a resurrection or ascension occurs!*

Most dispensational commentators see this 'catching up' as symbolic of the **'Rapture of the Saints'** (see page 169) particularly since the word *church* is not used again in Revelation until the last chapter. Like John, once the Church is "caught up" to heaven, the subject of the book changes to Israel and its salvation. Furthermore, the remainder of the book deals with the judgments of God toward an unbelieving world. If the Church escapes the wrath of God as many Bible verses convey, the *Church would not remain in the world during this period of judgment.* This assumption is a cornerstone for those that believe in the 'pre-tribulation' Rapture. As we mentioned before, the voice that John hears is *"like a trumpet"* (compare with I Thessalonians 4:13, I Corinthians 15:52). Just like the Rapture, this catching up occurs with a blast of a 'trumpet' (the 'last trumpet' to be precise.) Exactly what this trumpet amounts to is the subject of a later discussion. See **Chapter 25: the Voice of God – The Trumpet of God** on page 229.

Not everyone agrees that the timing of 'John's catching up' is precisely before the Tribulation period begins. Some see the chapters 4 through 7 dealing with the last two thousand years, future to John, but history to us. John's catching up doesn't picture the Rapture. Rather, it is to give John the opportunity to see the arrival of the Lamb of God, after completing his work of redemption upon the earth. Looking back to the beginning of the Book of Acts, Chapter 1, we recall that Jesus ascends to heaven. Then, it is as if the 'camera switches' to Revelation Chapter 4 to pick up the story in heaven. Jesus arrives on the scene and He is found worthy to break the seals of the *Seven Scrolls*. His death on the cross enables Him to accomplish what no one else was found worthy to do.

The Legacy of the Apostle John

John was the last of the original twelve Apostles to die. He was not only freed from the Isle of Patmos where he wrote *The Revelation*, but according to tradition also miraculously escaped death from being boiled in oil. John likely died a natural death[4] at a very old age and is believed to be buried in Ephesus, as is the Apostle Philip.

There are many stories about John's later life that we know about from Eusebius' history through *Polycarp* (one of the Church Fathers who John himself 'discipled' and who was also the first Bishop of the Church at Smyrna). Polycarp recorded a number of stories about John and communicated others to *Irenaeous*. Irenaeous, Poly-

> **THE KEY POINT TO PONDER:**
>
> *There is strong historical continuity between the Apostles and the Church Fathers into the second and third centuries. In addition, no ancient text has stronger extant manuscript support than the New Testament. The authenticity of the New Testament documents should be a matter of wonder not dispute!*

carp's famous pupil, was noted for his work *Against Heresies* and in particular his case for orthodox Christianity against *Gnosticism*. Eusebius indicates that Polycarp lived 86 years nearly up to the time of Marcus Aurelius (circa AD 166, 67). If so, it is noteworthy that eyewitnesses of the events of the Apostles lived up to 150 years after Christ's death and perhaps 70 years after the Apostles themselves passed away.

Because of this continuity, it would appear that the genuine teaching of Jesus and the Apostles should not be regarded with such skepticism. Coupled with the enormous textual support (thousands of extant fragments from the New Testament and from the Church Fathers), the authenticity of the Gospel should be the subject of wonder, not dispute. Please note: *No other ancient manuscript can be substantiated to the same extent as the New Testament.*

Recapping the Key Points Covered in This Chapter

- The author of the Revelation is traditionally John the Apostle.
- The Revelation is written while John is exiled on the Isle of Patmos (in today's Greek Islands).
- The sequence of 'which came first' – the Revelation of John or the Gospel of John is debated by scholars.

- Liberals and 'preterists' do not take the 'prophecies' of the Revelation as predictions; they see Revelation's purpose merely to encourage the early Christians who were suffering great persecution.
- The story begins with John and his first vision. He is overwhelmed at Christ's awesome appearance – this vision of Christ is identical to 'a man' in one of Daniels' visions, as the details of the description closely match.
- John writes letters to seven churches at Christ's dictation.
- The rest of John's vision occurs as he is 'caught up' into heaven.
- The visions of John and Daniel have many identical aspects, sharing symbols, numerology, and images throughout.
- John and his 'disciples,' Polycarp and Irenaeous, who testify to John's witness of Christ and His teaching, provide 150 years of 'message continuity' for the early church, often discounted by 'higher criticism.'

Technical Notes

[1] Some Covenantal or 'preterist' scholars believe it was earlier, before the destruction of Jerusalem, since no passage in Revelation insinuates the destruction of Jerusalem has already occurred. This is not the majority view.

[2] There are scores of examples in the Old Testament were the text reports that individuals encountered an angel, or the angel of God, and then the contextual verses identify the angel as 'God.' Just to list a few examples: Genesis 21:17, Genesis 31:11, Exodus 14:19, Judges 6:20, Judges 13:6. The appearance of God as a man or an angel is known in theology as a *theophany*. As we will see, a theophany was a 'safe' way for humans to 'see' God. Even still, those who saw a theophany were quick to conclude that they would die for having seen God!

[3] I have worked in a number of mainline Churches alongside many wonderful and highly committed Christians who have liberal theological beliefs. Such a characterization is unfair in many instances. I would rather draw a distinction between Liberalism as a system of theology and Christian believers who attend Liberal churches.

[4] I have always found it fascinating that all of the apostles were martyred except John. John (traditionally held to be the youngest of the 12), was the only Apostle who risked his life at the crucifixion, staying with Mary the Mother of Jesus and with Christ during his sufferings (all of the other Apostles fled, fearing for their lives, assuming the Romans would round them up and crucify them too). I believe these facts may not be coincidence. The resurrected Christ turned the cowardly disciples into heroes. John, who proved his courage and willingness to die 'as a lad,' lived to an age many believe of almost 100. Perhaps his long life was a reward for the courage he showed in his youth!

DD# 7 The Bible's Use of 'Popular' Terms

Sometimes in an effort to expound or explain an idea, a biblical writer will use a 'pagan' (or secular) term familiar to his audience. However, this is usually an occasion to clarify what the truth of a matter is and to distinguish it from a competing falsehood.

The *Logos* was a popular concept developed by a famous Jewish philosopher, Philo of Alexandria (Egypt), who was a contemporary of Jesus and the Apostles (20 BC-50 AD). Philo taught that the world was created not by God, for God is too pure, but by an intermediary, the *Logos of God*. Philo harkened to the 'Wisdom' literature of the Old Testament where (1) sometimes God's *words* and in other cases, (2) 'Wisdom' acting 'on its own,' appear to be synonymous with the action of God. (See Proverbs 8:1, 12, as examples). From a slightly different perspective, John, the author of the gospel, takes pains to clarify that while the Logos did create the world, the Logos was not only *"with God, but was God."* John 1:1-3 reads, *"In the beginning was the Word, and the Word was with God, and the Word was God. He was with God in the beginning. Through him all things were made; without him nothing was made that has been made."*

Knowing that Philo's philosophy was familiar to both the Jews of the 'Diaspora' and to the Greeks in Asia and Africa (most likely John's contemporary audience), John takes advantage of the term *Logos* to infuse it with new meaning: The *Logos* in his view includes the divine nature of Jesus Christ. John emphasizes that God didn't exist first and then create the Logos. The Logos was there at the beginning too.

It also infers that in contrast to certain Gnostic views, Christianity doesn't believe that there is any inherent 'evil' in the material of which the world is made. In contrast, most Gnostic belief is based upon this idea. Matter is 'corrupted.' Therefore, since Christ could never be composed of matter, His humanity must be illusory. In contrast, authentic Christianity believes in both the reality of matter and spirit. In addition, from the beginning of the Bible in Genesis 1, we read the daily news of what God created and how He declared it 'good.' At the end of day one we read, "And God saw that it was good." At the end of day two, we read the same thing: "And God saw this was good too." And so on. And so on.

If God wasn't omniscient, you almost could hear Him surprising Himself with how awesome His work was! He took a step back and gazed upon what He did and endorses it enthusiastically, "This is great!" That is going a bit overboard. Then again, that is one reason why He created human beings – so He could have intelligent and sentient beings that could enjoy His creation and praise His greatness.

Where evil comes from of course is another discussion! However, it isn't due to a flaw in the 'material the world is made of' or a faulty creator for that matter.

Paul in his letter to the Colossians talks about *'gnosis so-called'* and criticizes those who wish to base salvation upon receiving 'inner illumination' or hidden knowledge. He turns the word around to his purposes and discusses, *'epignosis'* or super knowledge which he indicates is the knowledge of Christ. He also clarifies that in Christ, *"the fullness of God is pleased to dwell bodily"* (NASV), pointing out that it was not abhorrent for the material and the spiritual to be united in the incarnation of Jesus Christ. In Chapter 1 of Colossians we read:

15 He is the image of the invisible God, the firstborn over all creation.

16 For by him all things were created: things in heaven and on earth, visible and invisible, whether thrones or powers or rulers or authorities; all things were created by him and for him.

17 He is before all things, and in him all things hold together.

18 And he is the head of the body, the church; he is the beginning and the firstborn from among the dead, so that in everything he might have the supremacy.

19 For God was pleased to have all his fullness dwell in him,

20 and through him to reconcile to himself all things, whether things on earth or things in heaven, by making peace through his blood, shed on the cross.

DEEP DIVE NUMBER 7

DD# 8 The Formation of the New Testament Canon

Several individuals were particularly important in deciding which books that were circulating in the early Church should be 'canonized' (made official and pronounced acceptable). One of the first was Eusebius.

Many believe Eusebius wrote his Church History in 324 A.D. just before the Council at Nicaea. While some of his reports are mistaken, most scholars regard his testimony to names, dates, and times invaluable in understanding what transpired in the first three centuries of the Church. In reading Eusebius on the issue of the canon, it becomes clear that the usage of the church was formative to the canon and not the other way around. 'Canonizing' books was merely formally recognizing what the Churches were already using—with few exceptions (for example, books like 'The Shepherd of Hermas' and the 'Epistle of Barnabas' were popular but not accepted). To be acceptable, the 'book' (1) must have found a place in the Church's use, (2) must not contradict *the apostolic teaching*, and (3) must be written by an Apostle or a close associate. Perhaps unexpectedly to some, Eusebius is quite candid about which writings he believes are authentic and which ones are not. He questions the authenticity of Second and Third John among a number of other books in the accepted New Testament. But to 'set the record straight,' Eusebius points out various 'lists' of acceptable 'gospels' and 'letters' from various authorities by tracing their history through the 2nd and 3rd centuries.

Most scholars associate the final determination of the canon associated with the Bishop of Alexandria, Egypt, St. Athanasius, in his 'Easter Letter' of 367 AD. We read in Wikipedia, "In AD 367, Athanasius of Alexandria authored the 39th Festal Letter, or Easter letter. In it, he listed the same 27 books of the New Testament that are in use today. The same letter defines a 22-book Old Testament. The epistle to the Hebrews is missing from some later lists, but the canon defined dogmatically at the Council of Trent matches Athanasius's list and includes the epistle. The New Testament writings founded in the Codex Vaticanus (A.D.340) and Athanasius' 39th Festal Letter were the first compilations of the present list of Roman Catholic New Testament writings, which were officially determined at the Council of Rome (A.D. 382), under Pope Damasus. This determination was then confirmed by the Third Council of Carthage (A.D. 397)." See: *http:// en.wikipedia.org /wiki/ Easter_letter.*

DEEP DIVE NUMBER 8

Chapter 15: The Living Creatures Before the Throne

To Understand Revelation, Know the Old Testament

The previous section introduced John, the author of Revelation, with background information about the timing and location of his writing. Additionally, we reviewed the first chapter of that book to provide additional context for our study. We also emphasized that the one who revealed to *John* 'what is soon to come' was the same 'man' who appeared to *Daniel* in his vision—namely, Jesus Christ. So it should be no surprise, that there is agreement among Christian scholars of all perspectives that these two books, Daniel and Revelation, should be read *together* because there are so many parallels. By reading both 'side-by-side,' one can achieve a much better understanding of each book in its own right.

Furthermore, we often talk about how difficult it is to understand the Revelation of John. We should realize that part of the reason we don't understand it is that we fail to link it to the Old Testament prophecies to which John refers—and by so doing, *we disclose our ignorance of what the prophecies of Old Testament teach*. This 'unbalanced' knowledge of the Old and New Testaments is a common problem for Christians and something those of us who are Christians should try to correct. I admit I need this counter-balance to my knowledge bank of the Bible as much as anyone does!

Parallels between Revelation and Ezekiel

Indeed, not only does Revelation tie to Daniel, there are also fascinating parallels between the Revelation and the Book of Ezekiel.[i] In this section, we will address the most intriguing one having to do with the *Living Creatures before the Throne* in Revelation 4.

---

[i] Ezekiel, a prophet of Israel, prophesied at the same period as Daniel, writing his manuscript from his captivity near Babylon.

What we will see, once again, is an exceedingly clear identification of the *Glory of God, a 'palpable and overpowering presence'* with the subject of the Revelation, Jesus Christ. As in the comparison between Revelation and Daniel, John's vision confirms beyond any doubt that early Christianity identified Jesus Christ with the most sacred and exalted visions of God in the Old Testament.

We read in Chapter 4 of John's Revelation:

¹ After this I looked, and there before me was a door standing open in heaven. And the voice I had first heard speaking to me like a trumpet said, "Come up here, and I will show you what must take place after this."

² At once I was in the Spirit, and there before me was a throne in heaven with someone sitting on it.

³ And the one who sat there had the appearance of jasper and carnelian. A rainbow, resembling an emerald, encircled the throne.

⁴ Surrounding the throne were twenty-four other thrones, and seated on them were twenty-four elders. They were dressed in white and had crowns of gold on their heads.

⁵ From the throne came flashes of lightning, rumblings and peals of thunder. Before the throne, seven lamps were blazing. These are the seven spirits of God.

⁶ Also before the throne there was what looked like a sea of glass, clear as crystal. In the center, around the throne, were four living creatures, and they were covered with eyes, in front and in back.

⁷ The first living creature was like a lion, the second was like an ox, the third had a face like a man, the fourth was like a flying eagle.

⁸ Each of the four living creatures had six wings and was covered with eyes all around, even under his wings.

⁹ Day and night they never stop saying: "Holy, holy, holy is the Lord God Almighty, who was, and is, and is to come."

Is it a coincidence that John's vision of the four living creatures has so many characteristics in common with Ezekiel's vision of four living creatures within the *"chariots of fire"?*[i] We read in Ezekiel, Chapter 1 (verses 5-11):

---

[i] From whence the 1981 British film, *Chariots of Fire*, gets its name.

132

5 ...and in the fire was what looked like four living creatures. In appearance their form was that of a man,

6 but each of them had four faces and four wings.

7 Their legs were straight; their feet were like those of a calf and gleamed like burnished bronze.

8 Under their wings on their four sides they had the hands of a man. All four of them had faces and wings,

9 and their wings touched one another. Each one went straight ahead; they did not turn as they moved.

10 Their faces looked like this: Each of the four had the face of a man, and on the right side each had the face of a lion, and on the left the face of an ox; each also had the face of an eagle.

11 Such were their faces. Their wings were spread out upward; each had two wings, one touching the wing of another creature on either side, and two wings covering its body.

The final verses of Ezekiel Chapter 1 are most instructive because they provide the interpretation of Ezekiel's vision:

25 Then there came a voice from above the expanse over their heads as they stood with lowered wings.

26 Above the expanse over their heads was what looked like a throne of sapphire, and high above on the throne was a figure like that of a man.

27 I saw that from what appeared to be his waist up he looked like glowing metal, as if full of fire, and that from there down he looked like fire; and brilliant light surrounded him.

28 Like the appearance of a rainbow in the clouds on a rainy day, so was the radiance around him. This was the appearance of the likeness of the glory of the LORD. When I saw it, I fell facedown, and I heard the voice of one speaking.

Many details correlate in the visions of John and Ezekiel. We can point out several important ones:

1. The throne appears deep blue like sapphire in Ezekiel and its surrounding color is like emerald in Revelation.

2. Seated on the throne is someone who appears 'like a man.' His appearance is reminiscent of the image of Christ from Chapter 1 of Revelation and the Son of Man from Daniel Chapter 10. Ezekiel

says plainly, *"This was the appearance of the likeness of the glory of the LORD"* (verse 28).

3.   In each case, 'four living creatures' possess a face of a man, a lion, an ox, and an eagle. In John's vision, each creature has only one of these faces; in Ezekiel's vision, each of the creatures possesses all four faces.

4.   In John's vision, (as in Isaiah's, see Isaiah 6:1-4), the creatures have six wings whereas in Ezekiel, they only have four. However, the creatures in John's vision are covered 'with eyes everywhere' which most scholars believe is a symbol of supernatural awareness and perception. We will see this same trait ('eyes everywhere') in Ezekiel's second vision (Ezekiel Chapter 10:12).

5.   Moreover, the ultimate attribute common to both visions—*the throne is brilliantly illuminated and surrounded by a rainbow.* What a fantastic sight it must have been!

However, what is the real purpose of these creatures? What are they seeking to convey?

Cherubim and the Glory of God

In Ezekiel, Chapter 10, Ezekiel eventually discloses to us that in his vision these creatures are *cherubim¹*—mighty angels—and while their appearance is the same as before, in this account we see them in action:

¹⁵ Then the cherubim rose upward. These were the living creatures I had seen by the Kebar River.

¹⁶ When the cherubim moved, the wheels beside them moved; and when the cherubim spread their wings to rise from the ground, the wheels did not leave their side.

¹⁷ When the cherubim stood still, they also stood still; and when the cherubim rose, they rose with them, because the spirit of the living creatures was in them.

¹⁸ Then the glory of the LORD departed from over the threshold of the temple and stopped above the cherubim.

¹⁹ While I watched, the cherubim spread their wings and rose from the ground, and as they went, the wheels went with them. They stopped at the entrance to the east gate of the LORD's house, and the glory of the God of Israel was above them.

20 These were the living creatures I had seen beneath the God of Israel by the Kebar River, and I realized that they were cherubim.

21 Each had four faces and four wings, and under their wings was what looked like the hands of a man.

22 Their faces had the same appearance as those I had seen by the Kebar River. Each one went straight ahead.

How should we interpret these visions? Some have suggested (perhaps going out on a limb), that cherubim move about via flying machines. In fact, they just might be 'flying saucers!' Certainly, Erich von Däniken (b. 1935-), in his book, (*Chariots of the Gods?* published in 1968), amassed some evidence along with considerable speculation along these lines (although his main point wasn't regarding those 'amazing angels in their flying machines'—instead it was that God was really an *ancient alien astronaut!*).

Nevertheless, closer to 'orthodoxy,' (yet still not quite 'down to earth' so to speak) some Christians suppose that angels may need some manner of spacecraft to move 'to and from heaven.' The great distance or dimensional 'transition' appears to involve travel in a way that we cannot imagine. However, is this supposition necessary or is it also 'over the top'?

Virtually all commentators agree that the visions of Ezekiel speak of the *Glory of God*. However, to verify this, we need to take note of other Old Testament stories concerning the appearances of God.

- God's glory is portrayed *"as a cloud by day and a fire by night"* in the wilderness wanderings of the Jews after the Exodus (Numbers 9:15).

- In the Temple of Solomon in Jerusalem, God's glory fills the template 'like a cloud.' I Kings 8:10 says, *"When the priests withdrew from the Holy Place, the cloud filled the temple of the LORD. And the priests could not perform their service because of the cloud, for the glory of the LORD filled his temple."*

- In the Holy of Holies, the innermost and most sacred portion of the temple, His glory 'resides' on the mercy seat on the Ark of the Covenant between the golden cherubim. However, the cloud always covers His glory (Leviticus 16:2) (see the Deep Dive below **The Glory of God and the Cloud,** page 142, for more details).

The cherubim appear to reside where the Glory of God is. We *normally don't see the Glory of God without cherubim nearby and we never see the Glory of God without the 'dark cloud' hiding it.* God's glory is associated with the cherubim and God must cloak his glory to protect nearly observers. Logically, we can also conclude that if a being has the cherubim keeping pace with him, we must consider the being in some sense divine and therefore, *full of glory too!*

The Meaning of the Vision

So in this vision of Ezekiel 10, what are we witnessing? What does it mean? Commentators suggest that God's Glory is departing from the Temple due to the sin of Israel. This occurs about 586 BC with the destruction of the Hebrew Temple by Nebuchadnezzar. God is communicating an elaborate and powerful vision to prepare Ezekiel to deal with the challenges of confronting Israel and its sin. This vision is to strengthen Ezekiel for his ministry.

However, what are we to make of the elaborate wheels and chariots of fire? Most interestingly (and unexplainably), the cherubim appear to be the means for God's Glory *to move from the Temple, pass through the East Gate of the City, and apparently to return to Heaven (verse 18).* Indeed, Ezekiel provides a detailed account of the movements of the 'whirling wheels' and the living creatures:

> *9 I looked, and I saw beside the cherubim four wheels, one beside each of the cherubim; the wheels sparkled like chrysolite.*
>
> *10 As for their appearance, the four of them looked alike; each was like a wheel intersecting a wheel.*
>
> *11 As they moved, they would go in any one of the four directions the cherubim faced; the wheels did not turn about as the cherubim went. The cherubim went in whatever direction the head faced, without turning as they went.*
>
> *12 Their entire bodies, including their backs, their hands and their wings, were completely full of eyes, as were their four wheels.*
>
> *13 I heard the wheels being called "the whirling wheels."*
>
> *14 Each of the cherubim had four faces: One face was that of a cherub, the second the face of a man, the third the face of a lion, and the fourth the face of an eagle.*

15 Then the cherubim rose upward. These were the living creatures I had seen by the Kebar River.

16 When the cherubim moved, the wheels beside them moved; and when the cherubim spread their wings to rise from the ground, the wheels did not leave their side.

17 When the cherubim stood still, they also stood still; and when the cherubim rose, they rose with them, because the spirit of the living creatures was in them.

While we can't go too far in our speculations about what Ezekiel saw, we can say that the image of 'wheels intersecting other wheels' is an image we've seen spacecraft sport in science fiction movies. However, what is radically different *is that these vehicles and the cherubim are somehow united – they are NOT separate and distinct.* We read that whatever direction the cherubim faced, the vehicle would go that direction. Each living creature had its own 'whirling wheel.' Likewise, the vehicles never left their side—wherever the machine was the cherubim was right there.

Then very specifically, in verse 17 we understand that the unified movement between the cherubim and the whirling wheels are linked because *"the spirits of the living creatures are in them." It appears that the union is "body and soul."* The whirling wheels are an extension of the image of the cherubim. Just as the cherubim showcase 'wings' they project whirling wheels too. It seems apparent that *the image of the whirling wheels must be the way the cherubim choose to appear in this particular vision.* We can conclude through this analysis that cherubim and 'their flying machines' are actually one and the same!

So what does this tell us about angels? We know from other situations that angels can appear in many different forms. Even Lucifer, a.k.a., Satan, can appear *"as an angel of light."* (II Corinthians 11:14) Moreover, in many situations, angels appear to be humans—so the writer to the Hebrews tells us we may have entertained *"angels unaware."* (Hebrews 13:2). We can go a little further and speculate that perhaps *angels don't really have wings*—they project an image in this way to communicate something to us about their nature and their purpose (in times past, wings symbolized *speed* and implicitly *distinction*). ⁱ

Are Objects of Visions Real?

This would suggest that what Ezekiel has witnessed is not what 'an impartial observer might be seeing.' Indeed, in the final analysis, the image of the whirling wheels may not be of a physical object at all—these celestial machines may just be what the cherubim want the observer to see! Furthermore, what the observer sees may be external (objective), or they may be purely subjective pictures placed within his mind. *If so, the perceiver is as important in creating the image as the 'projectors' of the image itself.* In other words, two separate observers may see the same thing, or they may not. The nature of visions isn't conducive to 'verifying the facts by comparing the stories of the eyewitnesses.' Two witnesses might both have visions of the same thing, see details differently, yet both are right!

There is certainly considerable speculation today about what UFOs actually are. It is easy to conclude from what we have just learned about the 'good angels', which appear with celestial machines in Ezekiel, that 'bad angels' could do the same. Indeed, many books have been written for the past three decades suggesting that UFOs and alien appearances are in fact a *grand deception* – the aliens and their flying machines may be nothing more than fallen angels intensifying their mission to deceive.[2] Even C.G. Jung commented substantively on this topic. Based upon his research with many patients who experienced these phenomena and through discussions with authorized government officials,[3] Jung questioned the popular verdict that flying saucers are necessarily physical objects from another planet! He suspected that in most cases they had a *spiritual* origin. The connection between their characteristics and standard human 'symbols' led him to this conclusion.[4]

ⁱ Today, continuing along this line of thought, we could conjecture that angels might choose to appear with a 'jet pack' attached to their back! After all, wings are so 'retro!'

The Meaning of the Four Living Creatures

But to return to the focus of the vision, it seems clear that with John's vision in Revelation and Ezekiel's first of two visions (in Ezekiel Chapter 1), we are viewing the *throne of God and those beings that help us 'see' God who sits on the throne.*

To elaborate: These four beasts, as we have learned from Ezekiel, are cherubim, which appear to be the highest rank of angel. In John's vision, they each have six wings and a unique face. He identifies the faces in a particular order that is significant: *A lion, an ox, a man, and a flying eagle.* Many scholars have postulated that these creatures represent a 'portrait' of Christ from each of *the four gospels.* It is interesting that each gospel presents a unique 'picture' of the Messiah. To expand upon this point, each of the four creatures conveys a primary aspect of the gospel central to its message:

- The first creature corresponds to a lion, a picture of Jesus as King of the Jews (and the lion of Judah) as depicted in Matthew's gospel;

- The next an *ox* symbolizing a servant represented in Mark's gospel where Christ comes *"to serve and not be served but to give His life a ransom for many"* (Mark 10:45);

- The third creature possesses the face of a *man* which is described in the third gospel, Luke's gospel, which traces the lineage of Christ all the way back to Adam; thus Jesus is seen as the 'new Adam' or perfect human being.

- Finally, the fourth creature, as symbolized in the gospel of John, has the face of an eagle, a being that dwells in the heavens, as John's gospel emphasizes the divine aspects of Jesus more than the other three. John's gospel begins with the Logos, the heavenly Word of God that creates the entire universe, and then, as Messiah, visits the creation He has made.

Assuming that God in fact intends this symbolism, it clearly portrays the nature of the Messiah symbolically hundreds of years before His first coming. It is a strong corroboration that God and Jesus are equals. Furthermore, it verifies that there was intent on God's part to have four gospels written each portraying a specific aspect of the Messiah's purpose. Likewise, it would refute the value of any other gospel that attempts to reinterpret the words and nature of Jesus Christ.[5]

One final curiosity related to the same phenomena: In noting the four 'fixed signs' of the Zodiac, isn't it interesting that the four are *Leo, Taurus, Aquarius,* and *Scorpio*? A famous biblical authority on 'the gospel in the stars,' E. W. Bullinger contended that we could trace the entire gospel story through all 12 of the common signs of the constellations. He contended that God 'wrote His story large' in the stars. This action was part of His 'general revelation' to human-kind of His nature and His plan.

If this is true, what we see are the four 'fixed signs' confirming the same four faces of Ezekiel and John: Leo is the lion, Taurus is the bull (or ox), Aquarius is a man (the cupbearer), and Scorpio represents the eagle. However, the reader might point out that Scorpio is a dragon not an eagle. This is true; but experts in this area point out that originally in ancient astrology predating the Greeks, Scorpio was an eagle or a phoenix (a bird resurrected). So is this just another coincidence?

Arthur C. Clarke once made a fantastic observation: "Any sufficiently advanced science is indistinguishable from magic." I submit the following might be a useful maxim to highlight how repeated coincidences reinforce the probability of providence.[i]

> *As coincidental phenomenon accumulates which confirms the improbable, the probability increases such phenomena aren't coincidental.*[6]

John's Unique Four Perceptions of Jesus

There is yet one more mystery: John the Apostle who sees the four creatures before the throne in Revelation (which reflects the 'four-fold gospel of Jesus Christ') has seen this same Christ 'with his own eyes' in *four different and unique manifestations*: Initially, John has seen Jesus as,

---

[i] A *maxim* is "a succinct or pithy saying that has some proven truth to it."

1.   Jesus of Nazareth over the three or perhaps four years as Jesus' disciple during Jesus' ministry (and perhaps, he grew up with Him);

2.   Transfigured on Mount Hermon appearing to James, Peter and to John (Jesus' 'inner circle), in brilliant light where his clothing appeared *"whiter than any launderer can make them"* (Mark 9:2-7)

3.   The resurrected Christ (how He appeared to the Apostles), did *not look like the man Jesus they knew before His death and resurrection.* Indeed, it was because of what He told them to do (something He had done at their first encounter—cast their fishing nets on the other side of the boat) which may have 'given Him away' (see John 21:1-7).

4.   Lastly, this final appearance is quite different still from his post-resurrection appearance and is the most exalted of all manners in which John saw his Lord. Christ has blazing eyes and hair white as snow with arms and legs that burn like metal in a hot furnace.

John is the only person recorded in the Bible to witness Jesus Christ in these four different ways. Did John's various encounters with Jesus correspond to that of a lion, an ox, a man, and a flying eagle? We could plausibly map the purely human Jesus to Mark, the Transfigured Jesus to Matthew, the Resurrected Christ to Luke, and the Christ whose eyes blaze to John. Is this correlation fair? I'll let the reader decide.

Therefore, what we must conclude is that the link between Christ and the 'man' enthroned in Revelation 4, surrounded by the four living creatures and the twenty-four elders,[7] underscores that the early Christians saw Jesus Christ not just as the promised *Messiah, but as a powerful divine being.* Indeed, they weren't afraid to tie the most exalted images of their Jewish LORD with the person of Jesus Christ! Simply put, *they had no problem identifying Jesus Christ as the Lord God Himself.*

Key Points Covered in This Chapter

- John's apocalyptic vision is closely associated with a number of prophecies from the Old Testament Prophets.
- Daniel is the principal connection, but Ezekiel's vision of the 'living creatures' is nearly identical to John's vision of these creatures too.
- The creatures have extraordinary characteristics – multiple faces, wings, and eyes that clearly seem to symbolize the glory of God.
- We learn later in Ezekiel that these living creatures are 'cherubim' – the highest rank of angels.
- A discussion among apocalyptic writers today is the linkage to UFOs – the visions of these creatures summon images of flying saucers. Do angels need flying machines?
- The cherubim's appearance gives us insight into the nature of angels and their method of disclosing themselves.
- God's glory is associated with cherubim, but also with a dense cloud.
- The nature of visions and the 'objects' of visions can be better understood by studying this particular one shared by John and Ezekiel.
- There are 'four faces:' A lion, an ox or bull, a man, and an eagle.
- These four faces also correspond to the four fixed constellations.
- John has a unique history of four different perceptions of Christ.
- The fourfold nature of the gospel appears intentional!

DD# 9   The Glory of God and the Cloud

So why does God choose to be hidden 'by a cloud?' When God descends upon Mount Sinai, he descends 'in a cloud' and His presence is like fire that, according to Bob Cornuke (through his adventurous visit to the probable Mount Sinai in Arabia), *chars* the top of the mountain, and turns it dark gray. (One can suppose that the heats' metamorphic affect upon the rock transformed the normal sand color).

When God guides the Israelites in the Wilderness, His presence is a *"cloud by day and a fire by night"* (Numbers 14:14). When God is present in the Temple, His Shekinah Glory that resides above the Mercy Seat of the Ark of the Covenant is so powerful that its brightness lights the inner Temple—and it is apparently so dangerous that it must be cloaked. The Scripture says that a cloud fills the Holy of Holies so that those who come near will not see God's Glory—for if they do, they will die.

Leviticus 16:2 says, "The LORD said to Moses: "Tell your brother

Aaron not to come whenever he chooses into the Most Holy Place behind the curtain in front of the atonement cover on the ark, or else he will die, because I appear in the cloud over the atonement cover." So the Old Testament teaches that no one can see God 'as He is' and live. It would seem that 'the cloud' intends in part to shield God's glory from those who would suffer should they behold it in its 'fullness.'

We should recall the story in Exodus where Moses asks to see God's Glory and God agrees but only under specific conditions. Moses can hide in a cleft of a Rock and look at God's shadow (or 'back side') as He passes by. God does this and Moses is able to experience God's glory in a dose that doesn't kill him! *"When my glory passes by, I will put you in a cleft in the rock and cover you with my hand until I have passed by. Then I will remove my hand and you will see my back; but my face must not be seen."* (Exodus 33:22, 23)

Our opportunity to 'see God' is restricted because it is apparently life threatening. For us to apprehend what God is, we must have a manifestation that is something we can literally 'live with.' Jesus Christ is of course the ultimate way we come to understand and appreciate what God is like—and via the incarnation (God in the flesh), what He 'looks like.' (*"Anyone who has seen me has seen the Father,"* John 14:9).

But the appearance of God's Glory in the Old Testament is so awesome, that it is a reminder—God has to 'filter' Himself in some manner for us to be able to encounter Him. Does this mean that Jesus Christ was then 'less than fully divine?'

Philippians 2:5-7 points out that something was 'diminished' (the Greek word Paul uses is *kenosis* or 'emptying') in order for God to become incarnate in Jesus:

"Have this attitude in yourselves which was also in Christ Jesus, who, although He existed in the form of God, did not regard equality with God a thing to be grasped, but emptied Himself, taking the form of a bond-servant, and being made in the likeness of men..." (NASV)

However, to be consistent with the main point of the Nicaean Creed, it is probable that this 'emptying' process was not metaphysical, but simply one of stature or respect. Christ willingly gave up His stature in heaven to become a human being.

To paraphrase C.S. Lewis: "It would be like one of us becoming a slug!"

DEEP DIVE NUMBER 9

Technical Notes

[1] Cherubim were not exclusive to the Hebrews. Mighty statues of angelic beings known as cherubim were frequently posted at the gates of pagan temples too, guarding the way into the temple. Oftentimes, they had two faces that differed—one a lion, the other a man. We see this in Ezekiel, Chapter 41:18, 19. (The cherubim here have only two faces!) This does not invalidate the idea of there actually being cherubim associated with the throne of God and His Holy temple. Pagans have memories too; from their cultural history, they may have associated cherubim with their pagan gods because of an 'archetype' that inspired them to maintain the connection even in their false religions – religions which were corrupted facsimiles of the true one from which they had fallen.

[2] The first book I read on the subject was John Weldon's and Zola Levitt's *UFOs: What on the Earth is Happening?* Published in 1976 by Bantam Books. A quick search on Yahoo! yielded a dozen books available on the subject of the Bible and UFOs. I predict there are more to come and this may in fact be the final and great deception of the False Prophet and the Antichrist. This is the main point of L.A. Marzulli, in his book, *Politics, Prophecy, and the Supernatural.* See **For Further Reading** for a synopsis of this work.

[3] Jung's view corroborates the position here that while the phenomena could not be dismissed neither could it really be proven to be objectively true. UFOs appear to be spiritual symbols perhaps more than they appear to be genuine spacecraft. Jung does allow for both possibilities however.

[4] See the book, *Flying Saucers*, C.G. Jung, Princeton University Press, 1978, which is a collection of numerous excerpts on the topic.

[5] Yet another Old Testament example comes from the alignment of how the Israelites camped during their wilderness wanderings. The 12 tribes were grouped into four camps (incidentally shaped in the form of a cross), under the ensigns of four of the tribes, which just so happened to be ensigns of a lion, an ox, a man, and an eagle. Fantastic!

[6] One of the greatest series of coincidental phenomena is how the ninth of Av, a date on the Jewish calendar typically occurring during August of the Gregorian calendar, was 'doomsday' for the nation of Israel. We know that both temples were destroyed on the ninth of Av (586 BC and 70 AD); the edict to cast all Jews out of Spain in 1492 (just before Columbus sailed) was the 9th of Av; and the mandate of Hitler in Poland to quarter the Jews in the ghetto began the process of the holocaust on the ninth of Av. We can discover many other 'bad things' which happen to the Jews on this date. Why? This was also the date that the 'minority report' was rejected (Joshua and Caleb) to 'go take the land' – the majority report was accepted of the 10 spies who believed that Canaan, dominated by the Rephaim (a.k.a., Nephilim – the *giants*) was impossible for the Jews to conquer. The repercussions reverberate down through history.

[7] The 24 Elders is another great story—but we won't tackle it here.

Chapter 16: The Mark of the Beast

The False Prophet Enforces the Mark

One of the most dramatic topics in Christian prophecy is the nature of the *Mark of the Beast*. Like the identity of the **Antichrist** (see page 65), speculation on this *Mark* has been the subject of many books and enlivened countless hours of discussion.

Revelation describes a 'mark' that everyone in the world must accept in order to be able to 'buy or sell'. John says of the **False Prophet** (see page 115) in Revelation Chapter 13,

> *16 He also forced everyone, small and great, rich and poor, free and slave, to receive a mark on his right hand or on his forehead,*
>
> *17 so that no one could buy or sell unless he had the mark, which is the name of the beast or the number of his name.*
>
> *18 This calls for wisdom. If anyone has insight, let him calculate the number of the beast, for it is man's number. His number is 666.*

The Beast will enforce his mark to be placed on the hand or forehead. The mark is associated with the number 666. Scholars relate 666 to biblical numerology, three being the number of God in the Scripture (related to the Trinity), and six being the number of humankind. What the number adds up to, quite simply is 'man making himself God.' This is perhaps the most conservative and safe assertion made about what the *Mark* means. However, there are many more guesses about the exact form of the Mark of the Beast that are far more sensational than the 'safe' one cited here!

Speculation on the Nature of the Mark

In the film, *The Omen* (1976), a priest tells the father of Damien that if his son is the Beast of Revelation, he will find a mark of three sixes somewhere on his body, perhaps on his head. Sure enough, Gregory Peck, playing Damien's father, finds a tattoo-like figure of three sixes on his scalp! This idea makes for a great film but doesn't have biblical support. It is unlikely that the Antichrist will bear 'the Mark' anywhere on his person. In other words, it may be 'his mark' but it doesn't mean it will physically identify him!

In stark contrast, the clearest sign of his identity is quite simply what the Antichrist says about himself. The Beast speaks blasphemies 'against the God of Heaven making Himself equal to God' according to Daniel and to John. His revealing is very clear-cut. There really isn't any mystery at all concerning how we learn who the Antichrist is.

Nevertheless, speculation has run rampant through the centuries. How can we identify the Beast 'beforehand' and what does the number of the Beast mean? Most attempts to link the Mark of the Beast to a particular man involve the use of either Greek or Roman numerals that compose his name. Since the Greek and Roman numerical systems used the letters of their alphabets to signify numbers (just as in Latin, 'I' represents one, 'V' five, 'X' represents 10, etc), it is traditionally believed it would be quick work to 'add up' the value of each letter and compute the value a particular candidate's name. If it equaled 666,[i] we would know to keep a close eye on him!

Early Christians believed that the Caesar Nero was the Antichrist (Nero burned Rome in 64 AD, and then falsely accused the Christians of the crime). His name added up to 666 based upon this simple calculation.[1]

In today's technology, one could imagine the *Mark of the Beast* implemented as bar code scanning system or an embedded smart chip. It is interesting that the bar code scanning system (with which we are accustomed when purchasing retail goods), uses the bar code for six, three times, which serves as a calibration mechanism to identify the width of the entire bar code and enable the scanning system to detect and interpret the entire set of numbers. Is this pure coincidence? Was it a joke played on us by IBM?[2] However the Beast chooses to implement his 'mark,' it's open to a great deal of educated speculation. Nevertheless, it is practically certain that once the

---

[i] This numerology provides an intriguing answer to the question often posed, "What's in a name?"

Beast reveals himself, we will easily confirm his number is 666 by resorting to one of these numerological techniques from times past.

A Recent Interpretation of 666

Some sources contend that in proto-Hebrew (the early language and alphabet that became Hebrew), the three characters that stood for three sixes resembled the characters that could be seen to convey 'a snake in the tree' (reminiscent of the evil talking snake in the Garden of Eden). Likewise, Arabs who have converted to Christianity point out that the three characters in their alphabet that identify the name of Allah in Arabic actually resemble three sixes. (See David Flynn, *The Temple at the Center of Time*, for further details). Not being an expert in these matters, I can't confirm such accounts to be factual, but I must admit the thought is intriguing!

The Mark of the Beast and God's Judgment

John warns us that to accept the Mark is to accept the Beast. Bearing *the Mark* will bring the judgment of God. *"So the first angel went and poured out his bowl on the Earth; and it became a loathsome and malignant sore on the people who had the mark of the beast and who worshiped his image."* (Revelation 16:2, NASV). Earlier in Revelation 14, John draws the distinction between those who receive the Mark and those that don't:

> *⁹ A third angel followed them and said in a loud voice: "If anyone worships the beast and his image and receives his mark on the forehead or on the hand,*
>
> *¹⁰ he, too, will drink of the wine of God's fury, which has been poured full strength into the cup of his wrath. He will be tormented with burning sulfur in the presence of the holy angels and of the Lamb.*
>
> *¹¹ And the smoke of their torment rises forever and ever. There is no rest day or night for those who worship the beast and his image, or for anyone who receives the mark of his name."*
>
> *¹² This calls for patient endurance on the part of the saints who obey God's commandments and remain faithful to Jesus.*

13 Then I heard a voice from heaven say, "Write: Blessed are the dead who die in the Lord from now on." "Yes," says the Spirit, "they will rest from their labor, for their deeds will follow them."

We also learn that many die in the Great Tribulation because they choose *not* to receive the Mark. We know this because we learn in Revelation 20:4, the power of God has resurrected many *out of this time of Great Tribulation to reign with Christ during the Millennium*:

"And I saw the souls of those who had been beheaded because of their testimony of Jesus and because of the word of God, and those who had not worshiped the beast or his image, and had not received the mark on their forehead and on their hand; and they came to life and reigned with Christ for a thousand years" (NASV).

The *Great Tribulation* is a time of *decision*. Those who are left alive during this period must make a frightening choice: (1) Either you choose to *receive* the Mark of the Beast to avoid the threat of death, or (2) you choose to *reject* the Mark and trust in the protection of God. However, understand that this stance will mean persecution not protection from the Beast. Instead, God's 'seal' shields you from the many forms of wrath and judgment that He will soon pour forth upon the earth. Happily, it will seal your fate too, but in a good way – to be a part of God's Kingdom! Nevertheless, John warns us that many will become martyrs during this time.[i]

Who Will Go Through the Tribulation?

Because the stakes are so high—because the possibility of martyrdom is so great during this period—the debate rages as to whether today's true believers in Christ will go through the Great Tribulation.

Those who believe the Church is 'raptured' before the Tribulation preach that by believing in Jesus now you can avoid the persecution of the Antichrist and avoid the choice between receiving the *Mark of the Beast* or the *Seal of God*. Those who teach that we will go through the Tribulation rely upon the promise of this Seal—the

---

[i] With this death, believers win a very special crown of martyrdom, but earned at the highest of costs.

protection of God during this especially horrible time. For this reason, the 'post-tribbers' criticize those who believe in the pre-
tribulation Rapture for counting on 'the great escape.' They argue
that martyrdom has always been a possibility for those who call
themselves Christian. The *'post-tribulationalists'* argue that we must
not count on a magical 'beam-me-up-Scotty' event that will save us
from this persecution. We must be ready to buckle our chinstrap, say
our prayers, and have faith in God to deliver us from evil. Indeed, we
know many Christians in various corners of the world that face possible martyrdom every day. They rely upon God's grace to get them
through and to stand their ground. These believers are an inspiration and model for us who 'remain safe at home.'[3]

Nevertheless, we can't settle the dispute based upon whether
one does or doesn't have such courage. The willingness to 'go the distance' for what we believe and to risk personal harm is admirable.
However, the matter of whether or not the Rapture happens before,
during, or at the end of the Tribulation is determined based upon
what the Scripture teaches. Ultimately, that teaching and that alone
is what resolves the debate. To argue otherwise, evangelicals from
all sides would declare, denies the authority of the Bible.

Recapping the Key Points Covered in This Chapter

- Like the Antichrist, the Mark of the Beast is the subject of much speculation.
- The False Prophet enforces the Mark of the Beast upon the entire
world – no one can participate in commerce without the Mark.
- Unlike the movies, the Mark isn't a tattoo on the body of the Antichrist; it is some form of marking or identification tag for everyone
who participates in the 'world system' of Antichrist.
- If you accept the Mark, you become a target for the judgment of God.
In contrast to the Mark of the Beast, God will 'seal' His chosen ones
with His own 'mark' on their foreheads.
- The time of the Great Tribulation is a time of judgment. Those upon
the earth must make a 'life and death' decision, for time and eternity.
- 'Pre-tribulation' believers are criticized for their 'blessed hope' that
purports the Rapture as an escape from Antichrist and the Mark of
the Beast. Is this a valid criticism?

Technical Notes

[1] Scholars label this methodology *Gematria*. It is also consistent with the Jewish cabalistic approach to Scripture, which asserted that there are hidden messages in the scriptures. It may surprise some that the magical incantation, 'Abracadabra' is actually a reference to the first four letters of the Hebrew alphabet which follows the same order as modern English and essentially the same as Greek: A, B, C, D, and Alpha, Beta, Gamma, Delta.

[2] IBM's first computer scanning system was model number 3666. The nomenclature: 3 stands for third generation and 666 to note the specific model! Perhaps this was just another joke. Burroughs Corporation (now Unisys) has continued to operate the massive computer system in Brussels, Belgium for over four decades. It handles the entire interbank financial transaction processing system for all the worlds' banks. Its nickname (since the 70's), is *The Beast!* How do I know this? I used to work for Burroughs right after graduating from college.

[3] Tim LaHaye has done a recent and complete analysis of the timing of the Rapture. I've included information about this book in the Section, **For Further Reading.** His analysis points out that not only are there strong scriptural arguments for the 'pre-tribulation Rapture,' there is also strong historical evidence that this view existed throughout the history of the Church and wasn't the invention of J.N. Darby.

FIGURE 6 – THE NUMBER OF THE BEAST IS 666,
WILLIAM BLAKE, 1810

Chapter 17: Mystery Babylon

The Woman of Revelation 17

One of the most challenging images used in the Book of Revelation is that of a woman supported by the Beast of Revelation Chapter 13 and 'drunk with the blood of God's people.' We know her as *"Mystery Babylon."* *This matter is one of the most debated topics in the entire series of apocalyptic subjects.*

Who is this woman? We read in Revelation 17:1-6:

¹ One of the seven angels who had the seven bowls came and said to me, "Come, I will show you the punishment of the great prostitute, who sits on many waters.

² With her the kings of the earth committed adultery and the inhabitants of the earth were intoxicated with the wine of her adulteries."

³ Then the angel carried me away in the Spirit into a desert. There I saw a woman sitting on a scarlet beast that was covered with blasphemous names and had seven heads and ten horns.

⁴ The woman was dressed in purple and scarlet, and was glittering with gold, precious stones, and pearls. She held a golden cup in her hand, filled with abominable things and the filth of her adulteries.

⁵ This title was written on her forehead:

> *MYSTERY*
> *BABYLON THE GREAT*
> *THE MOTHER OF PROSTITUTES*
> *AND OF THE ABOMINATIONS OF THE EARTH.*

⁶ I saw that the woman was drunk with the blood of the saints, the blood of those who bore testimony to Jesus.

The fact that the Woman *is a great city that sits on seven hills* discloses one of the clues to her identity. Another is a reference to a series of eight kings. *Mystery Babylon* therefore consists of both a 'place' and a 'person.'

The City of Seven Hills

As to location: Virtually all scholars identify the city of Rome as the city of seven hills and the location of 'Mystery Babylon.' Wikipedia states: "The historic centre of Rome was built on seven hills: the Aventine Hill, the Caelian Hill, the Capitoline Hill, the Esquiline Hill, the Palatine Hill, the Quirinal Hill, and the Viminal Hill."[1] Virgil and other Roman writers refer to Rome as the 'City of Seven Hills'. However, while the City seems unquestionably to be Rome, what *person, entity,* or *Kingdom* is *"the woman drunk with the blood of God's people"?* We read,

> [9] *"This calls for a mind with wisdom. The seven heads are seven hills on which the woman sits.*
>
> [10] *They are also seven kings. Five have fallen, one is, the other has not yet come; but when he does come, he must remain for a little while.*
>
> [11] *The beast who once was, and now is not, is an eighth king. He belongs to the seven and is going to his destruction." (Revelation 17: 9-11).*

A Reincarnation of Caesar?

This awkward but deliberate wording has led some commentators in times past to speculate that the *Antichrist* will in fact be a resurrected or reincarnated Caesar. Perhaps Domitian is a candidate. He was most likely the Caesar alive at the time when John penned the Revelation, who mercilessly persecuted the early church. He could be the king *who was, but is not, but is to come.* Although interesting, this position seems far-fetched to most commentators.

Thomas Horn, author of, *Apollyon Rising: 2012*, believes that the Antichrist is indeed a reincarnated being. Based upon his extensive knowledge of mythology and the clues he sees in various Masonic predictions and traditions, Horn speculates the spirit reincarnating Antichrist is *Apollo*, known as the *destroyer*. This is a fascinating conjecture to be sure.[2] John names the spirit of the abyss in Hebrew *Abaddon, the destroyer,* which he says in Greek, is *Apollyon*, another form of the name Apollo (see Revelation 9:11). According to Horn,

Satan himself will resurrect the spirit of Apollo and 'incarnate' it into the Antichrist.

The Protestant reformers from Luther to Wesley uniformly see the Roman Church as 'Mystery Babylon' and as I noted before, *the Pope as Antichrist.* Even today, many evangelical Protestant commentators still see Catholicism as the villain. Some commentators, especially Dave Hunt, have done extensive analysis in this area.[3]

While there is certainly no question that during the Reformation (and in the case of some other groups before the Reformation), Catholicism wrecked havoc upon those who claimed to be Christian but were outside the Catholic Church. However, it is doubtful that after the Church Council known as Vatican II (1965), that Protestants should hold Catholics in such contempt. Catholicism embraced many Protestant principles at that time. Other movements, such as the Charismatic Movement of the late sixties and early seventies, did much to 'personalize' the faith of many Catholics and reduce the differences between the two major Christian camps.[4] If 'baptized by the Spirit' and indwelt by the Holy Spirit, should there still be any doubt?[5]

FIGURE 7 – WHORE OF BABYLON, RUSSIAN ENGRAVING, 1800S

Possible Identities of the Seven (Eight) Kings

Some of those who see the fulfillment of these issues in the first century simply suggest that the Caesars of that time were the seven kings. There were six kings who were members of the family known as the *Julian-Claudian Dynasty*—Julius Caesar, Augustus, Tiberius, Caligula, Claudius, and Nero. Only five, however, were contemporary to Jesus and the Apostles (Augustus to Nero). These five would have fallen before John wrote Revelation. After Nero, we have the Flavian Dynasty of Vespasian and his two sons, Titus, and Domitian. Domitian in this scenario could be the eighth King, the Antichrist who caused great persecutions of the early Church as mentioned earlier. This would require overlooking the other Caesars between the two dynasties (Otho, Galba, and Vitellius), who reigned collectively for about one year. With a bit of historical license, this is a possible explanation. Liberalism likely ascribes to this position, as would amillennial 'preterists.'

Another possible solution identifies the eight kings (and the most compelling for many scholars). This viewpoint is that the eight kings represent the different Kingdoms that have ruled over Israel. These kingdoms include Egypt, Assyria, Babylon, Media-Persia, Greece, and Rome. Five have fallen but Rome, the sixth, is ruling at the time of Revelation's writing. At some point, the author infers that Rome will cease to rule in the same dominant way. However, it will arise again as the seventh Kingdom. The eighth (Antichrist) will actually be one of the seven. He will therefore be from Rome.

Note that John's description isn't very different from the way Daniel depicts 'the people' who destroy the city of Jerusalem and the Prince of the people who is to come (Daniel 9:24-27). While this interpretation seems more consistent with history, we must admit it is far from obvious. Nevertheless, this has been the majority view up to this point in time.

However, as mentioned earlier there is another perspective today that is gaining momentum. Chuck Missler, who espouses most of the traditional positions of *Dispensationalism*, sees the future world leader, the Antichrist, potentially coming from Assyria, the home of the world's first dictator, Nimrod. To Missler, Antichrist could be "Nimrod II."[6] Indeed, Assyria and nine other nations (adding up to ten) of the Middle East, were also part of the Roman Empire (the Eastern leg!) David W. Busch is his book, *The Assyrian* (Xulon Press, 2007, 330 pages), lays out this viewpoint in considerable detail.

Looking to Scripture, Micah uses this nomenclature (Micah 5:5). Likewise, Isaiah refers to the Antichrist in one messianic passage as 'the Assyrian' (Isaiah 7:17) and in several other places (e.g., 10:24, 30:32). These passages appear to speak of far-future times following the eighth century BC crisis with Assyria. If this viewpoint is correct, the Antichrist likely will be from Lebanon, Syria, or Iraq as ancient Assyria was comprised of these areas in today's world. Given our current political situation, interpreting the identity of the Antichrist in this way would yield a very different 'prophetic scenario.' If true, it would also seem to suggest that the Tribulation period could still be many years away.[7] If nothing else, it provides a warning to us once again that we are not likely to know exactly how prophecy will be fulfilled until we get very close to the moment in which it is.

Is Babylon Itself Mystery Babylon?

Those who speculate that the Antichrist is an Assyrian also contend that *Mystery Babylon* is the actual historical city of Babylon (about 60 miles south of Bagdad in Iraq). They assert that Babylon has never been 'as desolate' as the Bible seems to convey. Consequently, they propose that Babylon's total desolation is not yet accomplished. Therefore, they suggest that (1) Babylon must be restored and (2) become a significant capital for the Antichrist. Then (3) Babylon must be completely obliterated. Otherwise, they argue, Scripture has not been perfectly fulfilled.

On the other hand, most believe that what happened to Babylon historically amounts to complete destruction. These scholars ask, "So, if what has happened to Babylon isn't total destruction, *just what constitutes total obliteration?*" Babylon was once the most magnificent city in the world with attributes like no other. It was the capital for three of the four principal empires that dominated Israel (Nebuchadnezzar's Babylon, Media-Persia, and for Alexander's

Greek empire when Alexander was alive). It had massive walls hundreds of feet high and 40 feet across. Its *Hanging Gardens* was one of the Seven Ancient Wonders of the World. Moreover, the whole city along with its ziggurats (those infamous towers of Babel!) is no more. Why should we insist upon a more complete annihilation? Do we have serious doubts that Babylon was not "sufficiently destroyed?"

While it is true that some rebuilding occurred during the time of Saddam Hussein –Babylon remains unimpressive. Since the Bible says that it will never be rebuilt, one could argue that what has been done thus far doesn't qualify – little has been erected. Its appearance lacks "even a shadow of its former glory." Consequently, while a future gigantic building program is an intriguing possibility, it seems unlikely to most scholars.

Additionally, these experts point out that Revelation Chapter 18 conveys Mystery Babylon is a seaport as its smoldering ruins are visible from the Captains of the world's sea going vessels.[8] Finally, since the 'city of seven hills' is such an obvious reference to Rome, the location of Mystery Babylon isn't a mystery. Only the 'King' is in question.

Consequently, most scholars understand that the Beast and his kings comprise a 'revived Roman Empire.' Furthermore, *Mystery Babylon is just another name for this kingdom.* From their many comments we ascertain the early 'theologians' of the Church, the 'Church Fathers' who lived just after the apostolic period, 100 AD until St. Augustine – 354-430 AD – also believed the kingdom of Antichrist to consist of a newly partitioned set of nations from, if not 'revival' of, the Roman Empire.[9]

Of course, this view also ties to the Book of Daniel and his two visions describing a series of consecutive empires: The (1) Babylonians, whose most famous king was Nebuchadnezzar; (2) the Medes and the Persians, whose famous kings were Darius I and Cyrus; (3) the Greeks, Alexander and his kingdom split into four parts, and (4) finally, Rome. In both of his visions, Daniel discusses these empires, their characteristics, and their outcomes. The 'little horn' who becomes the Antichrist arises from 'the fourth kingdom' in Daniel's visions.

Lastly, some suggest that New York City is Mystery Babylon. They base such speculation on the economic language and the 'seaside' images used in Chapter 18 where Babylon is fallen and its doom discussed. What is the argument against this interpretation? The explanation is just too far afield from John's account.

While the pictures of the smoldering city on the eve of 9-11-01 matches the imagery used of Revelation, little else would justify this interpretation. Yes – New York is the capital of World Commerce. It could be a 'capital' for Antichrist also. However, again we say, the *location* isn't as much in question as *who leads the final empire*.

Recapping the Key Points Covered in This Chapter

- One of the most challenging images in the Book of Revelation is of the woman drunk with the blood of the Saints – 'Mystery Babylon.'
- There are two parts to the 'identity' – one is the location of the city, the other is the 'entity' that is being described. Who is she?
- The location seems to be Rome from the label, 'The City of Seven Hills,' which ancient writers such as Virgil used as a name for Rome.
- However, the identity remains hotly disputed. *Historicists* believe that the woman is the Roman Catholic Church. *Preterists* believe that the woman is one of the Caesars from the 1st century, possibly Domitian. Liberals would most likely agree with this latter position.
- Recent speculation focuses on the actual rebuilding of the city of Babylon. This is linked with the view that the Antichrist will actually be 'the Assyrian' and arise from the area around Babylon.
- The most common interpretation is that the woman represents a series of empires that have subjugated Israel for 2,500 years – Babylon is a city that was the capital of many of these empires.
- In the final analysis, Babylon may only symbolize the city of Antichrist, whereas Jerusalem is symbolically and literally the city of God.

Technical Notes

[1] See *http://Wikipedia.org/wiki/Rome# From_founding_to_Empire*

[2] See Thomas Horn, *Apollyon Rising: 2012*. Domitian himself believed he too was Apollo reincarnated.

[3] See Dave Hunt, *A Woman Rides the Beast,* Harvest House Publishers, 1994, 588 pages. This book is an extensive look at Catholicism as the world religion of the False Prophet and Antichrist.

[4] It is not within the scope of this study to discuss the views of Catholicism on eschatology and certainly not to debate the merits of those Protestant perspectives that continue to hold Catholicism in contempt. There is no question that many doctrines and traditions are very different between Protestants and Catholics to this day. My point here is that there have been substantial changes in Catholicism and many individual Catholics that now accept key elements of Protestant belief while still embracing much of what they hold dear in Catholicism.

[5] I have a number of wonderful Catholic relatives who are passionate for their faith. The 'trappings' of the 'old ways' such as the 'Mariology', the Rosary, etc., are much less prominent today, at least in the United States.

[6] Missler, *The Antichrist: The Alternate Ending*, Video, Koininia House, 2002.

[7] I say this because it would seem improbable that anyone from this region could be viewed with such high regard throughout the world given the turmoil today and the politics involved. The '*zeitgeist*' (the spirit of our age) must experience major changes for this outcome to occur.

[8] Missler believes that *Babylon* means Babylon in Iraq and that the woman is a symbol of wickedness and evil—and that wickedness will in fact 'come home to roost' in Babylon again in the last days. Babylon no doubt serves as the religious counterpoint to Jerusalem—Babylon is the origin of all evil from the perspective of the Bible.

[9] I cite Justin Martyr (100-165 AD) as but one example, "We should therefore concur with the traditional interpretation of all the commentators of the Christian Church, that at the end of the world, when the Roman Empire is to be destroyed, there shall be ten kings who will partition the Roman world among themselves. Then an insignificant eleventh king will arise, who will overcome three of the ten kings." (*Dialogue with Trypho,* Chapter 110) We see that this view is very old indeed.

Chapter 18: Parables of the Kingdom of God

The Call to the Kingdom – Today!

All Christians, Liberal, Covenantal, and Dispensational believe that *Jesus Christ calls us to live the principles of His Kingdom, not just in the 'hereafter' but today.* Indeed, the Kingdom of God was Jesus' *'clarion* call.'[i] For those that touched by His mercy, it is not enough just to be grateful. Those that comprehend the Grace of God desire to exhibit the characteristics of goodness themselves. Those that know His forgiveness are those that want to put into practice the Kingdom attributes that Jesus describes. What are those characteristics? Jesus teaches numerous lessons about the Kingdom of God through a number of famous parables. I have selected three that capture the essentials.

Jesus' Parable of the Master and the Talents

Jesus wove wonderful stories for his listeners concerning God's Kingdom, including what we must do to participate. *Most of us fail to grasp just how high the Kingdom's eligibility standard is!* Therefore, Jesus' words that follow could come as quite a shock. Be warned!

From Matthew 25, we read one of the more famous parables of Jesus, the *Parable of the Talents:*

> *14 "Again, it will be like a man going on a journey, who called his servants and entrusted his property to them.*
>
> *15 To one he gave five talents of money, to another two talents, and to another one talent, each according to his ability. Then he went on his journey.*

---

[i] A clarion was a medieval trumpet or organ stop that had a very high pitch but clear tone. It was a musical way to get everyone's attention!

16 *The man who had received the five talents went at once and put his money to work and gained five more.*

17 *So also, the one with the two talents gained two more.*

18 *But the man who had received the one talent went off, dug a hole in the ground and hid his master's money.*

19 *"After a long time the master of those servants returned and settled accounts with them.*

20 *The man who had received the five talents brought the other five. 'Master,' he said, 'you entrusted me with five talents. See, I have gained five more.'*

21 *"His master replied, 'Well done, good and faithful servant! You have been faithful with a few things; I will put you in charge of many things. Come and share your master's happiness!'*

22 *"The man with the two talents also came. 'Master,' he said, 'you entrusted me with two talents; see, I have gained two more.'*

23 *"His master replied, 'Well done, good and faithful servant! You have been faithful with a few things; I will put you in charge of many things. Come and share your master's happiness!'*

24 *"Then the man who had received the one talent came. 'Master,' he said, 'I knew that you are a hard man, harvesting where you have not sown and gathering where you have not scattered seed.*

25 *So I was afraid and went out and hid your talent in the ground. See, here is what belongs to you.'*

26 *"His master replied, 'You wicked, lazy servant! So you knew that I harvest where I have not sown and gather where I have not scattered seed?*

27 *Well then, you should have put my money on deposit with the bankers, so that when I returned I would have received it back with interest.*

28 *"'Take the talent from him and give it to the one who has the ten talents.*

29 *For everyone who has will be given more, and he will have an abundance. Whoever does not have, even what he has will be taken from him.*

30 *And throw that worthless servant outside, into the darkness, where there will be weeping and gnashing of teeth.'*

In Jesus' parable, the Master remains firm in his expectations—he has "high hopes" for his servants. By analogy, if we do not choose to take the talents given to us and invest them for the benefit of the Kingdom, Jesus declares that even what little we have will be taken away and given to a servant who already has more.

We complain, "Surely the Master is not justified in doing this. How is it fair to take even the little that the one has and give it to the one who has much more?" However, Jesus' lesson emphasizes that the Master does this precisely because he is a *"hard man, harvesting where (he has) not sown and gathering where (he has) not scattered seed."* Furthermore, the Master does not let his 'high expectations' serve as an acceptable excuse—it is the basis for the servant's condemnation: "So you knew about me as you readily admit. Well then, you should have at least done the minimum. But since you didn't even do the minimum, you will be thrown outside as a worthless servant."

Jesus teaches we must be about the business of the Kingdom, investing our time and talent when and where we can. If we don't invest ourselves, we have no right to expect commendation when the Master comes.

What We Do Unto Others

We learn a similar lesson in another famous parable. This parable, the *Parable of the Sheep and Goats,* is just as explicit in the fate of those who fail to meet the standard:

> [31] *"When the Son of Man comes in his glory, and all the angels with him, he will sit on his throne in heavenly glory.*
>
> [32] *All the nations will be gathered before him, and he will separate the people one from another as a shepherd separates the sheep from the goats.*
>
> [33] *He will put the sheep on his right and the goats on his left.*
>
> [34] *"Then the King will say to those on his right, 'Come, you who are blessed by my Father; take your inheritance, the kingdom prepared for you since the creation of the world.*

35 For I was hungry and you gave me something to eat, I was thirsty and you gave me something to drink, I was a stranger and you invited me in,

36 I needed clothes and you clothed me, I was sick and you looked after me, I was in prison and you came to visit me.'

37 "Then the righteous will answer him, 'Lord, when did we see you hungry and feed you, or thirsty and give you something to drink?

38 When did we see you a stranger and invite you in, or needing clothes and clothe you?

39 When did we see you sick or in prison and go to visit you?'

40 "The King will reply, 'I tell you the truth, whatever you did for one of the least of these brothers of mine, you did for me.'

41 "Then he will say to those on his left, 'Depart from me, you who are cursed, into the eternal fire prepared for the devil and his angels.

42 For I was hungry and you gave me nothing to eat, I was thirsty and you gave me nothing to drink,

43 I was a stranger and you did not invite me in, I needed clothes and you did not clothe me, I was sick and in prison and you did not look after me.'

44 "They also will answer, 'Lord, when did we see you hungry or thirsty or a stranger or needing clothes or sick or in prison, and did not help you?'

45 "He will reply, 'I tell you the truth, whatever you did not do for one of the least of these, you did not do for me.'

46 "Then they will go away to eternal punishment, but the righteous to eternal life."

The righteous clothe the poor, care for the sick, visit those in prison, and so win their invitation to enter into the Kingdom. The righteous do these things *without expecting reward*. It is simply their nature to be concerned about the welfare of others. Nevertheless, the King applauds the righteous for their good deeds, treating them as if what they did for the lowly ("*the least*") was done expressly for Him.

In contrast, those who failed to care for the sick, clothe the poor, and visit those in prison are separated from those that did. Their fate, harsh though it seems, is eternal punishment. Could that be true? After all, the parable seems to allow for the possibility that 'the goats' may have treated some people well, just not those who were most in need.

Nevertheless, Jesus' teaching is clear. The attributes of those who will inherit the kingdom must include *humility* and *compassion in action.* We must seek out those in great need. If the sheep don't have these attributes, they are only masquerading as sheep—they are "goats in sheep's clothing." Forgive another mixed metaphor, but as Jesus says elsewhere, *"You will know a tree by its fruit."* (Matthew 12:33).

Being Watchful—A Key to the Kingdom

Jesus' teaching on *watchfulness* in Luke Chapter 12, adds further insight into what we must do to be included in the Kingdom:

35 "Be dressed ready for service and keep your lamps burning,

36 like men waiting for their master to return from a wedding banquet, so that when he comes and knocks they can immediately open the door for him.

37 It will be good for those servants whose master finds them watching when he comes. I tell you the truth, he will dress himself to serve, will have them recline at the table and will come and wait on them.

38 It will be good for those servants whose master finds them ready, even if he comes in the second or third watch of the night.

39 But understand this: If the owner of the house had known at what hour the thief was coming, he would not have let his house be broken into.

40 You also must be ready, because the Son of Man will come at an hour when you do not expect him."

41 Peter asked, "Lord, are you telling this parable to us, or to everyone?"

42 The Lord answered, "Who then is the faithful and wise manager, whom the master puts in charge of his servants to give them their food allowance at the proper time?

43 It will be good for that servant whom the master finds doing so when he returns.

44 I tell you the truth, he will put him in charge of all his possessions.

45 But suppose the servant says to himself, 'My master is taking a long time in coming,' and he then begins to beat the menservants and maidservants and to eat and drink and get drunk.

46 The master of that servant will come on a day when he does not expect him and at an hour he is not aware of. He will cut him to pieces and assign him a place with the unbelievers.

47 "That servant who knows his master's will and does not get ready or does not do what his master wants will be beaten with many blows.

48 But the one who does not know and does things deserving punishment will be beaten with few blows. From everyone who has been given much, much will be demanded; and from the one who has been entrusted with much, much more will be asked.

Watchfulness is the attribute highlighted in this lesson. Watchfulness happens when our priorities are set straight and when we focus on the right things. Watchfulness is a result of faith—recognizing that the Master could return at any moment. There is no time to bully those whom we oversee, nor is there time to eat to excess and to get drunk (verse 45). The Master can return at any time. That's why those who will inherit the Kingdom aren't surprised—they will be dressed for service and 'keep their lamps burning' (verse 35). The *Parable of the Wise and Foolish Virgins* (Matthew 25:1-13), another Kingdom parable, conveys the same message.

Can We Obtain the Kingdom?

These words should not be discouraging to us, difficult though they be. Jesus assures us in Luke Chapter 12:

27 "Consider how the lilies grow. They do not labor or spin. Yet I tell you, not even Solomon in all his splendor was dressed like one of these.

28 If that is how God clothes the grass of the field, which is here today, and tomorrow is thrown into the fire, how much more will he clothe you, O you of little faith!

29 And do not set your heart on what you will eat or drink; do not worry about it.

30 For the pagan world runs after all such things, and your Father knows that you need them.

*31 **But seek his kingdom,** and these things will be given to you as well.*

32 "Do not be afraid, little flock, for your Father has been pleased to give you the kingdom.

33 Sell your possessions and give to the poor. Provide purses for yourselves that will not wear out, a treasure in heaven that will not be exhausted, where no thief comes near and no moth destroys.

34 For where your treasure is, there your heart will be also.

Cheap Grace and the Kingdom of God

Dietrich Bonheoffer, a great Christian theologian and martyr in World War II, talked about the idea of 'cheap grace.' Bonheoffer was disturbed that oftentimes Christians are so quick to preach the goodness of God, that Christ's message is 'watered down', and God's grace devalued.

After all, if there are no consequences for what we do, especially when we do evil, isn't God's grace unnecessary? On the other hand, if there are consequences when we do wrong or fail to do what's right, it's only because of God's grace that we can have hope. Paul tells us, *"For all have sinned and fall short of the glory of God and are justified freely by his grace through the redemption that came by Christ Jesus"* (Romans 3:23, 24).

Christ's teaching of the Kingdom also reminds us that those who inherit the Kingdom will do so because they have prepared themselves, they are watchful, they are compassionate, they are humble, and they seek to do what is right. They cannot justify themselves—but they can be justified by God's "free gift" through the redemption that is in Jesus Christ.

To be perfectly clear (and to let all of Scripture inform our interpretation of these parables): Those that exhibit such Kingdom traits do so because *they have been justified by God's gift.* Because they have experienced this redemption, they bear much fruit (John

167

15). Because they have been redeemed, the Spirit dwells in them producing the fruit of the Spirit (Galatians 5:22, 23). *These kingdom attributes are the result, not the means to be justified.*

If you count yourself a Christian, through these parables Jesus challenges you to respond to these questions: Are you bearing fruit? What kind of tree are you? Are you proving yourself worthy of the Kingdom?

Key Points Covered in This Chapter

- The Kingdom of God is the 'clarion call' of Jesus Christ.
- All Protestants believe that Jesus' parables on the Kingdom teach us what life is supposed to be like when we all live with a Kingdom 'mindset.'
- The three parables selected here provide us with a challenging outlook on how difficult it is to be invited to participate in the Kingdom.
- The first, the *Master and the Talents,* points out that the Master has very high expectations of His servants. If they do not invest their talents wisely, they will forfeit their right to join in the Kingdom.
- The parable of the *Sheep and the Goats* teaches that those who inherit the Kingdom are distinguished from those who do not.
- The last parable teaches watchfulness, comparing the coming of the Second Advent to the coming of the Master from a wedding feast. Those that are watchful and awake will join the Master when He arrives.
- The Kingdom is not an exclusive club for the rich or highly regarded from a human perspective – Jesus teaches that God strongly desires to grant the Kingdom to all His children.
- We must learn the lesson of 'cheap grace' taught by Dietrich Bonheoffer during World War II. The death of God's Son cost God dearly. If we believe it is easy to enter into the Kingdom, we deny the price paid for us, making God's grace, *cheap.*

Chapter 19: The Rapture of the Saints

Harpazo and Raptere

Evangelical scholars explain that the Rapture is the 'catching away' of believers from the earth to join Christ in the Heavens at the sound of the *'last trumpet.'* Rapture comes from a Latin verb, *raptere,* used in Jerome's Latin translation of the Bible, the *Vulgate* (c. 400 AD), and referencing I Thessalonians 4:17. I cite the entire passage below.   Note the New International Version translation uses the words 'caught up' (no single word conveys the exact meaning in English):

> *¹³ Brothers, we do not want you to be ignorant about those who fall asleep, or to grieve like the rest of men, who have no hope.*

> *¹⁴ We believe that Jesus died and rose again and so we believe that God will bring with Jesus those who have fallen asleep in him.*

> *¹⁵ According to the Lord's own word, we tell you that we who are still alive, who are left till the coming of the Lord, will certainly not precede those who have fallen asleep.*

> *¹⁶ For the Lord himself will come down from heaven, with a loud command, with the voice of the archangel and with the trumpet call of God, and the dead in Christ will rise first.*

> *¹⁷ After that, we who are still alive and are left will be* **caught up together with them in the clouds to meet the Lord in the air.** *And so we will be with the Lord forever.*

> *¹⁸Therefore encourage each other with these words.*

The term *rapture* has become the de facto English equivalent of the Greek word *harpazo,* meaning 'caught up' or to 'snatch away.'

True—the Greek text does not use the word *rapture*. Curiously, some commentators don't take the concept seriously simply for this reason.[i] This seems odd in that there are some doctrines of Scripture collectively labeled by a particular term but which require

---

[i] Using this logic, the problem would be eliminated if instead of using the Latin transliteration of *raptere,* an English word were coined using *harpazo,* perhaps it could be *harpaze*? I'll leave the pronunciation of this to the reader.

explanation to make their meaning clear. Even the famous term *Logos*, the Greek word used for Christ in the first chapter of John's gospel, has a depth of meaning that the mere word itself doesn't convey. Without its 'extra-biblical' background, the word used in Scripture would have very little significance.

However, is coining a term as a means to translate the Scripture, a term that provides a meaning consistent with Scripture, an infraction of the rules? Few scholars would argue that. Instead, they would ask hypothetically, "Isn't the real issue whether or not the meaning of the term is consistent with what the Bible teaches? Are we so literally-minded that the failure of one language to have a term that maps perfectly to a word in another language (whose meaning is identical) invalidates any attempt to translate it?"

Indeed, the example of the limited meaning of our English word 'love' compared to the Greek language which had a multiplicity of words for love points out the difficulty in properly translating almost any Scripture.[i] Likewise, using the term 'rapture' is quite acceptable if the audience understands the Bible's correct meaning. (See the deep dive, ***The Bible's Use of 'Popular' Terms,*** page 128).

Many dispute the timing of this term's first usage in which it was consistent to its usage today. Most believe John Nelson Darby, the Father of Dispensationalism, first popularized the term in the 19th century (c.1827-40).

> *"Listen, I tell you a mystery: We will not all sleep, but we will all be changed—in a flash, in the twinkling of an eye, at the last trumpet. For the trumpet will sound, the dead will be raised imperishable, and we will be changed."* (I Corinthians 15:51, 52)

Darby taught that Christians would not go through the Tribulation period; Christ would take them out of the world before it happened. As mentioned before, we know this as the 'Pre-Tribulation Rapture'; obviously, it's the view upon which Tim LaHaye and Jerry Jenkins based the "Left Behind" series.

---

[i] (See C.S. Lewis' book, *The Four Loves*, which highlights the four different meanings of love in Greek: (1) *'storge'* for affection'; (2) *'eros'* for sexual love; (3) *'philia'* for brotherly love; and (4) *'agape'* for unconditional love).

Who Is Included in the Rapture?

In the Apostles Creed, one of the creedal assertions is that "we believe in the resurrection of *the quick* and the dead." Immediately after Christ has resurrected the dead, then "the *quick" (which* refers to the *raptured* believers) meet Christ in the air. As the Scriptures cited above teach, believers alive at the time this event occurs do not die; God *transforms them* from one mode of physical life that is mortal to another form of physical life that is immortal. This concept was clearly present very early in the life of the Church (and not as some might suppose *a later invention*). It was in Paul's earliest letters to Thessalonica and Corinth, letters that even liberal scholars consider authentically Pauline.

Indeed the Rapture doesn't just pertain to those that are alive. It covers two different circumstances. First, there are those that have already *'fallen asleep'* who He resurrects. Then, there are those that are alive at that moment and are *'caught up.'* Since these actions happen only a split second apart, while apparently important to Paul, the distinction is lost on us. To speak of the Rapture, one should be talking about both (1) the resurrection and *transformation* of the dead and (2) the *transformation* of living believers. *"Behold, I shew (show) you a mystery; we shall not all sleep, but we shall all be **changed"** (I Corinthians 15:51, King James Version).

Because of the immediate transformation of the 'quick' as well as the dead, the Rapture is also known as *'the translation of believers'*— a metamorphous of the most special sort, from a corruptible (mortal) body to an incorruptible (immortal) existence. The Apostle John also points out the unique change believers will experience.

THE KEY POINT TO PONDER:

The Judeo-Christian view of the afterlife is quite unique – the resurrection of the body begets an immortal being more like our popular view of 'super-heroes' than the stereotype of angels sitting on a puffy cloud.

"Dear friends, now we are children of God, and what we will be has not yet been made known. But we know that when he appears, we shall be (become) *like him, for we shall see*

him as he is." (I John 3:2). The resurrected body of Christ, as depicted in the Gospel of John provides many hints as to what this existence will be like (see John 20 and 21). Indeed, unlike most other
religions, Judaism and Christianity assert *the bodily resurrection*—
not to a ghostlike spirit, but to a corporeal, spectacular existence—
certainly *more akin to our concept of superheroes than our stereotypi-
cal depiction of angels!* Therefore, if you are planning to play a harp,
sprout wings, and sit on a puffy cloud, *you had better find a different
religion.* True Christianity will admit no such destiny!

When Does the Rapture Occur?

There has been considerable debate among evangelicals over
the past 50 years as to when (before, during, or after the Tribulation
period), the Rapture occurs. Most dispensationalists believe it can
occur at any time—even well before the Tribulation period (this is
the doctrine of *'imminence'*—that implies nothing has to happen, before the Rapture occurs). Christ tells his followers, "Be ready!"

In contrast, Covenantal theologians teach that the Rapture and
the Second Coming are synonymous events. The Rapture comes at
the end of the world as we know it before it is recreated into the final
eternal Kingdom—the coming of the *New Jerusalem,* a *new heaven
and a new earth.* Because it is a non-historical event (history does
not flow beyond it), the *Rapture* for the Covenantal theologian has a
very different character. Obviously it is a realization of salvation,
perhaps coming at the end of a period of tribulation (the *post-
tribulation* Rapture viewpoint); but because it lacks the quality of
imminence (where it could happen at any moment) it portends much
less drama in the meantime.

Is Revelation's Seventh Trumpet the 'Last Trump'?

The key event specifying the exact moment of the Rapture is
'the trumpet call of God' or the 'last trump' or 'trumpet.' We will discuss in a later section the explicit *nature* of this 'trumpet call' (it may
not be a trumpet at all, but the *Voice of God!*) Here, we will analyze
the exact *timing* of this trumpet.

A minority view regarding 'the last trumpet' relates to the blowing of the *Seventh Trumpet* in Revelation 11:15. As mentioned in the discussion of the two witnesses, an *angel* blows this trumpet, the *last of seven trumpets*. He blows this trumpet at the culmination of the time of tribulation. We read:

> *The nations were angry; and your wrath has come.*
> *The time has come for judging the dead,*
>   *and for rewarding your servants the prophets*
> *and your saints and those who reverence your name,*
>   *both small and great—*
> *and for destroying those who destroy the earth."* (Revelation 11:18)

For this reason, those who believe that the Rapture happens concurrently with the visible Second Coming *('the Glorious Appearing'*—Titus 2:13), would see this seventh and final trumpet as *'the last trumpet.'* To say it slightly differently: Only if the Rapture happens concurrently with the physical appearing of Christ Jesus, is the seventh trumpet of Revelation 11 the 'last trumpet' spoken of by Paul. This would be the position of the Covenantalist. It is a very logical position—but as pointed out elsewhere, there are other interpretations as to the meaning of the Seventh Trumpet that may invalidate this as, the 'last trump.'

Instead, the purpose of this trumpet appears intended to ready those in heaven for the culmination of the judgments of God soon to take place. Revelation 10:7 says, *"But in the days when the seventh angel is about to sound his trumpet, the mystery of God will be accomplished, just as He announced to His servants the prophets."*[1] By the time of the Seventh Trumpet, the events described in Revelation are ending. There is no mention of 'multitudes that cannot be counted' before the throne. Instead, we read of the opening of the *Temple of heaven* and the appearance of the *Ark of the Covenant in the heavenly Temple*, which clearly mean something else.[2]

Nevertheless, here, let's drill down into the question of 'when' the trumpet sounds. To do this, we will need to understand much more about the *Jewish holidays* or festivals (some of which we know

173

as 'high holy days' and all of which the Bible labels, *convocations*[i]). Please study **Figure 8** on page 176 below.

This study is highly fruitful because most Protestants believe that Jesus Christ fulfills each of these Jewish festivals in a 'literal' way. Also, please note, that there are exactly *seven* of these feasts. The number seven stands for *completion* in the Bible. If we see these festivals as a *typology* for their fulfillment in Jesus Christ, the number seven conveys a complete picture of the nature and work of Jesus Christ.

Rosh Hashanah, Pentecost, and the Jewish Holidays

The traditional view links the *last trumpet* with the blowing of the Shofar, the ram's horn, *on Rosh Hashanah*. Rosh Hashanah is the Jewish New Year. Rosh Hashanah is also known as 'the Feast of the Trumpets' – so there is a logical suggestion that the Rapture (which includes the resurrection of the dead), would take place on this day. The argument is that 'the last trump' is the final blowing of the Shofar (one hundred times on each of the two days – unless it concludes on a Sabbath! Then the horn blows 100 times only on the first day). If so, this would tie the Rapture to *Rosh Hashanah* as the fulfillment of this key Jewish *High Holy Day*.

Indeed, the term officially used for all of the Jewish holidays is *convocation* (see Leviticus 23:2, 4, 37). Is Rosh Hashanah the day of the Rapture? Perhaps – but it is not the only candidate 'holiday' that could be fulfilled by the Rapture event as we will see.

Since we have begun with the first of the *three fall feasts*, let's continue to describe the other two.

- *Yom Kippur*, the second fall holiday (literally 'holy day') Jews know as the *Day of Atonement*. It is the most solemn of the Jewish holidays. On this day, according to priestly tradition, the High Priest enters the Holy of Holies and makes atonement for all the people by

---

[i] Convocations are 'formal assemblies' but may also have the meaning of 'dress rehearsals' as we will discuss. I owe this insight to Mark Biltz, a 'messianic pastor' in Tacoma who has provided wonderful instruction on the Jewish traditions and their fulfillment in Christianity. See his website, *www.elshaddaiministries.us*.

sprinkling blood on the Mercy Seat of the Ark of the Covenant. The Priests would refer to this act as 'propitiation,' in which God is satisfied with the offering and forgives the nation's sin. This day is also the day that many speculate will be the coming of the Messiah to rescue the nation from the Antichrist and the armies that surround it (His visible appearing).

- *Sukkot (The Feast of the Tabernacles)* is the final fall holiday. It commemorates the dwelling of the people in tents during their wilderness wanderings for 40 years. It is also a reminder that God will dwell with the people in the Kingdom of God upon this earth, when David (and/or Christ) sits on the throne of God's Kingdom in Jerusalem. Dispensational Christians see the *Feast of the Tabernacles* symbolizing the Millennial Reign of Christ upon the Throne of David in Jerusalem. It is this feast, the Bible tells us, that all nations must observe during the Millennium – otherwise, their nation will experience drought! (Zechariah 14:18, 19).

There are the *three spring festivals*: (1) Passover, (2) Feast of Unleavened Bread, and (3) Feast of First Fruits.

- *Pesach (Passover)* is of course the holiday reminding all Israel how the Angel of Death 'passed over' the houses of the Hebrews in Egypt, sparing their first born but killing the first born of the Egyptians. This event finally caused the Pharaoh to 'let the Hebrew people go.' Christians see Passover as a symbol of Jesus, as God's firstborn, sacrificed on the cross redeeming not only Israel's firstborn, but also all humankind!

- The *Feast of Unleavened Bread* is a period of seven days which reminds the people how quickly they had to leave Egypt—they would not have time to use leaven—there was no time to allow their bread to 'rise.' The Jews considered leaven a symbol of *sin*. To avoid leaven is a personal sacrifice, as unleavened bread is not as tasty or soft as leavened bread. Symbolically, to not use leaven is to avoid sin! Christians see this period as speaking to the sinless nature of Christ and the sacrifice he made to bring salvation to us.

- *Omer*, the festival of First Fruits, is a time to celebrate harvest. The people gather the initial sheaves of the harvest during this 10-day period, bring them to the Priest, and then wave them before the Lord. Upon completing this event, harvest occurs for the next seven weeks. First Fruits is also seen by Christians as a symbol of the resurrection of Christ, in which Christ's rising is a symbol of being the 'first among many brethren' to be resurrected. He is the first fruits of those rising from the dead.

Jewish Name	Common Name	Meaning of the Jewish Holy Day	Possible Christian Fulfillment
The Spring Festivals			
1. Pesach	Passover	First full moon after the blooming of Almond trees. Redemption of Israel through the Angel of Death 'Passing over' the Jews and striking the Egyptians' first born. Individual salvation.	Crucifixion of Christ that redeems all humankind.
2. Pesach	Unleavened Bread	Seven days eating unleavened bread—reminiscent of Exodus' quick departure. Leaven = sin.	Pictures sinless life of Christ—His death and burial.
3. Omer	First fruits	Celebration of initial harvest—First sheaves waved before the Lord.	Resurrection of Christ—The 1st of Many Brethren.
4. Shavuot	Pentecost Festival of the Harvest Festival of Weeks	Giving of Law at Sinai. The Grain Harvest is Completed. 50 days after 'Omer.' The festival of the Bride and Bridegroom—Ruth.	Coming of the Holy Spirit and the Birth of the Church (Acts 2). The Rapture of the Church?
The Fall Festivals			
5. Rosh Hasha-nah	Feast of the Trumpets	Day of Creation. *Seven days afterwards are the Days of Awe.* Also, Jewish New Year. Time to Examine Oneself.	The Rapture of the Church? Return of Christ to Mount of Olives? Days of Awe—the Tribulation Period?
6. Yom Kippur	The Day of Atonement	10 days after Rosh Hashanah. High Priest enters the Holy of Holies in the Temple to make restitution for sin of the people. National salvation.	Judgment Day. The Battle of Armageddon 10 days after the return of Christ to Mount of Olives?
7. Sukkot	Feast of Taber-nacles	5 days after Yom Kippur. Lasts for 7 days. The people are to dwell in 'booths' or tents to remind them of their dwellings in the wilderness. God will dwell with mankind in the kingdom.	The Millennial Reign of Christ. The Holiday that all nations must honor in the Millennium.

FIGURE 8 – TABLE OF JEWISH FESTIVALS & POSSIBLE CHRISTIAN FULFILLMENT

Lastly, we come to the Festival of the Harvest, or *Pentecost*, occurring in springtime, but seen as 'the middle festival', lying between the fall and spring holidays. Pentecost happens 50 days after the 10 Days of Omer. The possibility of Pentecost being 'the day of the Rapture' would be symmetrical in that the church began on Pentecost and would conclude on that same day. It would be appropriate to interpret both dates figuratively as 'days of harvest.'

According to most scholars, God gave the Law to Moses on the day of *Pentecost*. Some traditions suggest that *David the King was also born on Pentecost*. I speculate that this is the actual birthday of Jesus.[3] As noted earlier, a few scholars suggest that the various *dispensations always commence on a Pentecost*. For Christians, Pentecost is indeed a major holiday! Orthodox Jews are to celebrate Pentecost by staying up all night, studying Scripture, and praying. I doubt many Christians follow this tradition![i]

Additionally, the story of the Book of Ruth, associated with Pentecost, is a story that has probable *typology* involving the Rapture of the Church. The book is about a gentile woman, Ruth, a Moabite, redeemed by a 'kinsmen redeemer,' Boaz. In order to propose marriage between Ruth and Boaz, at the coaching of her mother-in-law from her prior marriage (Naomi), Ruth goes to the upper loft of the 'threshing floor' and quietly lies down at the feet of Boaz where he is sleeping, uncovering his feet, and resting with him. Upon discovering Ruth, Boaz understands the 'petition' and quickly marries Ruth. Tradition has it that this event occurs on the day of Pentecost. In fact, it is a story normally read on Pentecost by orthodox Jews. It symbolizes the marriage between God and Israel. Christians of course see in this story a symbol of the marriage between Jesus Christ and His Church—especially since Ruth, the bride, *is a gentile.*

The date is also known as the only festival date *that cannot be established on a fixed date,* due to the fluctuation of Passover. The sequence: Passover occurs on a particular date of a full moon (which

---

[i] This tradition is reminiscent of Jesus' parable in which he mentions that the Master may return from the wedding feast in the 2nd or 3rd 'watch of the night.' So stay awake! (Luke 12:38) The Greek Church actually has this tradition too. Therefore, some Christians do stay vigilant on Pentecost.

varies depending upon the blooming of the Almond Tree); (2) Omer is offered on the first day (Sunday) after the Sabbath (Saturday) after the Passover (which varies); (3) Pentecost or Shavuot was to be exactly seven weeks after the day following Sabbath (Sunday), immediately after Passover (50 days after Omer).

In contrast, during Jesus' day the Pharisees fixed the date as the sixth day of Sivan (typically late May or early June). However, biblically, the date was always to be a Sunday and a 'variable date' holiday. Christians of course supported Sunday as the holy day as it was a memorial to the day of Jesus' resurrection. Additionally, the fact that the date of the festival couldn't be officially 'known' until the blossoming of the Almond Tree, it infers that *'no man knows the day.'*

So it is that many Christian scholars believe that the Rapture of the Church will happen either on *Rosh Hashanah* (due to the correlation with the *Feast of Trumpets*) or on *Pentecost* (due to the various typological factors implied in this festival).

No Man Knows the Day nor the Hour

However, we must also point out that scholars agree that Jesus taught that humankind won't know when He will return (Matthew 24:36)—specifically, we are told that we will not know *the day nor the hour*—therefore, we should always be *alert and ready*.

However, in a slightly non-traditional way, many argue this caution applies only to *the year* of His coming. The fulfillment of these festivals will indeed happen on the day of the festival (just as have all the others), but because we do not know the year, by inference *we won't know the day or the hour either*. Others would say that the statement that, "we won't know when He is coming" is really directed *at those who are not earnestly watching*. Those who are watching are not surprised when He comes *"like a thief in the night"* because we are sons of the light. We read in I Thessalonians 5: 2-5:

¹ Now, brothers, about times and dates we do not need to write to you,

*² for you know very well that the day of the Lord will come **like a thief in the night.***

3 While people are saying, "Peace and safety," destruction will come on them suddenly, as labor pains on a pregnant woman, and they will not escape.

4 But you, brothers, are not in darkness so that this day should surprise you like a thief.

5 You are all sons of the light and sons of the day. We do not belong to the night or to the darkness.

6 So then, let us not be like others, who are asleep, but let us be alert and self-controlled.

On the one hand, the Bible teaches that the *'Day of the Lord'* (which is usually understood as the *entire period of God's wrath* upon the earth) will come like a thief in the night (verse 2). On the other hand, Paul tells us that this should not shock us because we *are sons of light and sons of the day* (verse 5). The Scripture charges us, nonetheless, to be alert and in control of ourselves (verse 6). Overall, *because we are alert* it suggests that *we may know the 'holiday' when the Lord is coming.* So it is not necessarily the 'Rapture' that the Lord suggests will come 'like a thief.' Instead, *it is God's judgment or the Day of the Lord* that will overtake those who do *not* understand the 'signs of the times.' They believe peace and safety is coming when destruction looms (verse 3).

What Comes After the Rapture?

For the Covenantal theologian, immediately after the Rapture *eternity begins* (Revelation 21). For the Dispensationalist, there are many more events yet to come (from Revelation 19 and 20):

1. The return of Christ will occur at the Battle of *Armageddon.*

2. After defeating his enemies with the help of His Saints, Christ throws the *Antichrist* and *False Prophet* into the Lake of Fire.

3. All believers will be united and attend 'the marriage supper of the Lamb.'[4]

4. Satan is bound and thrown into a bottomless pit.

5. Immediately thereafter, the Millennium commences and continues for 1,000 years.

6. It is followed by yet another battle. In this battle, Satan is loosed from the bottomless pit for a little time and stirs up the nations of

the world once more. He leads the armies of Gog and Magog to Jerusalem for yet another battle against the Messiah.

7. Satan fails once more and is thrown into the Lake of Fire, joining the Antichrist and the False Prophet.

8. 'The Great White Throne Judgment' takes place immediately after 'the Second Resurrection.' Only those unfavorably judged are resurrected here. These have not been redeemed by the blood of the Lamb and are judged according to their works. Since their names are not found in the Lamb's Book of Life, they are also thrown into the Lake of Fire.

9. Coming forth like a new bride, New Jerusalem appears along with the new heavens and new earth.

10. Eternity begins!

Dispensationalists are obliged to point out that there are many events that *must be spiritualized*, if (1) the Rapture and the (2) 'Glorious Appearing' and (3) the appearance of the New Jerusalem take place *at virtually the same instant.* Looking at the list above of 'Ten things that happen after the Rapture,' we would eliminate many of them. If so, might we be taking too much interpretive liberty?

Key Points Covered in This Chapter

- Rapture comes from the Latin term used by Jerome in translating the Greek New Testament into Latin.
- Some deny the meaningfulness of the Rapture due to its failure to be a word used in the original Greek manuscripts.
- When the Rapture occurs in relationship to the Tribulation period (the final 7 years leading to the Second Advent) is a hotly debated issue. One position supposes the seventh Trumpet of Revelation is the 'last trumpet.'
- There are four distinct positions: 'Pre-trib,' 'mid-trib,' 'post-trib' and the fourth, 'no-trib Rapture,' those who believe in no Rapture at all.
- The 'quick and the dead' refers to the two types of believers that will be 'caught up in the clouds' – those 'dead and buried' and those still alive at that moment when the Rapture happens.
- The translation into a new body is a distinguishing feature of Christianity over most other religions (that is, a view to a *physical* resurrection).
- The Jewish Festivals may provide clues for the timing of the Rapture.
- These holidays, many Christians believe, serve as a typology for later fulfillment in the life and work of Jesus Christ and His coming again.

- What of the warning, 'No man knows the day or the hour?' It may not refer to the Rapture, but to 'the Day of the Lord' – the Day of Judgment.
- For the Dispensationalist, there is a long list of events 'still to transpire' after the Rapture. For the Covenantalist, most of the 'final events' happen concurrently or in a tight sequence when New Jerusalem appears.

Technical Notes

[1] Although this statement concerns the passage in Chapter 10 of Revelation with another 12 Chapters to go, it appears to be clear that Revelation cycles through the events generally in Chapters 8 through 10 and then returns to the events in the next cycle in detail. This follows a pattern of the first book of the Bible, Genesis, which employs the same literary device. For this reasons, Chapter 10 may be 'near the end' of the Tribulation although John will begin to 'drill down' on details in Chapter 11 and thereafter.

[2] Commentaries on this verse suggest that the 'opening of the Temple' and the ability to see the Ark of the covenant in the Holy of Holies points to the accessibility that Christ has now made available to all who call upon His name. The lightning and peals of thunder likewise illustrate, according to some commentators, the vindication by God of His people. Humankind has access to God and God is well pleased.

[3] I also speculate that Jesus' birthday is on Pentecost. According to the star charts, if we take the statement in Revelation 12 about where the sun and moon are in relation to the "virgin" (Virgo—"at the feet of the virgin"), the annunciation to Mary by the Angel Gabriel, likely occurred in September 2 BC, possibly on Rosh Hosanna. Assuming that the conception of Jesus in the womb of Mary occurred at this moment, nine months later would bring us to June. The earliest that Pentecost can occur using our Gregorian calendar is May 10. The latest is June 13. My educated speculation is that Jesus' birth may have occurred then, probably in 1 BC.

[4] Almost as if reinforcing the corporeal nature, the first thing that believers do after being 'translated' apparently is eat. This is certainly consistent with most churches I have had the pleasure to be a part of! Seriously, there is a strong argument that the Marriage Supper does not actually occur until after the Second Coming and immediately before the Millennial Reign begins. In this view, the 'Saints' of both Old and New Testament times will sit together at this event. In the former view, only New Testament Saints would be present.

DD# 10   *Without 'Imminence' Why Bother to be Watchful?*

Dispensationalists argue the *Doctrine of Imminence* is very important—otherwise, Jesus' admonition to remain 'alert' doesn't make sense. If the Rapture can't happen until *after* the Tribulation concludes, it would seem that Christians shouldn't worry about Jesus making a surprise visit!

Since the Rapture is not imminent for the Covenantal Theologian, the Dispensationalist would point out that Covenantal believers can't take Jesus literally when He instructs them 'to watch' and stay alert—*"for you know not when the Son of Man cometh!"* (Matthew 25:13, *King James Version*). Moreover, if we can't take Jesus' words seriously, why did He bother to utter them?

Instead, according to the Dispensationalist, the Covenant theologians should advise their followers not to watch for Christ, but to watch for the revealing of the Antichrist and the Great Tribulation. According to the Covenantal view of when the Rapture occurs, these other apocalyptic events must come first! Even then, if the chronology of Daniel and John is correct, we still have at least 42 months to go before we see the Lord! In this context, the argument that Paul put forward to the Thessalonians would appear to be meaningless.

The Dispensationalist would transliterate II Thessalonians 2:1-8 as follows: "Why are you thinking that we are in the Tribulation Period? We can't be. The Antichrist has not revealed Himself yet. And you know he can't appear until what restrains him, the Spirit of Christ, which indwells you as members of the Body of Christ, is removed from this earth."

On the other hand, the Covenantalist could challenge the Dispensationalist as to whom Jesus' admonition is addressed. They could point out that the admonition to stay alert refers only to 'the Day of the Lord' and not to the Rapture. If you follow the verses closely, this argument holds water. Both schools believe that the Day of the Lord is predictable and evident to anyone who literally follows the Bible's predictive prophecy when it comes to the timing laid out in Daniel's 70 Weeks. If the Lord's warning only refers to the Day of the Lord, then the Doctrine of Imminence as taught by Dispensationalists is mistaken. The warning isn't for Christians but for unbelievers. When Jesus says, "Watch," He is talking about something else, not the Rapture.

DEEP DIVE NUMBER 10

DD# 11 A Practical Argument for a Separate Rapture Event

If one strongly believes there will be a 1,000 year Millennium and that it is populated by believers still remaining on the earth at the time that Christ comes (at the *"glorious appearing"* of Titus 2:13), the question is who remains on the earth in human form to begin the process?

Some contend that all unbelievers will perish leading up to and including the return of Christ at the Battle of Armageddon. Others suggest that unbelievers will be cast out of the Kingdom at the so-called 'separation of the sheep and goats' at the beginning of the Kingdom. This 'judgment event' affects those that did not profess an active living faith (Matthew 25:31-34). To be more specific, the story teaches us that at the outset of the Kingdom, the 'goats are disqualified' and *"go away to eternal punishment"* and therefore, can't enter in. In contrast, the Sheep are invited to enter into the Kingdom.

Logically if the Rapture happens at the same time as the Second Coming, all of the Sheep will already be transformed into new immortal creatures! They won't be able to procreate. Consequently, neither the Sheep nor the Goats are available to populate the earthly Kingdom. This creates a prohibitive dilemma. How do you create a new population of people if you don't have any mortals left to beget children? If repopulating the earth during the Millennial Kingdom is to happen, it would seem undeniable that there must be *a separation* between 'the secret coming of Christ,' (a.k.a., the Rapture), and the physical, 'glorious appearing of Christ,' visible to all on the earth.

This is a practical argument that some have advanced.

On the other hand, the Covenantalist is likely to say this conjecture is just as silly as believing there is to be a literal Kingdom on earth in the first place! Such an argument is built upon a misunderstanding arising from the mistaken view that 'life goes on' in the Kingdom to follow. For the Covenantalist, life does go on. However, it is a very different type of life.

DEEP DIVE NUMBER 11

Chapter 20: Seven Seals, Seven Trumpets and Seven Bowls of Wrath

Sevens, Sevens, and More Sevens

We have already read about the *Seven Lamp Stands* and the *Seven Spirits of God* in Revelation Chapter 1. In general, the number seven represents *fullness, perfection,* or *completion* in the Bible. We can interpret the meaning of 'seven' in both of these instances to refer to the 'totality' of the Churches and the 'perfection or completeness' of the Spirit of God.

Starting in Chapter 4 and throughout the rest of Revelation, we will encounter many other 'sevens.' One of the most interesting numerological issues in Revelation is the frequent use of 'seven' associated with trials, tribulation and judgment. Unlike the reference to 'lamp stands' and the 'spirits of God,' these 'sevens' always bring bad news (at least to the inhabitants of the earth!) The first set of 'seven' we encounter is the *'Scroll'* with *'Seven Seals'* to be broken so that the scrolls can be unrolled. Let's turn to this 'seven' first.

The Seven Seals

The Seven Seals (1-6 in Revelation Chapter 6, Seal Seven in Chapter 8) include the account of the *Four Horsemen of the Apocalypse* corresponding to Seals One through Four. As each seal is broken, one of the riders comes forth and creates some manner of havoc in the world. We read about these horses and their inauspicious equestrians in Chapter 6. Appearing in order is:

- A white horse that portends nation conquering nation – causing oppression among the peoples of the world;

- A red horse that brings war to the world – peace is snatched away;

- A black horse that causes great financial distress;

- A pale horse that brings suffering from death, illness, plague, and from attacks by the creatures of the earth.

Then we come to Seal number five. It is different from the first four. As it is broken, it causes the souls of those who have endured tribulation to appear beneath the throne of God and to ask for justice. They are comforted and told to wait until the full number of their fellows is completed. Next, an even more eventful seal is broken. The *Sixth Seal* is broken open causing a great earthquake and great signs to appear in the heavens. We hear calls from those that are hiding in caves because of this earthquake: *"The time of God's Wrath has come. Who will be able to withstand it?"* Could this be the moment when the Tribulation (Daniel's 70th Week) begins?

Next, 144,000 special emissaries of the Lamb are commissioned and sealed by God from each of the 12 tribes of Israel. In contrast to those who receive the Mark of the Beast, these 144,000 receive the 'seal of God' on their foreheads—a marking that will both set them apart and empower them during the tribulation period to follow. Immediately after this occurrence, we read that an 'innumerable multitude appears before the Throne of God' which wears white robes and gives glory to the Lamb. They appear in heaven after a great earthquake that shakes the foundation of the entire world. Following this intriguing event, the Seventh Seal is broken—30 minutes of silence result (no doubt, it is a somber if not solemn moment!). Immediately after the silence, John describes the awful judgments of God. Could this be the start of the Great Tribulation (the final three and one-half years) and the final judgments of God? The 'cave dwellers' appear to state this unequivocally. The 'Day of the Lord' has begun!

The traditional pre-millennial view is that the 'Seven Seals' address judgments transpiring during the first three and one-half years of the Tribulation period. This would be the position of Tim LaHaye and most dispensational scholars. Those that appear before the throne are believers 'who have come out of *great tribulation.*' The 144,000 are Jewish special agents of the Lamb that are earmarked (or *forehead* marked!) between the Sixth and Seventh Seals and begin to preach the gospel to the world. The multitude is *the persecuted and martyred believers* who come out of the *Tribulation* period. The entire sequence happens after the *Tribulation* has begun, but before the *Great Tribulation* (the final three and one-half years) commences.

When Does the Tribulation Begin in Revelation?

Another possible interpretation begins by asking, "Who is this multitude that stands before the throne?" An alternative position that I find compelling: *The multitude is the resurrected and raptured of the Church of Jesus Christ.* If so, it appears the first six of the '*Seven Seals'* happen *before* the Tribulation period; therefore, they are not truly judgments of God. They are 'trials' but not *the Great Tribulation.* Note: It isn't until this multitude appears in heaven that the Seventh Seal can be broken and the wrath of God 'poured out.' Does this provide a typology[i] for the 'pre-tribulation Rapture?'

David W. Lowe makes this argument in his book, *Then His Voice Shook the Earth,* (Seismos Publishing, 2006, 167 pages). He contends that Revelation, Chapters 4-7, is in fact covering the time known as 'the Church Age' that begins with Christ's ascension and concludes with the 'Rapture of the Church.' The timing of the breaking of the First Seal is immediately after the Lamb of God appears in Heaven and shows Himself uniquely qualified to break the Seals. John tells us Jesus' personal sacrificial death enables Him, and Him alone, to open the Seals. Thereafter, Jesus opens the seals one by one, beginning in Chapter 5. In his view, the actual period of Tribulation (Daniel's 70th Week), doesn't begin until Chapter 8. Lowe believes the multitude mentioned in Chapter 7 (the 'multitude that cannot be counted') includes both the raptured and resurrected believers comprising the 'New Testament Church.' These who are resurrected or translated, are 'caught up' come out of 'great affliction, suffering, and persecution.' Again, Lowe interprets the meaning of the passage differently than the 'standard' pre-millennial and pre-tribulation positions. This multitude did not come out of '*the great tribulation'* – which is the way this verse is usually translated by scholars who subscribe to the 'millennial' viewpoint. Rather, the multitude consists of 'the Saints' who have been spared from 'further tribulation' or suffering in the normal course of the past 2,000 years.

---

[i] Microsoft Word's dictionary defines 'typology' as "the study of religious texts for the purpose of identifying episodes in them that appear to prophesy later events."

Lowe's position hinges on a number of elements including an analysis of the Greek word *thlipsis*, which can be translated *tribulation,* but also translated as *affliction, persecution, suffering, anguish,* or *burden* – and is translated these many different ways throughout the New Testament.[i] Lowe's viewpoint is that 'all Christians pass through affliction and tribulation.' *Thlipsis* could easily be translated *'the great affliction'* or *'the great persecution'* not just 'the great tribulation.' Consequently, the passage doesn't necessarily talk about believers martyred specifically during the *Great Tribulation.* Given the context of the entire section of Revelation 4-7, this interpretation is logical. If so, the 'Four Horsemen of the Apocalypse' are not riding at the beginning of the Tribulation as most commentators contend. Instead, they are actually riders who have been on their horses for almost two thousand years, creating war, oppression, financial distress, plague, and death throughout the age. Therefore, these four riders are to blame for the pain and suffering experienced by the resurrected believers during their sojourn on earth.[ii] Now in heaven, these Christians no longer face such trials— God wipes away every tear!

To recap: *While the Seven Seals include oppression, war, financial crisis, and disease, The Seals are not necessarily judgments from God. For this reason, it would appear that they might **not** be associated with the final seven-year period of tribulation.*

The Seven Judgments of Revelation

Finally, the Seventh Seal concludes the first 'set of seven.' As it is broken the judgment of God officially commences – depicted by the symbolism of the 'Seven Trumpets' and the 'Seven Bowls (or Vials) of Wrath.' Since the Seventh Seal initiates the Seven Trumpets and Bowls of Wrath, it appears to bridge the former 'trials' to the final 'tribulation.' Certainly, the Book of Revelation contains the greatest number of references to judgment and the wrath of God. The Book of Revelation possesses much more detail than any other section of

---

[i] See Lowe's chart in his book, pages 138, 139, for the various counts – how many times – this word is translated these different ways.
[ii] Perhaps we could rename them the *Four Horsemen of the Church Age!*

Scripture concerning the various trials, plagues, and destructive events that take place during this horrible time. To follow the detailed account of these events, we must study the descriptions of the *Seven Trumpets* and the *Seven Bowls of Wrath*.

Since these 'sevens' are confusing and hard to follow, I have 'streamlined' their presentation for the reader, creating two tables to make the details more evident. As you read through these two tables, take note of the *similarities* and the *results of these judgments* (see **Figure 9 and 10** below).

Revelation, Chapters 8 and 9 describes the *Seven Trumpets* in detail. John depicts the judgments known as of the *Seven Bowls of Wrath* (containing the *Seven Plagues*) in Revelation, Chapters 15 and 16. A review of these judgments 'side-by-side' does raise the question: Should we understand these lists as *separate and distinct*, or are they speaking of the *same seven judgments*? Note that the Trumpet judgments appear to match the Bowl judgments in the second, third, fourth, fifth, and sixth instances. The first Trumpet judgment and the first Bowl of wrath judgment are both dealing with issues 'on the land.' The Bowl judgment description adds that sores plague those who accepted the *Mark of the Beast*. The seventh Trumpet and Bowl judgment also seem to relate in part to events at the 'heavenly Temple.'[i] But the Seventh Bowl Judgment relates much more detail about the most severe of all judgments causing all the cities of the world to collapse, every island to disappear and every mountain 'to be laid low' in the poetic words of the prophet. As a result, it appears that the descriptions may not refer to fourteen separate judgments, but only to seven distinct judgments whose descriptions are provided in the first list and supplemented in the second.[ii]

---

[i] The concept of a Temple in Heaven that is the model for the Temple on earth is based upon information in the Book of Hebrews (See Hebrews, Chapters 8 and 9), as well as this mention in the Book of Revelation. It is a platonic idea as some liberal commentators have pointed out (such as William Barclay), but apparently, also true.

[ii] Sir Isaac Newton also concludes in his commentary on Revelation that the two lists really comprise only one set of judgments.

The Trumpet	The Judgment	The Result of the Judgment
1st	Hail and fire mixed with blood	1/3rd of the earth burned up, 1/3rd of trees burned up, all green grass burned up.
2nd	Huge mountain, ablaze thrown into the sea	1/3rd of sea turned to blood, 1/3rd of living creatures in sea died, and 1/3rd of the ships in the sea destroyed.
3rd	A great star, Wormwood, blazing like a torch fell on 1/3rd of the springs and 1/3rd of the rivers	1/3rd of waters turned bitter, and many people died from the bitter water.
4th	1/3rd of Sun, Moon and Stars struck	1/3rd of the stars turned dark; the sun did not shine 1/3rd of the day, nor the moon 1/3rd of the night.
5th	A star that had fallen to earth was given the key to the shaft of the Abyss. This is the first WOE.	Smoke rose like a giant furnace. Sun and sky were darkened by the smoke. Locusts came out of the smoke to sting like scorpions for 5 months those who did not have the seal of God on their foreheads. Their king is Abaddon / Apollyon.
6th	Four angels at the river Euphrates released. Fire, smoke, and sulfur come from the mouths of the great army as plagues upon humankind. This is the second WOE.	1/3rd of humankind killed by the 3 plagues of the army of 200 million.
7th	Loud voices in heaven proclaim the kingdom of the world is ready to become the kingdom of Christ. The third WOE is implied.	God's temple is opened and the Ark of the Covenant is seen. There are flashes of lightning, thunder, a hail storm and an earthquake.

FIGURE 9 – THE SEVEN TRUMPET JUDGMENTS

The Bowl	The Judgment	The Result of the Judgment
1st	Bowl poured out upon the land.	Ugly and painful sores broke out on those with the Mark of the Beast.
2nd	Bowl poured out upon the sea.	Sea is turned to blood and every living thing in the sea died.
3rd	Bowl poured out on the rivers and springs.	Rivers and springs turned to blood.
4th	Bowl poured out on the sun.	People were scorched by the intense heat of the sun causing them to curse the name of God.
5th	Bowl poured out upon the throne of the Beast.	His kingdom was plunged into darkness. Men gnawed their tongues in agony.
6th	Bowl poured out on the river Euphrates.	The waters are dried up. 3 evil spirits go forth to gather up the kings of the earth for the great battle on the great day of God Almighty.
7th	Bowl poured out into the air.	A loud voice from the Temple cries out "It is done!" Flashes of lightning, rumblings, peals of thunder and a severe earthquake. The great city splits into 3 parts. Every city in the world collapses. Every island fled away. No more mountains could be found. 100 pound hailstones fall from the sky.

FIGURE 10 – THE SEVEN BOWL OR VIAL JUDGMENTS

Whether or not I have demonstrated that there are in fact only seven judgments, what we see described in Revelation is an amplification of Old Testament passages proclaiming the nature of the 'Day of the Lord.'

Revelation gives much more detail and interweaves the stories recounting of these judgments by providing descriptions of 'the *Two Witnesses*,' 'the Beast', 'the *Woman*' (Israel) of Revelation Chapter 12, 'the *False Prophet*,' 'the *Prostitute*' (*Mystery Babylon*), and 'the *Coming of the Lamb with His Saints*.' We can hardly present the Book of

Revelation fairly unless we are willing to admit the book addresses an unpopular warning: Judgment is coming. The language is 'apocalyptic.' However, the severity of the pictures painted here stands unequaled in any other religious literature. All people on earth suffer great torment and anguish. However, as with so many other images in the Book of Revelation, we still can ask, "Are these judgments literal? Will they happen in 'space-time'? Do these passages depict real events?"

This is where applying the correct *hermeneutic* is critical. If we believe these judgments are inconsistent with the rest of what the Bible teaches, we can spiritualize them in such a manner to nullify their horror. Nevertheless, if we base our interpretation on 'the plain meaning' of the Bible, it seems inevitable that we take the warnings seriously.

Recapping the Key Points Covered in This Chapter

- Revelation is infused with numerology. The number seven appears many times – particularly concerning sequencing the trials and tribulations experienced on the earth.
- The first Four Seals unleash the 'Four Horsemen of the Apocalypse'.
- The Sixth Seal heralds the appearance of 144,000 special representatives of the Lamb originating from each of the 12 tribes of Israel.
- A great multitude appears before the Throne of God.
- The traditional view proposes these events happen during the first part of the Seven Years of Tribulation (Daniel's 70th Week).
- A new view proposes that the first Six Seals are opened *before* the Tribulation. The opening of the Sixth Seal is timed to coincide with the resurrection of the dead and the rapture of the living.
- The Seventh Seal leads the way to the Wrath of God.
- The 'Seven Trumpets' and 'Seven Bowls of Wrath' convey the details about these horrendous judgments.
- The two lists appear to follow the same sequential path and therefore, may be two different descriptions of the same seven judgments. If so, there are in fact only a single set of seven judgments.

Chapter 21: The Third Temple

A Brief History of the First Two Temples

Perhaps the most specific prediction not yet fulfilled, which appears to be a *precursor* to the return of Christ, *is the rebuilding of the Jewish Temple on the Temple Mount.*

There have been two previous temples: The *Temple of Solomon* completed according to tradition in 962 BC and the *Temple of Herod* completed in the first century AD. Solomon's Temple was one the Seven Ancient Wonders of the World.[1] The building of the second Temple commenced in 536 BC when a contingent of Hebrews taken prisoner to Babylon (beginning in 606 BC, the first of several exiles) returned to rebuild the Temple under Zerubbabel's leadership and with King Cyrus' permission. The second Temple was a shadow of the first Temple—those who remembered the glory of the first Temple wept at the sight of the second Temple they constructed and completed in 516 BC (see Haggai 2:3). However, King Herod commenced a dramatic rebuilding program in 20 BC; laborers worked for over 60 years to complete vast improvements. It was still under construction when Jesus walked there. Ironically, within 25 years of its completion, Titus destroyed Herod's Temple in AD 70, just as Jesus predicted (see Matthew 24).

Why the Temple is Key to Prophetic Matters

All of the authors of major apocalyptic sections of the Bible (Daniel, John, and Paul), are in agreement that the Antichrist will desecrate the Temple during the Tribulation Period (the *abomination of desolation*). Since there is no Temple today, logically the nation of Israel must build a third Temple in the future. As mentioned earlier, there is no public policy in Israel today indicating intent on the part of the Government to support or even allow the Temple to be constructed. Tensions on the Temple Mount are so strong that it seems impossible to contemplate this possibility. Nevertheless, many preparations have been made to facilitate Temple worship and to reinstate the ancient Jewish custom of animal sacrifice. Many utensils and vessels[2] have been constructed, a Levitical order of Priests have been established and trained, the Sanhedrin has been re-established and met, and numerous artifacts from the Second Temple have been discovered in caves and beneath the Temple Mount itself—helped by a virtual treasure map known as 'the Copper Scroll.' This metallic, eight-foot scroll was one of the more significant artifacts discovered at Qumran in 1947 when archaeologists, through the lead of a shepherd boy, stumbled upon the *Dead Sea Scrolls.*

Can The Temple Be Rebuilt Today?

Of particular importance is whether the Muslim holy places, the Dome of the Rock and the Al-Aqsa Mosque, must be removed before the Temple can be constructed. Grant Jeffrey in his recent book, *The New Temple and the Second Coming* (2007), indicates that based upon his research and many discussions with rabbinical experts in Jerusalem today, the actual location where the Temple should stand is directly west of Jerusalem's East Gate, approximately 150 feet directly north of the Dome of the Rock. (The East Gate is sealed today and according to tradition will remain so until the coming of the Messiah—See Ezekiel 44:2, 3). If true, it would appear that Israel could erect the Third Temple and the existing religious shrines could remain undisturbed. David Flynn in his recent book, *The Temple at the Center of Time*, identifies a similar scenario. The 'Dome of the Spirits' (a.k.a., the Dome of the Tablets), a small cupola in the northwest portion of the Temple Court, actually may stand over the 'foundation stone' of the Temple, the sacred place where the Art of the Covenant itself rested in the Holy of Holies.[3]

From the perspective of Hebrew religious orthodoxy, recovering the essential elements of worship including 'the Oil of Anointing' and 'The Ashes of the Red Heifer' are matters of upmost importance. Without these, sacrificial worship in the Temple cannot be undertaken. Jeffrey's findings indicate however, that the Oil of Anointing has already been found and the breeding of 'red heifers' has been underway for years (although a perfect heifer with 100% red hair may still not be exist). An entity known as 'The Temple Institute,' has already rebuilt most of the required vessels like the *Ark of Incense.* Even more intriguing, the location and recovery of the *Ark of the Covenant,* made famous in modern times by the movie, *Raiders of the*

Lost Ark (1981), seems very close. If all of these findings are accurate, the primary hindrance to the rebuilding of the Third Temple is now purely political. Therefore, those who believe we are on the verge of seeing the Third Temple look for a dramatic shift in the geopolitical climate that will allow Israel to commence its building.

Why Rebuilding the Temple Doesn't Matter to Some

For Covenantal believers, the possible rebuilding of a third Temple in Jerusalem is of no real interest. Since they interpret the third temple figuratively to be the resurrection of the Body of Christ, whether or not Israel rebuilds a new house of worship and reconstitutes its sacrificial system makes no difference. No longer do they view that God holds any special significance for the people of Israel. Indeed, it would be viewed as counterproductive in that it would likely lead Judaism to continue its rejection of Christ and keep individual Jews from realizing salvation through a personal belief in Jesus Christ.

**FIGURE 11 – THE SACKING OF THE TEMPLE BY TITUS,
TITUS VICTORY ARCH IN ROME**

On the other hand, Dispensationalists appear enthusiastic about the prospects of building this Third Temple. However, since Christ has fulfilled the sacrificial system, this enthusiasm exposes Dispensationalists to a valid criticism from Covenantal believers. Christians could see reinstituting the sacrificial system as a massive *denial of the atoning work of Christ on the cross.* Since Jesus died "once and for all" (Hebrews 7:27), to reinstate this system is a strong rebuttal to Christianity's assertion that Christ is the 'Passover lamb.' If one believes that the sacrificial system is reinstated and carried out through the Millennium as the latter chapters of Ezekiel appear to state (see Chapters 40-48), the Dispensationalist faces an interpretive challenge.[4] This is no small matter.

However, the other side of this argument is also very powerful: If the Messianic Kingdom is not realized, the final eight-chapter section of Ezekiel has no relevance whatsoever. We must consider all of Ezekiel's predictions 'contingent' and now superseded. However, when reviewing this section of Scripture, no warning appears that what Ezekiel predicts and describes in such minute detail is conditional. Quite to the contrary, the words of the Prophet seem consistent with the Kingdom promises made elsewhere to the Jews: God will fulfill his covenant with the nation of Israel.

Let's consider some of the detail prospects outlined by Ezekiel in these fascinating Chapters:

1. In Chapter 44, Ezekiel discussed provisions made for those Priests that served the Lord faithfully and those that did not. This implies a resurrection. It also suggests, as some Jewish scholars believe, that both the righteous and the sinful have an inheritance in the future Kingdom – something that is foreign to Christian doctrine and tradition.

2. We read in 44:4 that the *Glory of the Lord returns to the Temple.* If God does not fulfill His promise, why would Ezekiel see His Glory return? In regards to the cherubim, their presence is a key theme of his book as we saw in studying Ezekiel Chapters 1 and 10. Their reappearance here reinforces the interpretation from the earlier portions of Ezekiel.

3. In Chapter 45, Ezekiel proclaims that there will be Princes who do not oppress the people any longer, who rule over the land, newly divided into gigantic parcels. This implies that the people will overcome their past failures and enjoy just rulers. Even Dan has an inheritance in this list – and Dan is often dropped from the list of the 12 Tribes because of their refusal to take possession of their portion of the land during the time of the Judges.

4. In Chapter 48, verses 30 through 35, the future gates of the city are named and a new name is given to Jerusalem: *'The Lord dwells there.'* It has been God's desire to live among men. Ezekiel indicates God's ultimate desire is fulfilled in the age to come.

If the coming of the 'New Jerusalem' fulfills the prophecy of the Kingdom, we are left with the need to gut a large section of Scripture—Ezekiel 40-48—for the details of the New Jerusalem in Revelation and the 'renovated Jerusalem' in Ezekiel 40-48 are not consistent. One way or another, the prophecies are unfulfilled and thus the Word of God appears 'broken.' However, if we allow both to be true, the differences are easily reconciled: Ezekiel is speaking of Jerusalem on earth during the Millennium—John in Revelation is speaking of the New Jerusalem immediately after the Millennium.

The key to decide which scenario is more likely—what transpires in the future and what Christians should believe—returns once again to the matter of biblical interpretation. Do we need to reconcile these two different views of the Kingdom? Alternatively, is it the case that one view simply replaces the other? Can they both be true? To the Dispensationalist, they must be reconciled and both must be true. To the Covenantalist, the Kingdom of Ezekiel will no longer come about – the rejection of Israel forfeits their right to see this Kingdom fulfilled. They reconcile the two by selecting one Kingdom and discarding the order.

Recapping the Key Points Covered in This Chapter

- From the dispensational perspective, the most specific prophecy yet fulfilled that appears to be a precursor to the Second Advent is the rebuilding of the Jewish Temple in Jerusalem.
- This is third such temple: The first was built by Solomon (c. 960 BC); the second was built in two stages: Zerubbabel started the second temple (c. 536 BC) and King Herod completed it (c. 45 AD).
- The key event that must occur in the Temple is the *abomination of desolation*, when the Antichrist reveals himself to the world as God.
- There are many obstacles to rebuilding the temple today.
- Much work has been accomplished over the past 30 years, however...

> - The implementation of Temple worship could happen quickly due to two scenarios that don't require rebuilding a full-scale Temple.
> - There is an extensive passage in Ezekiel about the restoration of Israel and its temple worship.
> - Covenantalists are not interested in the possible rebuilding of the Temple – they interpret the Temple being rebuilt to be the resurrection of Jesus Christ (Jesus said, "Destroy this body and in 3 days I will rebuild it").

Technical Notes

[1] According to Grant Jeffrey, a researcher and author on subjects related to the Second Coming of Christ, Solomon built the first temple with 100,000 talents of gold and 1,000,000 talents of silver. A talent was a unit of mass ranging from 26 to 32 Kilograms (approximately 65 pounds). At today's pricing, the cost of the gold and silver alone would be approximately $70BB. See Grant Jeffrey, *The New Temple and the Second Coming* (listed in **For Further Reading**).

[2] Such vessels would include the seven-foot brass Menorah, the Silver Trumpets, the Altar of Incense, and the Table of Showbread. Note **Figure 11** on page 195 where several of the original vessels from Herod's Temple (captured and taken to Rome by Titus) are easily seen.

[3] See David Flynn, *The Temple at the Center of Time*, Anomalous Publishing, Crane, MO., pp. 152, 153).

[4] What might be the Dispensational response? It has been suggested that whereas the former Temple worship and sacrificial system 'looked forward' to Christ, if reinstated and carried out during the Millennium, in some manner it would serve as a memorial to remind everyone that the sacrifice of Christ was achieved to fulfill the pictures inherent within this manner of worship. The 'sacrifice' and Temple worship would be, 'looking backward' to the work of Christ. If the 'Dispensational' viewpoint is in fact correct, we don't know today what the nature of the Temple worship will be during the Millennium. The latter part of the Book of Ezekiel provides many clues but its meaning in light of the death of Christ (which certainly doesn't appear to be contemplated by Ezekiel) is obscure to us at best.

DD# 12 Do We Know Where the Ark of the Covenant Is?

One of the most popular prophecy writers, Grant Jeffrey, relates a story confirmed by three different credible sources that the Ark of the Covenant has already been recovered by Israel from Ethiopia where it has been protected for almost 3,000 years and is today stored in the tunnels under the Temple Mount. Jeffrey, like many others, believes that the return of the Ark of the Covenant is a major event in end time's prophecy and should receive all the attention that it's getting. (See Grant Jeffrey's book, *The New Temple and the Second Coming*, listed in **For Further Reading**.)

The History Channel and National Geographic channels aired documentaries (in 2009), asserting the possible location of the Ark in Aksum, Ethiopia. Graham Hancock provided much of the original work on this hypothesis in his book, *The Sign and the Seal: The Quest for the Lost Ark of the Covenant* (Toronto: Doubleday, 1992). In stark contrast, David Flynn offers a very compelling view which states the authentic Ark and possibly the Tabernacle of Moses (the tents that comprised the 'mobile temple' during the wilderness wandering), are today located on Mount Nebo in Jordan. Flynn goes so far as to give an exact spot where authorities should go look based upon a number of somewhat esoteric, but compelling calculations, from history and scripture (See *Flynn*, op. cit., pg. 154).

Randall Price, a scholar with impressive seminary and archeological credentials, provides a third alternative. Price contends that the best bet is that the Ark remains hidden under the current Temple mount. He relates a number of discussions with key Jewish religious leaders who have been working on the recovery of the Ark of the Covenant for decades. Price, like Flynn, challenges Jeffrey's research and claim that the Ark was in Ethiopia. Flynn doubts Jeffrey's story of the Ark being 'air lifted' out of Ethiopia and returned to Israel.

However, unlike the other researchers and writers mentioned, Price doesn't' claim that the Ark has or will be found. While the Jewish authorities he has talked with contend adamantly that they know where the Ark is, the reality is that they have been digging for years, without the permission of either Jewish or *Waqf* government officials, and they have not found it. See Randall Price's book, *Searching for the Ark of the Covenant*, details in **For Further Reading**, page 305.

Finally, in personal discussions in June 2009 with Chuck Missler, noted prophecy teacher and writer, I listened intently as he contended that the Ark remains in Ethiopia. He has sojourned with Bob Cornuke following the supposed path of the Ark from Jerusalem to Elephantine Island and finally to Aksum, Ethiopia. Missler shared with me that he considers the archeological evidence strong and that in his view the Scripture suggests in many places that the Ethiopians will provide a gift to the Messiah when He returns to set up his Kingdom. That gift Missler believes may be the Ark or at least the golden covering, the Mercy Seat! Missler supposes that the Ark itself has decayed since it was made of wood. Merely covering it with gold would not secure it against the passage of 3,300 years! The Mercy Seat, however, is pure gold. It should be in fine shape.

In any event, the adventure and the search continue!

DEEP DIVE NUMBER 12

Chapter 22: The Tribulation and the Great Tribulation

When the Tribulation Begins

Evangelicals regard the *Tribulation* as a final seven-year period transpiring immediately before the Second Coming of Christ. It is considered synonymous with the Prophet **Daniel's 70th Week** (see page 97) presented in Daniel 9:24-27.

Most conservative scholars who believe in a 'Tribulation period,' believe the Tribulation formally commences with an agreement of some sort (perhaps a treaty or a covenant) between the Antichrist (who is not yet revealed as the Tribulation begins) and the leaders of Israel, promising peace or an alliance for seven years (Daniel 9:27). The Tribulation ends at the **Battle of Armageddon** (page 79) seven prophetic years (7 times 360 days) later.

Most scholars make a distinction between the Tribulation period and 'the Great Tribulation', which is thought to be the final three and one-half years of the seven-year period (Revelation 13:5). Both Daniel in the Old Testament and John in Revelation talk of 'a time, times, and half a time' (1,260 days), as the duration of the Great Tribulation period. The Book of Jeremiah calls this final period, *'the Time of Jacob's Trouble.' "How awful that day will be! None will be like it. It will be a time of trouble for Jacob, but he will be saved out of it."* (Jeremiah 30:7)

The Great Tribulation and the Time of Jacob's Trouble appear to refer only to the final three and one-half years of Daniels 70th week. However, others believe that many judgments spoken of in Revelation begin before the Antichrist reveals himself. Consequently, they believe that the proper way to label the seven-year period is *'The Tribulation' period* (synonymous with Daniel's full 70th week), and then the final three and one-half years of this seven-year period, as *the Great Tribulation.*

The Tribulation: A Time of Judgment

Most of the Book of Revelation describes the many calamites and judgments that transpire during this time of tribulation. We read of the *Seven Seals,* the *Seven Trumpets,* and the *Seven Bowls of Wrath.* Most of these occurrences connect to a specific judgment against an unbelieving world. I covered these in depth in **Chapter 20: Seven Seals, Seven Trumpets, and Seven Bowls of Wrath,** on page 185).

Scholars see the time of Tribulation as a *time of God's wrath.* Because the Tribulation is seen primarily as a time of judgment and wrath, for some it forms the strong rationale for 'the Pre-Tribulation Rapture.' The dispensational premise is that *believers should not experience God's wrath.* Therefore, the Rapture happens specifically to remove believers *from the earth prior to these events. "(I know) how you turned to God from idols to serve a living and true God, and to wait for His Son from heaven, whom He raised from the dead, that is Jesus, who rescues us from the wrath to come"* (I Thessalonians 1:9b, 10, NASV).

Today, some pre-millennialists have modified this position, referring to it as the 'pre-wrath' Rapture, similar to a position known in times past as the 'mid-Tribulation Rapture.' In this view, Christians alive when the 70th week begins will still be present on the earth. This is the case because there is no *theological imperative* to remove them before God releases His wrath. If wrath doesn't occur until much later in the seven-year Tribulation period, there is no need for the Rapture! Hence, the pre-wrath Rapture theory asserts that there is no judgment until immediately before or after the Antichrist reveals himself at the halfway point of the final seven-year period.

Does the Rapture Happen Before the Tribulation?

The matter of God's wrath and its connection to the timing of the Rapture bears additional scrutiny. As stated above, the key assumption made by all who believe the Rapture occurs prior to the Great Tribulation (the final three and one-half years), is that God will not bring His judgment upon the earth until He has removed *His redeemed first.* This assumption is not without biblical precedent.

There are many 'pictures' or fore-types in the Old Testament that suggest this reassuring principle to be true. Before God destroyed Sodom and Gomorrah his angels (possibly Christ Himself in a form known as a *theophany*), went to the city and rescued Abraham's brother Lot and his family. This is the famous story where Lot's wife turned around, looked back at Sodom and Gomorrah, and then turned into a pillar of salt.[i] She had been warned not to look upon the city when the wrath of God was poured out upon it—but she did anyway. Another possible picture is the 'rapture' of Enoch before the flood of Noah. The Scripture says, *"Enoch walked with God; then he was no more, because God took him away."* (Genesis 5:24). Enoch could be a figure of the Church, as God "takes him" from the earth before the Great Flood. Noah and his family (safely passing through the flood within the Ark), would prefigure Israel, which is protected through the Tribulation. Finally, the unbelieving who perished in the Great Flood, would be the analogous to those unbelievers during the Tribulation who perish because of God's wrath upon the earth.

To reiterate: As God told Abraham, he would spare Sodom and Gomorrah even if there were only five righteous souls there! *First, God removes his people, and then His judgment comes.* We could cite other passages to support the view that the Rapture happens before judgment falls.

1. Paul says to the Thessalonians in his second letter, *"For God chose to save us through our Lord Jesus Christ, **not to pour out His anger on us.** Christ died for us so that, whether we are dead or alive when He returns, we can live with Him forever. So encourage each other and build each other up, just as you are already doing."* (I Thessalonians 5: 9-11, *New Living Translation*)

2. John quotes the resurrected Jesus addressing the Church at Philadelphia, *"Since you have kept my command to endure patiently, I will also **keep you from the hour of trial** that is going to come*

---

[i] Jesus called Christians the 'salt of the earth.' Therefore, we should point out that Lot's wife was not a prototype!

upon the whole world to test those who live on the earth." (Revelation 3: 10)

Tim LaHaye asserts in his book, *The Rapture* (See **For Further Reading,** page 305, for details), that many of the judgments of God happen in the first half of the seven-year period, not just in the final three and one-half years. As a result, there is *not* a strong argument for a 'pre-wrath' or mid-tribulation viewpoint, *if* the rationale is that God will save Christians *"from the wrath to come."*

Since these 'pre-wrath' proponents argue that God's judgment does not commence until sometime in the final three and one-half years of this seven-year period, there is a sound theological basis for the 'pre-wrath argument.' On the other hand, the pre-wrath advocates still have to address the 'doctrine of Imminence'. If we view the doctrine of Imminence important, we must conclude that *the seven-year agreement between the Antichrist and Israel can't precede the Rapture.*[i] On the other hand, to say the inverse, the Rapture must precede the seven-year covenant with Antichrist.

When Will It Take Place?

We know the Great Tribulation by many other names: *The Day of the Lord*, the *Day of Jesus Christ*, and the *Day of Wrath*. Of course, we must interpret the concept of 'day' as a period different from the normal 24-hour period (II Peter 3:8). Day and 'days' are used almost interchangeably in some instances. Jesus said, *"Unless those days had been cut short, no life would have been saved; but for the sake of the elect those days will be cut short"* (Matthew 24: 22). We could interpret this comment to mean that the period of Great Tribulation will be exactly the number of days prophesized (1,290— Daniel 12:11) and no more, lest humankind go extinct. Furthermore, those who become believers during the Great Tribulation will literally be able to count down the days until Christ returns.

---

[i] With the 'pre-wrath' position, if the Rapture occurs *during the Tribulation period,* logically we must disregard the 'doctrine of Imminence' because other events that we can watch for will take place first and the timing of Christ's return can be calculated to the very day.

The final verdict on the timing of the Rapture in respect to the Tribulation period is likely best determined not as a result of any one single point, but by the totality of evidence on what the Bible teaches regarding all the issues of eschatology including the distinction (or not) between the Church and the spiritual 'nation' of Israel.

We should keep in mind that the Prophets do not teach the 'Rapture' to Israel. This event is part of the "mystery hidden in Christ" that Paul reveals. Rather, Israel must await the Messiah, rejoice at His appearance, have their hearts changed with God's Spirit dwelling in them, and then inherit the earthly Kingdom. In contrast, the Apostles teach their flocks to look forward to meeting Christ in the clouds and forever being with the Lord. We see all those saved by God are set for in the same destiny, but take different paths to get there!

Recapping the Key Points Covered in This Chapter

- Many scholars consider the Tribulation Period to be synonymous with the 70th Week of Daniel's Prophecy.
- The Tribulation is a time of great distress and destruction, commenced when a league of nations covenants to protect Israel. It culminates with at the Battle of Armageddon.
- This time is also known in Jewish tradition as *'The Time of Jacob's Trouble.'*
- The final three and one-half years (perhaps all seven years) are considered a time of God's judgment. Most scholars would equate this period with 'The Day of the Lord' as discussed in the Old Testament and 'The Day of Jesus Christ' in the New Testament.
- Pre-tribulation Rapture believers contend that the Rapture must happen before the tribulation because this seven year period is a time of judgment – and God does not inflict judgment on His elect. He rescues them first before He sends judgment.

Figure 12 - THE APOCALYPSE, RUSSIAN ICON, AUTHOR UNKNOWN, 1ST HALF OF 16TH CENTURY

Chapter 23: The Two Witnesses

The Insurgency against Antichrist

During the final seven years of tribulation, two fascinating characters come on the scene to oppose the **Antichrist** (see page 65). They are the so-called *Two Witnesses*. We read their story in Revelation, Chapter 11:

¹ I was given a reed like a measuring rod and was told, "Go and measure the temple of God and the altar, and count the worshipers there.

² But exclude the outer court; do not measure it, because it has been given to the Gentiles. They will trample on the holy city for 42 months.

³ And I will give power to my two witnesses, and they will prophesy for 1,260 days, clothed in sackcloth."

⁴ These are the two olive trees and the two lamp stands that stand before the Lord of the earth.

⁵ If anyone tries to harm them, fire comes from their mouths and devours their enemies. This is how anyone who wants to harm them must die.

⁶ These men have power to shut up the sky so that it will not rain during the time they are prophesying; and they have power to turn the waters into blood and to strike the earth with every kind of plague as often as they want.

⁷ Now when they have finished their testimony, the beast that comes up from the Abyss will attack them, and overpower and kill them.

⁸ Their bodies will lie in the street of the great city, which is figuratively called Sodom and Egypt, where also their Lord was crucified.

⁹ For three and a half days men from every people, tribe, language and nation will gaze on their bodies and refuse them burial.

¹⁰ The inhabitants of the earth will gloat over them and will celebrate by sending each other gifts, because these two prophets had tormented those who live on the earth.

11 But after the three and a half days a breath of life from God entered them, and they stood on their feet, and terror struck those who saw them.

12 Then they heard a loud voice from heaven saying to them, "Come up here." And they went up to heaven in a cloud, while their enemies looked on.

13 At that very hour there was a severe earthquake and a tenth of the city collapsed. Seven thousand people were killed in the earthquake, and the survivors were terrified and gave glory to the God of heaven.

Attributes of the Two Witnesses

The story begins indicating that the two witnesses will 'trample' on the Holy City (Jerusalem) for 42 months (verse 2), reiterated as 1,260 days (in verse 3), and which is three and a half years.

Trample is a colorful word. The dictionary defines it as, 'treading heavily,' which means to walk upon something in such a way as to crush it. However, another possible definition is even stronger: *To walk in such a way to show contempt for those in your presence.* Clearly, the Two Witnesses aren't taking a stroll in the park. Jerusalem appears to be one of several Antichrist capitals (Rome and Babylon may be the other two). *This suggests that the Two Witnesses will take every step in literal spite of Antichrist's government!*

We read in verse 3 that they will prophesy, clothed in sackcloth. Sackcloth is the 'homespun wool' the prophets wore when protesting the actions of the Kings and the people. It was also the clothing worn when in repentance. John the Baptist, the greatest prophet according to Jesus, wore sackcloth throughout his ministry identifying with the repentance he called for from the people of his day.

John the 'revelator' refers to them in verse 4 as the two olive trees and the two lamp stands. This is a direct reference to Zerubbabel and Joshua, (a.k.a., Joshua the High Priest at the time of Zerubbabel, circa 536 BC). (See Zechariah's vision of the two olive trees and lamp stands of Zechariah 4:11-14). One is a *Prince* the other is a *Priest.* They are also the first (of two exiles listed in Ezra 2:1) who return to the Holy Land from Babylonian captivity.

FIGURE 13 – MEASURING THE COURTYARD,
LA MESURE DU TEMPLE C. 950

However, the next bit of descriptive information suggests that their identities may be quite unexpected. *They have fantastic powers to defend themselves*—if anyone tries to harm them, they are able to breathe fire and consume them. These powers are reminiscent of Moses and Elijah. Moses could turn water into blood and send plagues upon his enemies. Elijah once shut up the heavens and kept rain from falling for three and a half years (there is that three and one-half years again!) At the battle on Mount Carmel with the prophets of Ahab and Jezebel, Elijah called down fire from heaven that fully consumed his sacrifice to God in a single moment.

The Two Witnesses apparently work these miraculous signs during this Tribulation period; the world apparently blames them for all the horrible judgments tormenting the earth.

The Death and Resurrection of the Two Witnesses

John tells us that upon completing their time of testimony, the Antichrist will finally overcome them—killing them in "Sodom or Egypt" – which is still most likely *Jerusalem*, as the city where their Lord, Jesus, was crucified as these verses state (verse 2 references the *Holy City*).[i] For three and a half days, their dead bodies will lay untouched. Middle Eastern culture sees this as a tremendous insult and illustrates the disdain that their enemies feel toward them. We read that the entire world will be watching (on television no doubt, although as you might guess that detail is not specified by John!). Their deaths will be a happy occasion among the supporters of the Antichrist: *They send gifts to one another because the Two Witnesses and their harmful signs are finally stopped.*

Then something amazing happens: *They are resurrected!*

We can visualize the television networks 'interrupting their normal programming' as the newscaster begins: "There is an amazing development in Jerusalem regarding the death of these two despicable tormentors of our world." We see the scene switch, perhaps to the courtyard of the Temple, to the dead bodies of the Two Witnesses, as their fingers start to twitch and as they slowly begin to take breaths. The cameras zero in on the Two Witnesses and they slowly rise to their feet. Then, like thunder, a voice is heard that shouts *"Come up here"* and immediately the Two Witnesses are powerfully resurrected and ascend upwards into a cloud (which as noted earlier, the 'shouting voice that sounds like a trumpet' and the appearance of a 'cloud' is the *modus operandi* for resurrections and ascensions in the Bible!). As the ascension transpires from within

---

[i] Perhaps John refers to Jerusalem as Egypt or Sodom because the city is under the control of Antichrist at the time the Two Witnesses prophesy.

the Temple courtyard, a strong earthquake hits. John tells us that 7,000 persons die in this quake—a small number for Revelation—indicating that it may be the persons in the crowds immediately surrounding the witnesses (the worshippers the Angel told John to count when he measured the Temple courtyard). Those that live through the quake are trembling and fearful and recognize that the power these witnesses possessed was from God—and reluctantly perhaps, they give Him credit for what has happened.

FIGURE 14 – THE TWO WITNESSES, PROPHETS AND BEAST

Identifying the Two Witnesses

Who are these Two Witnesses? Scholars have proposed a number of possibilities: Some have suggested that they represent the *Church* and *Israel*—the two 'nations' that have given witness to God throughout history. This seems unlikely because we read that they possessed powers that are not characteristic behaviors for the Church or Israel. Moreover, we know from what we have already studied that the Antichrist does not put either the Church or Israel to death. In fact, the Church may be already 'out of the way' (if the Rapture has taken place *before* the Tribulation period). As for Israel, God is caring for her with a special affection. God protects many of her people; she will survive through the Tribulation period. We see this in Revelation, Chapter 12, which provides detail regarding how God protects Israel from Satan and the Antichrist.

Therefore, most authorities believe these witnesses are actually two individuals. A few suppose that they are only supercharged evangelists acting in the spirit of the great prophets of old. However, most pundits contend this doesn't do justice to the story.

There are three names mentioned as candidates by prophecy scholars: Elijah, Enoch, and Moses. All scholars usually agree Moses is the first of the two. Most identify the second witness as Elijah.

However, why are these individuals such good prospects to serve as the Two Witnesses? As mentioned before, their miracles are characteristic of Moses and Elijah. We see here the same power performed to the same effect as during their previous 'ministries' in the Old Testament. So it would be logical to think that based upon these 'signs and wonders,' John discloses their identity.

These two are also logical choices because they once appeared alongside Jesus on the *Mount of Transfiguration* (which is probably Mount Hermon in today's Golan Heights, near Syria – see Mark 9:2-11) where they talked about Jesus 'departure' (i.e., death), which He was soon to accomplish at Jerusalem. Moses represents 'the Law' while Elijah represents 'the Prophets.' As noted back in the *Introduction*, when scholars refer to the Old Testament 'in its entirety,' they often speak of it as *the Law and the Prophets*.

Candidates Because of Their Mysterious Departures

Nevertheless, another reason scholars speculate about all three candidates is that in all *three* cases God was directly involved at the 'end' of their lives, and in two cases their ascension into heaven. Two of the three, if not all three, may not have suffered death.

Moses' death is indeed mysterious. Moses is the traditional author of the first five books of the Bible, the *Torah,* or *Pentateuch.*[i] If we believe he authored these books, it seems apparent that Joshua wrote the final verses, which indicate that Moses died upon seeing the lands of Canaan (the 'Promised Land') as God indicated he would. Immediately afterwards, the Bible says that 'God buried Moses.' We read in Deuteronomy Chapter 34:

> *4 Then the LORD said to him, "This is the land I promised on oath to Abraham, Isaac and Jacob when I said, 'I will give it to your descendants.' I have let you see it with your eyes, but you will not cross over into it."*
>
> *5 And Moses the servant of the LORD died there in Moab, as the LORD had said.*
>
> *6 He buried him in Moab, in the valley opposite Beth Peor, but to this day no one knows where his grave is.*

However, there is also a tradition that Moses wrote about his own death to keep others from speculating regarding what happened to Him – why he simply *disappeared.* Could it be that he was 'raptured' or ascended into heaven? Since *"no one knows where his grave is,"* we might dare to speculate. However, in the Book of Jude, verse 9, we learn that Michael and Lucifer vied 'for the body of Moses.' Was Satan attempting to block the possibility that Moses might return as one of the Two Witnesses? Notwithstanding this possibility, all biblical indicators, as tradition holds, appear to attest to the death of Moses and his burial, by God's own 'hands'. With the other two characters, we know that the Scripture is clear in its testimony that they did not die, but were 'taken up' into heaven.

---

[i] The Torah can refer either to the Pentateuch, the first five books of the 'Old' Testament, or to both the Pentateuch and the Talmud, which is a collection of these books including commentary by Jewish sages through the ages.

With *Elijah*, we know that he was 'taken up in a whirlwind' and that he ascended leaving Elisha behind, apparently without experiencing death. "As they were walking along and talking together, suddenly a chariot of fire and horses of fire appeared and separated the two of them, and Elijah went up to heaven in a whirlwind. Elisha saw this and cried out, *"My father! My father! The chariots and horsemen of Israel!" And Elisha saw him no more. Then he took hold of his own clothes and tore them apart."* (II Kings 2:11, 12)

The 50 prophets who were with Elijah and Elisha tried to find Elijah after his 'catching up' searching the hillsides nearby (although Elisha tried to prevent this explaining that Elijah was no longer 'with them'). Previously, Elijah told Elisha that God soon would take him to heaven and that Elisha must carry on without him. Of course, Elisha does continue. He works miracles in the same spirit as Elijah according to the history of II Kings.[1]

The Story and Book of Enoch

Lastly, we have the story of *Enoch*. Enoch was a one-of-a-kind character who lived before the Flood of Noah. Many extra-biblical stories have arisen about Enoch. The Book of Jubilees contains some of these. However, most are from the book that bears his name. We know that about two hundred years ago, archeologists discovered several complete copies of the book of Enoch in Ethiopia. The *Book of Enoch* had been lost for almost 1,300 years. Its disappearance was partially because it never became an accepted part of the canon of Scripture. Although not preserved throughout the church age, the *early* Church still honored and loved the book. Some held it to be divinely inspired. We know that Jude in his short epistle in the New Testament quotes from the Book of Enoch,[2] discussing the **Advent** (see page 35) of the Messiah:

> *It was also about these men that Enoch, in the seventh generation from Adam, prophesied, saying, "Behold, the Lord came with many thousands of His holy ones, to execute judgment upon all, and to convict all the ungodly of all their ungodly deeds which they have done in an ungodly way, and of all the harsh things which ungodly sinners have spoken against Him" (Jude 1:14, 15).*

Scholars who have spent time with the Book of Enoch believe that it may be older than any book in the Bible. Some suggest that it Enoch wrote the book and Noah carried it on the Ark to protect it from the Flood. Others dismiss the book as nothing more than fascinating story telling, reflecting a mythical interpretation of pre-diluvium events, and clearly a *pseudonym*. Nonetheless, it's an incredible book! Whether inspired or not, it discusses in detail the events mentioned in Genesis 6 concerning the *Nephilim*, the children begotten by the 'watchers'[3] and the 'daughters of men.' These were the 'men of renown,' the offspring of fallen angels that were born mortal but had amazing strength and grew to be giants.

However, the intent of the book was not just to chronicle the story of these fallen angels – the audience of the book is actually those *persons living during the final tribulation upon the earth!* If so, it is remarkable that one of the oldest written books (perhaps before the time that Moses first began to write the Torah), addresses those times and people who will be living so far into the future – perhaps near the chronological end of the Bible's subject matter.

However, concerning Enoch, we read in Genesis 5:24, *"And Enoch walked with God and was not, for God took him." In Hebrews 11:5, we read, "By faith Enoch was taken up so that he would not see death; AND HE WAS NOT FOUND BECAUSE GOD TOOK HIM UP; for he obtained the witness that before his being taken up he was pleasing to God."*

So, we have in each case one or more scriptural indications that these two very important Bible personages did not die—but were 'translated' or *raptured* in a way similar to what the Dispensationalist proclaims will be true for all Christians living just before the beginning of the Tribulation.

Of the two characters that were "taken," which is the more likely? One authority points out that Enoch is disqualified to be one of the witnesses because he was not a Hebrew. This would be quite true because he lived perhaps more than 1,000 years before Abraham, Isaac, and Jacob (Jacob of course, after wrestling with God, became *Israel* and thereafter had twelve sons, fathering the 'twelve tribes' of the Hebrews – circa 1850 BC). Perhaps we should eliminate Enoch from contention for this reason.

Why Bring Moses and Elijah to the Fray?

However, if the Two Witnesses are in fact Moses and Elijah, why are they 'called for' in this situation? Why would they make an appearance in the Tribulation? It would seem that because this time is the 'time of Jacob's trouble,' a time of tribulation unlike and incomparable to any other time of desperation for the Jewish nation, that it is time to call on *the special forces!* The two witnesses are dealing directly with Satan and with his Antichrist. This is the culmination of the ages. All of history has been moving to this moment. We can imagine that if Moses and Elijah are to make this appearance that they have been counting down the days until they can engage with the nemesis of God on the world stage.

The Timing of Their Appearance

The last issue has to do with 'when' the Two Witnesses make their appearance. Tim LaHaye in his book on the Rapture indicates that their ministry is in the first half of the Tribulation period. This is a common view. However, I find this unlikely for several reasons:

1. This event comes between the sixth and seventh trumpets in Revelation. The angel blows the seventh trumpet appears very near the time *that Christ returns to the Mount of Olives.* Revelation 11:18 states:

    The nations were angry; and your wrath has come.
    The time has come for judging the dead,
    and for rewarding your servants the prophets
    and your saints and those who reverence your name,
    both small and great—
    and for destroying those who destroy the earth."

    If my suggestion regarding the timing of the 6th and 7th Trumpets is correct, it would clearly specify the timing of the Two Witnesses is during the final three and one-half years.

2. The language, both before and after this chapter, suggests the Two Witnesses appear *at the culmination of satanic deception. The An-*

tichrist doesn't reveal himself until the first three and one-half years are finished.

3.   If the Two Witnesses appeared during the first half of the seven-year period, their deaths (even considering their quick resurrection three and one-half days later) would occur at the very moment the Antichrist appears. To me, this provides a *'mixed message' about who was really winning the battle.* If they cannot withstand the Antichrist any longer than this, why did God bother having them show up for the fight? The ability of the Two Witnesses to exercise their powers and to forestall their deaths would seem *far less impressive if not meaningless if the Antichrist appears on the scene and immediately puts them to death.*

4.   The covenant already exists between Israel and a league of nations committed to protect Israel. However, the Antichrist does not reveal himself fully until he commits the **abomination of desolation** (page 73) halfway through the Tribulation period. The Two Witnesses would have been prophesying right up to the time that he appears. This would mean that their testimony was not during 'the time of Jacob's trouble.' This seems unlikely and inconsistent with the emphasis on Jerusalem, the Temple Court, and the role the Two Witnesses appear to play in serving as a counter-point to the false religion of Antichrist and his False Prophet.

5.   If the Two Witnesses provide their testimony for 1,260 days, this most likely occurs after the Antichrist reveals himself—the *Two Witnesses become the 'thorn in his side' throughout his reign.* That is why they 'tramp around' in the Holy City!

Daniel indicates that the second half of the Great Tribulation is 1,290 days (See Daniel 12:11). There may be a 30-day overlap between these periods in which the total number of days of Tribulation is 2,520 days, or there may be two periods together totaling 2,550 days, one of 1,260 days and one of 1,290 days. Perhaps their death and resurrection is exactly 30 days before Christ returns to the Mount of Olives! For our purposes, it isn't necessary to be dogmatic about when the witnesses carry out their mission or when it concludes. However, it is worthy to make note of their activities. They appear to instigate an effective 'insurgency' against the government of the Antichrist and lead a tremendous evangelistic endeavor that encourages Israel and believers throughout the Great Tribulation.

Recapping the Key Points Covered in This Chapter

- The story of the Two Witnesses is an intriguing account of two evangelists who oppose the Antichrist during the Tribulation.
- Their identity has caused much speculation through the years.
- They have great powers, reminiscent of Moses and Elijah!
- Who are these future Prophets? Some scholars believe they are only powerful individuals who act in the spirit of Moses and Elijah. Others believe there is much more to the story than this.
- Virtually all scholars identify Moses as one of the Two.
- Most consider Elijah and Enoch the other possible candidates.
- All three share mysterious circumstances surrounding the conclusion of their mortal lives upon on this earth. God "translated" both Elijah and Enoch into heaven!
- Scholars debate the timing of their appearance in the Tribulation.
- The Antichrist manages to kill the Two Witnesses, possibly in the courtyard of the rebuilt Third Temple in Jerusalem.
- However, the Voice of God resurrects the two Witnesses. An earthquake accompanies this event. This may foreshadow details about the resurrection and rapture, an event that we will study later.

Technical Notes

---

[1] In response to the van Däniken scenario of alien astronauts, the details of the story don't seem to support an 'alien abduction.' Elijah apparently tosses out his cloak to Elisha to assure him that he will have a 'double portion' of Elijah's spirit, a sign they had prearranged to confer that twice as much power would be available to Elisha to work miracles!

[2] For the Scripture to quote any non-canonical book, such a book must have very special qualities. Perhaps this book did carry some degree of inspiration. No doubt, it was revered. Being *'an Old Testament'* source, it would not have been declared a part of the Christian canon, and for whatever reason, the Jews who completed their canon in the 2nd century AD, chose not to make it a part of their Bible. Today, most consider the book a *pseudonym*. That is the safe position to promote!

[3] The term 'watchers' is fascinating because it appears to be a synonym for 'angels' in the Bible. It is specific enough to convey some information about the role of angels, but vague enough to leave us asking more questions. Daniel uses the term one place in his book and it appears in the Book of Enoch throughout. I am not aware of its usage anywhere else in the Bible. I understand its meaning to be essentially those who 'watch out' for us! The fallen angels ceased being 'watchers' and became 'players' and received severe condemnation as a result.

Chapter 24: The Valley of Dry Bones

Ezekiel's Vision to Restore Israel

Some might say, "Give me one argument that says all this apocalyptic stuff is about to happen – *what the key sign is* that the Second Coming is about to happen." There is such a sign. This key is the *restoration of the nation of Israel.*

It is a true miracle. No other group of people in the history of the world have survived without a homeland for 2,000 years and maintained their own language, culture, and religion. It is a 'one of a kind' phenomenon.

Ezekiel Chapter 36 tells of God's promises to bring all Israel together again, to put a new spirit within them, to make their land blossom, and to restore both Judah (its two tribes) and the ten northern tribes (known as Israel in the 9th through 7th centuries BC), making them one nation once again.

In Chapter 37, the Lord God gives the famous vision to His prophet Ezekiel:

¹ The hand of the LORD was upon me, and he brought me out by the Spirit of the LORD and set me in the middle of a valley; it was full of bones.

² He led me back and forth among them, and I saw a great many bones on the floor of the valley, bones that were very dry.

³ He asked me, "Son of man, can these bones live?"
I said, "O Sovereign LORD, you alone know."

⁴ Then he said to me, "Prophesy to these bones and say to them, 'Dry bones, hear the word of the LORD!

⁵ This is what the Sovereign LORD says to these bones: I will make breath enter you, and you will come to life.

⁶ I will attach tendons to you and make flesh come upon you and cover you with skin; I will put breath in you, and you will come to life. Then you will know that I am the LORD.' "

⁷ So I prophesied as I was commanded. And as I was prophesying, there was a noise, a rattling sound, and the bones came together, bone to bone.

8 I looked, and tendons and flesh appeared on them and skin covered them, but there was no breath in them.

9 Then he said to me, "Prophesy to the breath; prophesy, son of man, and say to it, 'This is what the Sovereign LORD says: Come from the four winds, O breath, and breathe into these slain, that they may live.' "

10 So I prophesied as he commanded me, and breath entered them; they came to life and stood up on their feet—a vast army.

11 Then he said to me: "Son of man, these bones are the whole house of Israel. They say, 'Our bones are dried up and our hope is gone; we are cut off.'

12 Therefore prophesy and say to them: 'This is what the Sovereign LORD says: O my people, I am going to open your graves and bring you up from them; I will bring you back to the land of Israel.

13 Then you, my people, will know that I am the LORD, when I open your graves and bring you up from them.

14 I will put my Spirit in you and you will live, and I will settle you in your own land. Then you will know that I the LORD have spoken, and I have done it, declares the LORD.' "

The Restoration of Israel—the Key Prophetic Milestone

Most commentators believe that the restoration of Israel sets the stage for the many occurrences surrounding the Second Coming. May 14, 1948, was the birth of the modern nation of Israel. It culminated the Zionist movement that began late in the 19th century. Formed through the help of the United Nations, Israel managed to fight its way into existence overcoming remarkable odds and the armies of its Arab neighbors.

There is a phrase often used among prophecy teachers, 'the time of the Gentiles,' which is used in Luke's version of the 'Olivet Discourse.' *"And they shall fall by the edge of the sword, and shall be led away captive into all nations: and Jerusalem shall be trodden down of the Gentiles, **until the times of the Gentiles be fulfilled"*** (Luke 21:24, King James Version).

Covenantalists (*preterists*, specifically) believe that Jesus' prediction of the destruction of the Temple within one generation of His death fulfilled this prophecy. Jesus died in 32 AD. Titus destroyed the Temple in 70 AD (38 years later). This prophecy, like all the others in Matthew 24 (the 'Olivet Discourse'), is now 'history.' We await no future fulfillment. Futurists, like the Dispensationalists, disagree. This 'time' or epoch (the 'time of the gentiles'), is thought to encompass the duration of time in which gentiles control or govern Jerusalem. Some regard the time of the Gentiles concluded with the birth of the nation in 1948. Most usually relate the end of the time of the Gentiles with the Six-Day War of 1967 in which Israel recaptured eastern Jerusalem, the 'West Bank,' and most notably, the Temple Mount. As we will see, determining *when* the 'time of the gentiles' ends is an important *marker*.

What is the Length of a Generation in the Bible?

Jesus indicates that all events associated with His Second coming will occur *in the life span of a single generation* (Matthew 24:34). Many Bible teachers assert a biblical generation is 40 years. When the Hebrews did not go forth and take the land upon the report of the 12 spies, God judged them and said that no one in that generation (except Caleb and Joshua) would 'enter into the land.' Every single person in that generation would die during his or her *forty years* of wanderings in the wilderness.[1]

Likewise, in Matthew 24, Jesus indicated that the generation that witnesses the beginning of the signs (which notably began with His presence as Messiah) until the destruction within the city of Jerusalem, would be no longer than one generation. (Missler points out the timing of the 'wilderness wanderings' and the period from Jesus' death to the destruction of the Temple in 70 AD were both *38 years*, *within one generation* as foretold, and coincidentally exactly the same length of time!) Others suggest that the life span of a person, set at 70 years, or if by grace, 80 years (according to Psalm 90:10), is in fact the duration of a generation. Certainly, the Psalmist does give us a standard for the length of a normal life. Nevertheless, is this the same as the length of a generation?

This issue of when the time of the Gentiles ends and when a generation concludes is probably the greatest impetus influencing today's prophecy teachers to 'set dates' and prognosticate when Christ will return. *As such, it is the most problematic concept in recent prophetic studies, which has discredited many proponents of predictive prophecy.* [2]

To be precise, there are actually two different issues to distinguish: (1) Biblically speaking, how long is a generation? (2) When does the clock start so we can predict exactly when it ends?

As to generations and their length: My view is that a generation is most likely 40 years. When Matthew provides the genealogy of Christ, necessary to demonstrate that he was of the lineage of David (and thus could sit on David's throne), he points out the symmetry of 14 generations that span each of three consecutive periods. *"So all the generations from Abraham to David are fourteen generations; from David to the deportation to Babylon, fourteen generations; and from the deportation to Babylon to the Messiah, fourteen generations."* (Matthew 1:17). The span of time divided by 14 in each of these periods is reasonably close to 40 years. Here is the detail:[i]

- Abraham to David, about 900 years (average of 64 years—from 1950 BC to 1050 BC);

- David to the Babylonian deportation, about 470 years (an average of 34 years—from (1050 BC to 580 BC);

- From the deportation to the time of Messiah, about 580 years (average of about 41 years—from 580 BC to 1 BC).[ii]

The earliest period, from Abraham to David, is influenced by the curiosity that the patriarchs lived longer lives—almost 50% longer than the normal time span. Abraham, according to the Bible, lived to be 175 years old and Moses 120 years. In addition, Matthew's generations may be missing some entries as both liberal and conservative scholars have pointed out.

However, from what date do we start the clock running so we know the 40 years are up? As indicated before, some say the 'clock' starts in 1948. Others say it started in 1967. Additionally, do we

---

[i] This is using the traditional dating (rounded) of when each of these events took place or when these characters walked the earth.

[ii] If the entire period of 1950 years is divided by 42 for all 3 groupings (3 x 14), the resulting average generation length is about 46 years.

really know whether the time of the gentiles has ended? The fact that the Jews still do not control the Temple Mount[3] as I write this in 2009; this may mean that the Time of the Gentiles continues.[i] In fact, the Time of the Gentiles may continue until the return of Christ at the *Mount of Olives*. The Antichrist is to dominate Jerusalem until the Messiah returns and secures Jerusalem (Zechariah 14).

For all these reasons, I contend the starting time is simply not clear and cannot be a point about which anyone should be dogmatic. Indeed, since we cannot be perfectly sure about the length of a generation in the Bible or when to start the clock, we should avoid setting any date—especially attempting to use this marker (the 'time of the gentiles'), which has already been a frequent source of error.

The Nation of Israel is a Fact—But What Does It Mean?

The advocates of 'replacement theology' (those that see the Church replacing Israel as 'the apple of God's eye'), have an especially hard time understanding what the meaning of *modern Israel* is. If the Church is now 'spiritual Israel', why do the Jewish people persist? How do we interpret the Scriptures that promise such a restoration after the vast dispersion of the Jewish peoples across the world for the last 2,500 years? Isn't this coincidence a bit too much to explain away? [4]

To this point, Dispensationalists insist that the very presence of modern Israel proves that God never dissolved His special relationship with Israel and His Covenant with the Children of Abraham continues to this day. In contrast, Covenantal scholars are willing to say that God continues to honor the Jews because of His love for the patriarchs. However, they would *not* agree that the revival of the Jewish people 'in the last days' is evidence that God is still at work in the salvation of the Israel *as a nation*.[5] So can we make the Bible's position clearer?

We read from Deuteronomy Chapter 4:

---

[i] This was the position of John Wolvoord, noted Dispensational Theologian and former President of Dallas Theological Seminary.

25 After you have had children and grandchildren and have lived in the land a long time—if you then become corrupt and make any kind of idol, doing evil in the eyes of the LORD your God and provoking him to anger,

26 I call heaven and earth as witnesses against you this day that you will quickly perish from the land that you are crossing the Jordan to possess. You will not live there long but will certainly be destroyed.

27 The LORD will scatter you among the peoples, and only a few of you will survive among the nations to which the LORD will drive you.

28 There you will worship man-made gods of wood and stone, which cannot see or hear or eat or smell.

29 But if from there you seek the LORD your God, you will find him if you look for him with all your heart and with all your soul.

30 When you are in distress and all these things have happened to you, then in later days you will return to the LORD your God and obey him.

31 For the LORD your God is a merciful God; he will not abandon or destroy you or forget the covenant with your forefathers, which he confirmed to them by oath.

We read this passage and can plainly see that Moses predicted that the nation of Israel would go through all of these experiences including apostasy and the *Diaspora*, but would then be 're-gathered together' *"in the latter days"* (the same wording we see in Ezekiel's passage on **The Battle of Gog and Magog,** see page 85). It is clear that the 'return' was not contingent upon their faithfulness. It seems apparent that *God knew beforehand that the Jews would reject Him—but that their rejection of **Him** would not be a reason that He would reject **them.*** *"For the LORD your God is a merciful God; he will not abandon or destroy you or forget the covenant with your forefathers, which he confirmed to them by oath" (Deuteronomy 4:31).* The language appears to indicate that it is impossible for God to *not* make good on His promises. The Jews will return and be re-gathered. The Dispensationalists raises a predictable question: "If the re-gathering happens, wouldn't this indicate that the rest of the predictions about the 'end times' and restoration of Israel also must come to pass?"

However, Haven't We Heard It All Before?

When naysayers suggest that there is nothing special or determinant that infers the end times may be drawing close, certain evangelicals argue that the re-emergence of Israel and its place among the nations testifies just the opposite.

> **THE KEY POINT TO PONDER:**
>
> *The restoration of Israel is the single most unique and important event underscoring the possibility that Christ may soon return. It is a historical fact that Dispensationalists argue strongly validates their perspective.*

The restoration of Israel is the single most unique and important event underscoring the possibility that Christ may soon return. Because this is an unparalleled event, the restoration of a nation dispersed for almost 2,000 years, the rebirth of Israel appears to be undeniably *providential*. Since it does not square with those who espouse 'replacement theology', it also lends strong credence to the alternative viewpoint. Dispensationalists would argue that it is indeed a *strong historical basis upon which to build one's hermeneutic* for how we should interpret the Bible. To the Covenantalist, it mostly remains an unsolved puzzle.

The Meaning of the Fig Tree's Budding

Another related element often talked about in prophetic circles is the *Parable of the Fig Tree*. Likewise, this parable comes from Matthew 24, Jesus' discourse with His Apostles. Matthew quotes Jesus as follows:

> *"Learn a lesson from the fig tree. As soon as its twigs get tender and its leaves come out, you know that summer is near. In the same way, when you see all those things happening, you know that the end is near. It is right at the door. What I'm about to tell you is true. The people living at that time will certainly not pass away until all those things have happened. Heaven and earth will pass away. But my words will never pass away"* (verses 32-35).

Is there anything special about the *Fig Tree?* Many scholars say there is. They believe the Fig Tree represents *the nation of*

Israel. Their interpretation is that when Israel blooms, then we should know that 'the end is near.' Other scholars disagree with this interpretation however, and don't believe the 'budding of the Fig Tree' implies the formation of Israel.

Grant Jeffrey, in a research note on his website,[i] provides sound evidence through a quotation in the apocryphal book, *The Apocalypse of Peter—Ethiopic edition (circa 120 AD),* that the early Church did indeed understand the Fig Tree to represent Israel. Consequently, its 'budding' is significant. Quoting from Jeffrey's citation of the *Apocalypse of Peter:*

> And ye, receive ye the Parable of the fig-tree thereon: as soon as its shoots have gone forth and its boughs have sprouted, the end of the world will come." And I, Peter, answered and said unto him, "Explain to me concerning the fig-tree, [and] how we shall perceive it, for throughout all its days does the fig-tree sprout and every year it brings forth its fruit [and] for its master. What (then) meaneth the parable of the fig-tree? We know it not." And the Master answered and said unto me, "Dost thou not understand that the fig-tree is the house of Israel? Even as a man hath planted a fig-tree in his garden and it brought forth no fruit, and he sought its fruit for many years. When he found it not, he said to the keeper of his garden, 'Uproot the fig-tree that our land may not be unfruitful for us.' And the gardener said to God, 'We thy servants wish to clear it (of weeds) and to dig' the ground around it and to water it. If it does not then bear fruit, we will immediately remove its roots from the garden and plant another one in its place.' Hast thou not grasped that the fig tree is the house of Israel? Verily, I say to you that when its boughs have sprouted at the end, then shall deceiving Christs come, and awaken hope (with the words): 'I am the Christ, who am (now) come into the world.'[6]

Whether or not the Fig Tree is an ancient symbol of Israel, the words of Christ are clear that when *certain events happen,* within a *generation,* however we settle that period, *all things shall happen.*

---

[i] Which is to be made a part of a new book with the title, *Triumphant Return: The Coming Kingdom of God.*

Recapping the Key Points Covered in This Chapter

- One of the clearest prophetic milestones is the return of Israel to its homeland.
- This event is also a strong proof for the prophetic accuracy of the Bible.
- The *Vision of the Valley of Dry Bones* talks about how dead the nation of Israel is, yet how God will resurrect the nation in the last days.
- Bible scholars generally take Jesus' words literally that within one generation of the end of the 'time of the gentiles' all that is predicted will come to pass.
- There isn't agreement on the length of a generation. Some view it as a period of 40 years; others suggest 70 to 80 years.
- The evidence sides with those who believe in a 40-year time-frame. However, it is approximate based upon the Biblical data.
- The image of the fig tree and its budding suggests a generational timeframe tied to the return of Israel. A recent discovery of an apocryphal book supports this view.
- Dispensationalists believe the restoration of Israel is strong empirical evidence supporting their position.
- The restoration of Israel does appear to be providential!

Technical Notes

[1] The land of today's Saudi Arabia is the 'wilderness'—*not the Sinai Peninsula as is traditionally thought.* See Galatians 4:25. One of Bob Cornuke's books and videos, *In Search of the Real Mount Sinai*, documents this fact with compelling evidence.

[2] Hal Lindsey was insistent (in *The Late Great Planet Earth*), that 1948 was the end of the time of the Gentiles (Luke 21:24), and since a generation in the Bible was forty-years we could count on His return before the end of 1988. However, when Christ didn't return in 1988, it became clear that at least one or both of these assumptions were incorrect. Jack Van Impe, a TV preacher popular in the 1980's, predicted that the year 2000 was the date of the Second Coming. The date came and went. He now suggests 2012 may be the date, but indicates he doesn't know. What is the lesson learned? We can know the seasons, we shouldn't be caught off guard, and we are commanded to be watchful—but *we best abstain from setting a date.*

[3] Israel controlled the Temple Mount for only moments after the Six Day War of 1967. Moshe Dayan, the general of the Israeli army made the decision that a Jewish takeover of the Temple Mount would create an enormous upheaval in the world and turn many nations against Israel. Consequently, the Israelis gave the Temple Mount to the *Waqf*, a trust of Jordanian Muslims that oversee the area. This governance continues to this day.

[4] Scholars call this scattering of Israel, the *Diaspora*. Most Christians mistakenly believe that the Jewish Diaspora began with the destruction of Jerusalem in 70 AD. However, this overlooks the realities of the destruction of the Jewish Nation over 600 years earlier and the resulting dispersion of the Jews throughout the world that commenced at that time. The dispersion of the Jewish people actually began with the Assyrian destruction of the Northern Kingdom of Israel in 722 BC; it continued further with the Babylonian captivity in 606 BC of the Southern Kingdom. (Perhaps as many as one million Jews never returned from this captivity, but remained in what are today Iraq and Iran—thus giving rise to sizeable Jewish populations there even today). The destruction of Jerusalem in 70 AD by the Romans and their later quashing of the Bar Kochba Rebellion (Bar Kochba means *Son of the Star* in Aramaic) of 132-136 AD completed the desolation of Israel and the carrying away of the Jews from the land of Palestine.

[5] The placement of this prophecy immediately *before* the *Battle of Gog and Magog* in Ezekiel (chapters 38 and 39, see below) has also suggested to commentators that the restoration of Israel must take place before this future war can occur.

[6] See *www.grantjeffrey.com/article/ancient_manuscript.htm.*

Chapter 25: The Voice of God – The Trumpet of God?

An Alternative View to the Last Trumpet of the Rapture

One of the most interesting new ideas put forward in recent years is the possibility that the 'last trumpet,' which sounds immediately before the Rapture (and that signals the resurrection of the 'quick and the dead'), is not a trumpet at all, but is the *Voice of God*.

We have called attention before to some of the groundbreaking insights of David W. Lowe in his book: *Then His Voice Shook the Earth*. This work examines the possibility that the 'last trumpet' is in fact the 'voice of God' and he offers this opinion as a compelling alternative view. We will draw upon this source liberally along with other biblical analysis for the information presented in this section.

The Rapture Verses Revisited

Let's first review the traditional verses associated with the Rapture of the church to begin exploring the possible meaning of the *'Trumpet of God.'* First, we read Paul's comment as he is discussing the nature of the resurrected body in I Corinthians 15. He tells us that the resurrection and the Rapture will happen 'at the last trumpet:'

51 Listen, I tell you a mystery: We will not all sleep, but we will all be changed—

*52 in a flash, in the twinkling of an eye, **at the last trumpet.** For the trumpet will sound, the dead will be raised imperishable, and we will be changed.*

Then we read the classic passage regarding the 'blessed hope' of the Church—the Rapture—in I Thessalonians 4:

13 Brothers, we do not want you to be ignorant about those who fall asleep, or to grieve like the rest of men, who have no hope.

14 We believe that Jesus died and rose again and so we believe that God will bring with Jesus those who have fallen asleep in him.

15 According to the Lord's own word, we tell you that we who are still alive, who are left till the coming of the Lord, will certainly not precede those who have fallen asleep.

*16 For the Lord himself will come down from heaven, with a loud command, with the voice of the archangel and **with the trumpet call of God**, and the dead in Christ will rise first.*

17 After that, we who are still alive and are left will be caught up together with them in the clouds to meet the Lord in the air. And so we will be with the Lord forever.

18 Therefore encourage each other with these words.

In this passage, Paul's words are most descriptive: Here he tells us the signal is like (1) a *loud command*; (2) with the *voice of the archangel* and (3) with the *trumpet call of God*. Having employed all of these descriptors, we sense that there is much more to 'the trumpet' than merely the blowing of the Shofar!

Revelation's Use of the Phrase 'Voice of God'

The words in Revelation compare 'the Voice of God' to a trumpet. In Chapter 1, John relates the following:

9 I, John, your brother and companion in the suffering and kingdom and patient endurance that are ours in Jesus, was on the island of Patmos because of the word of God and the testimony of Jesus.

*10 On the Lord's Day I was in the Spirit, and I heard behind me **a loud voice like a trumpet**,*

11 which said: "Write on a scroll what you see and send it to the seven churches: to Ephesus, Smyrna, Pergamum, Thyatira, Sardis, Philadelphia and Laodicea."

John indicates that hearing the voice of God is like hearing *the sound of a trumpet*. This simile appears again in Chapter 4:

*1 After this I looked, and there before me was a door standing open in heaven. And **the voice I had first heard speaking to me like a trumpet** said, "Come up here, and I will show you what must take place after this."*

2 At once I was in the Spirit, and there before me was a throne in heaven with someone sitting on it.

And then in Revelation 11 regarding the resurrection of the **'Two Witnesses'** (see page 207) we note that the voice isn't compared to a trumpet but utters the same words John heard in Chapter 4, this time as a 'loud cry:' *Then they heard **a loud voice from heaven saying** to them, "Come up here." And they went up to heaven in a cloud, while their enemies looked on."* (Revelation 11:12). In addition, we immediately hear tell of an earthquake in verse 13: *"At that very hour there was a severe earthquake and a tenth of the city collapsed. Seven thousand people were killed in the earthquake, and the survivors were terrified and gave glory to the God of heaven."*

In this instance, either (1) the voice of God, or (2) the resurrection of the Two Witnesses is responsible for an earthquake that kills 7,000 in the city of Jerusalem. As I mentioned previously, if we compare this number to the numbers Revelation uses elsewhere (describe the horrific judgments of God), we note that it's quite small. Accordingly, this earthquake may be immediate to the location of the onlookers in the Temple Courtyard where this event appears to take place. Perhaps a portion of the Temple area itself experiences this earthquake.[1] The verse goes on to say that a 'tenth' of the city falls down because of this calamity.[2]

God's Voice as the Last Trumpet

David W. Lowe points out that *all of these phenomena should be considered together* to understand the true meaning of 'the *Trumpet of God.*' Lowe points us to the meeting of Moses and God on Mount Sinai as the Ten Commandments are being presented in Exodus Chapter 19:

> *[9] The LORD said to Moses, "I am going to come to you in a dense cloud, so that the people will hear me speaking with you and will always put their trust in you." Then Moses told the LORD what the people had said.*
>
> *[10] And the LORD said to Moses, "Go to the people and consecrate them today and tomorrow. Have them wash their clothes*
>
> *[11] and be ready by the third day, because on that day the LORD will come down on Mount Sinai in the sight of all the people.*

12 Put limits for the people around the mountain and tell them, 'Be careful that you do not go up the mountain or touch the foot of it. Whoever touches the mountain shall surely be put to death.

*13 He shall surely be stoned or shot with arrows; not a hand is to be laid on him. Whether man or animal, he shall not be permitted to live.' Only when the ram's horn sounds a long blast may **they** go up to the mountain."*

*16 On the morning of the third day there was thunder and lightning, with a thick cloud over the mountain, **and a very loud trumpet blast.** Everyone in the camp trembled.*

17 Then Moses led the people out of the camp to meet with God, and they stood at the foot of the mountain.

*18 Mount Sinai was covered with smoke, because the LORD descended on it in fire. The smoke billowed up from it like smoke from a furnace, **the whole mountain trembled violently,***

*19 and **the sound of the trumpet grew louder and louder.** Then Moses spoke and the voice of God answered him.*

20 The LORD descended to the top of Mount Sinai and called Moses to the top of the mountain. So Moses went up

21 and the LORD said to him, "Go down and warn the people so they do not force their way through to see the LORD and many of them perish.

The trumpet on Mount Sinai apparently was not just the Shofar. There is an instruction as to the acceptable time when the people can approach the holy mountain. We read in verse 13 that if the Shofar is blown in a 'long' blast, the people are to come up onto the Mountain. However, on the third day (verse 16), we read that there was a very loud trumpet blast that appears to be something more. Moses led the people per the direction to the foot of the mountain. However, the blast of the trumpet continues and grows louder and louder. At the sound of this trumpet, the entire mountain shook and the people experience tremendous fear. We learn later in Hebrews 12:19 that the sound was so terrible that it caused the people to plead with Moses to tell God to stop. Was the trumpet they heard the Shofar, or was it something more?

Turning to Chapter 12 of Hebrews, the writer provides an extended explanation of the meaning of the *Mount Sinai* experience and exhorts us to understand that we are no longer need to be terrified, for we are not at Mount Sinai. Instead, we are at *Mount Zion in a heavenly Jerusalem*:

> *¹⁸ You have not come to a mountain that can be touched and that is burning with fire; to darkness, gloom and storm;*
>
> *¹⁹ **to a trumpet blast or to such a voice speaking words** that those who heard it begged that no further word be spoken to them,*
>
> *²⁰ because they could not bear what was commanded: "If even an animal touches the mountain, it must be stoned."*
>
> *²¹ The sight was so terrifying that Moses said, "I am trembling with fear."*
>
> *²² But you have come to Mount Zion, to the heavenly Jerusalem, the city of the living God. You have come to thousands upon thousands of angels in joyful assembly,*
>
> *²³ to the church of the firstborn, whose names are written in heaven. You have come to God, the judge of all men, to the spirits of righteous men made perfect,*
>
> *²⁴ to Jesus the mediator of a new covenant, and to the sprinkled blood that speaks a better word than the blood of Abel.*
>
> *²⁵ See to it that you do not refuse him who speaks. If they did not escape when they refused him who warned them on earth, how much less will we, if we turn away from him who warns us from heaven?*
>
> *²⁶ At that time his voice shook the earth but now he has promised, "ONCE MORE I WILL SHAKE NOT ONLY THE EARTH BUT ALSO THE HEAVENS."*
>
> *²⁷ The words "once more" indicate the removing of what can be shaken —**that is, created things**—so that what cannot be shaken may remain.*
>
> *²⁸ Therefore, since we are receiving a kingdom **that cannot be shaken,** let us be thankful, and so worship God acceptably with reverence and awe,*
>
> *²⁹ for our "God is a consuming fire." (Emphasis mine)*

The writer of the Book of Hebrews is quoting a passage from the prophet Haggai, Chapter 2. The context (timing) of Haggai's passage is near the initial completion of the rebuilding of the second temple (the first stage) circa 521 BC. [3]

233

¹ On the twenty-first day of the seventh month, the word of the LORD came through the prophet Haggai:

² "Speak to Zerubbabel son of Shealtiel, governor of Judah, to Joshua son of Jehozadak, the high priest, and to the remnant of the people. Ask them,

³ 'Who of you is left who saw this house in its former glory? How does it look to you now? **Does it not seem to you like nothing?**

⁴ But now be strong, O Zerubbabel,' declares the LORD. 'Be strong, O Joshua son of Jehozadak, the high priest. Be strong, all you people of the land,' declares the LORD, 'and work. For I am with you,' declares the LORD Almighty.

⁵ 'This is what I covenanted with you when you came out of Egypt. And my Spirit remains among you. Do not fear.'

⁶ "This is what the LORD Almighty says: **'In a little while I will once more shake the heavens and the earth, the sea and the dry land.**

⁷ **I will shake all nations, and the desired of all nations will come,** *and I will fill this house with glory,' says the LORD Almighty.*

⁸ 'The silver is mine and the gold is mine,' declares the LORD Almighty.

⁹ 'The glory of this present house will be greater than the glory of the former house,' says the LORD Almighty. 'And in this place I will grant peace,' declares the LORD Almighty."

Lowe proposes that the *Voice of God* that shakes the nations is in fact metaphorically the 'last trumpet' (the *"once more"* of Hebrews 12:26) that we also read about in Revelation 6:

¹² I watched as he opened the sixth seal. **There was a great earthquake.** *The sun turned black like sackcloth made of goat hair, the whole moon turned blood red,*

¹³ and the stars in the sky fell to earth, as late figs drop from a fig tree when shaken by a strong wind.

¹⁴ The sky receded like a scroll, rolling up, and every mountain and island was removed from its place.

¹⁵ Then the kings of the earth, the princes, the generals, the rich, the mighty, and every slave and every free man hid in caves and among the rocks of the mountains.

16 They called to the mountains and the rocks, "Fall on us and hide us from the face of him who sits on the throne and from the wrath of the Lamb!

17 For the great day of their wrath has come, and who can stand?"

Does this great worldwide earthquake, result from the *Voice of God?* We read that it affects both the earth and the heavens, as stated in the prophecy from Haggai:

- The sun turns black like sackcloth.

- The moon turns to blood (red in appearance).

- The stars fall to earth.

- The sky recedes like a scroll, rolling up.

- Every mountain and every island are 'moved' from their place.

However, there is more to the story. Lowe ties the 'voice' to the physical action he believes will transpire *when the resurrection of the dead occurs.* He conjectures that perhaps there are a billion or more Christian believers who have died throughout history (and will be resurrected). Upon the command to 'arise,' their bodies transform. With their resurrection, the great earthquake occurs. As a precedent, we know that when Christ was resurrected there was an earthquake in Jerusalem and that the bodies of many holy people came out of their tombs. The resurrected then appear *"to many"* in the holy city. Matthew 27 recounts:

*51 At that moment the curtain of the temple was torn in two from top to bottom. **The earth shook and the rocks split.***

52 The tombs broke open and the bodies of many holy people who had died were raised to life.

*53 They came out of the tombs, and **after Jesus' resurrection** they went into the holy city and appeared to many people.*

Matthew does 'run together' the story of the crucifixion and the resurrection events, which makes the sequence more difficult to pin down. At the crucifixion, (1) 'the curtain in the temple was torn in two;' which is also recorded in the Gospels of Mark and Luke (Mark 15:38,

Luke 23:45). However, in Matthew we read something entirely different and unique: (2) *"The earth shook and the rocks split"* and (3) *"The tombs broke open"* such that there was a resurrection of many holy people. However, Matthew goes on to clarify that their appearance was **"after Jesus' resurrection."** Exactly what happened before or after the Resurrection is a bit unclear. Could the resurrection have created the earthquake in Jerusalem? This is Lowe's supposition.

> **THE KEY POINT TO PONDER:**
>
> *We frequently see a pattern between resurrections, earthquakes, and the Voice of God that commands each resurrection. The possibility that the Trumpet of God is truly the Voice of God with a powerful 'side affect' is a phenomenal new insight.*

There is some scriptural support for this perspective and the possibility is fascinating. Whether the resurrection coincides with the future Rapture and somehow 'generates' the earthquake; or whether the *Voice of God* alone causes the entire earth to tremble, it does appear by analogy, that the 'last trump' may not be a trumpet at all, but the *awesome and 'august' voice of God*—calling up all believers whether 'asleep or alive' to heaven. *"Come up here"* (Revelation 4:1, Revelation 11:12) may be the simple words we hear. However, these words may reverberate as if spoken from *a colossal trumpet*, just as John and the *Two Witnesses* in the Book of Revelation experience, causing them to be swept up immediately into heaven.

One last connection worthy of calling out: When Jesus stands in front of the tomb of Lazarus and calls out to him to arise, it is worth noting the force with which He speaks the command: "Lazarus, come forth!" His shout is like a military order. Did the ground shake at the command? Was there another example of the phenomena when Lazarus came forth?

Finally, it is worth mentioning once again *that Pentecost was the date God gave His law to the Jews.* This means that when the Voice of God sounded as if *it was a terrifying trumpet*, it was on the day of *Pentecost.* Therefore, as Pentecost approaches, no doubt we would do well to remember what happened in the ancient past and its potential implication for our future. To quote Jerry Lee Lewis, who I'm sure is no scholar on the Bible–on some future Pentecost, a 'whole lot of sha-kin' may be going on!'

Key Points Covered in This Chapter

- Is the last trumpet actually a trumpet at all?
- The standard verses speaking of the Rapture both refer to a trumpet that signals the event – but the verse in I Thessalonians 4, suggests it may be more than just the blaring of the trumpet.
- The story of the *Two Witnesses* suggests that a loud cry or the Voice of God may in fact be the signal.
- The story of the giving of the Law on Mount Sinai is the interpretive key. The writer to the Hebrews in the New Testament speaks distinctly about the fact that the Voice of God has shaken the earth once before and it will shake the earth yet again.
- There is a connection to the Voice of God and earthquakes in these stories.
- There may be a connection to the resurrection and the massive earthquake spoken of in Revelation 6.
- The resurrection of Christ also illustrates the same 'connection.'

Technical Notes

[1] From the Christian perspective, believing that Islam is not the true religion, it is interesting to suppose that the earthquake might in fact affect only the Muslim section of the Temple courtyard. This assumes that Israel rebuilds the Temple alongside the Dome of the Rock and the Al-Aqsa Mosque, rather than waiting for them to be cleared out of the way. Nevertheless, I don't wish to be accused of hoping for bad things to happen to the Islamic shrines!

[2] Jerusalem is actually quite small (inside the walls). As such, it would not necessarily be a large area that is harmed. This earthquake, with its limited impact, stands in contrast to the vast and horrible worldwide earthquakes mentioned elsewhere in the Book of Revelation. Hence, it would seem that this attention to detail makes this particular event all the more definite and the 'specifics' to be literally fulfilled.

[3] It would appear that the LORD is speaking of the Temple in the Millennium, not the Temple built by Zerubbabel. For this glory will be accompanied by peace which does not come about until the Millennium. Most scholars agree that the return of the exiles was far from complete and the promises made do not apply to the second temple for the people's repentance was not sufficient. The promises made must refer to the *Third Temple*.

DD# 13 Speculating on 2012, the Rapture, and the Great Earthquake

David W. Lowe speculates in his book, *Then His Voice Shook the Earth*, that the act of resurrection may well be like a 'mini-nuclear explosion' that creates an earthquake we read about in the instance of the Two Witnesses in Revelation Chapter 11 (which might be the cause for 7,000 deaths predicted there). This supposition stems from the continued 'enhanced study' of the *Shroud of Turin* that at least one scientist is now saying could only have been made (the image on the shroud) by some form of 'nuclear singularity event' that allowed the image to be formed three-dimensionally. Otherwise, this could only occur if the shroud were lying perfectly square to the body of Christ both above and below the body—something that would be practically and physically impossible in the tomb where Jesus was laid.

In the video, *The Fabric of Time* (Grizzly Adams Family Entertainment, Spokane, WA. 120 minutes), the particle physicist who proffers this view is Dame Isabel Piczek from Hungary. The impetus of her work was her discovery of the 'total absence of distortion of the image' of the crucified man on the Shroud of Turin. She indicates that the image formed there was accomplished in a situation akin to the 'Big Bang' in which the normal rules of physics are not in effect. She indicates, "As quantum time collapses to absolute zero in the tomb of Christ, the two event horizons (*apparently, one stopping events from above and the other stopping the events form below*) at the moment of the zero time collapse going through the body, get infinitely close to each other and eliminate each other," thus generating intense energy causing the image to print itself perfectly and three-dimensionally on the two sides of the Shroud. Is this really possible? Is the image on the Shroud a hologram?

We will continue to see experts perform more research in the years ahead to consider this theory. Lowe goes further in speculating how the earth would be physically impacted with a simultaneous resurrection of perhaps more than a billion dead believers at the time of the Rapture. Perhaps this explains the mighty earthquake of Revelation 6:12. If this supposition is correct (and admittedly it is highly speculative), we could see how a billion resurrections occurring simultaneously worldwide could create an earth shaking experience! If Lowe is correct, this event prior to the beginning of the Tribulation could create such havoc that the many millions of disappeared believers will be assumed 'missing' because of this worldwide earthquake.

Further supposition suggests that this calamity itself may be the plausible explanation for the disappearance of so many through the Rapture event.

Lowe points out that during the second largest volcanic event in recorded history in 2004 (a seismic event near Indonesia that registered over 9.1 on the Richter scale), it generated devastating tsunamis that killed over 300,000 persons (many that were officially classified first as 'missing' and then 'dead' one year later). It also adjusted the magnetic north pole slightly and shortened our days by a few seconds. Speculating on this event with these characteristics is very much like the 2012 'apocalypse' projected by modern-day interpreters of the Mayans. This destruction predicted by several secular sources (oftentimes tied into UFOs and spiritualist 'cults' which should give us pause), hinges upon a reversal of the North and South poles—wreaking havoc on marine life and other animals who migrate based upon an innate sense of the earth's magnetism. If this disaster took place, could the world begin to spin faster around its axis? Could it thereby shorten the days and be a fulfillment of Jesus' prophecy? *("that unless those days were shortened no life would be left upon the earth"*—Matthew 24:22) This is also highly speculative, but it could be a literal meaning of the 'shortening of days,' completing the Tribulation period sooner.

However, please note that this interpretation is not something that I have seen any other author suggest. It would be best to take my suggestion with a grain of salt. Note also: I don't agree that the Mayan prophecy of the 'end of the world' stands up to scrutiny. The fact of the matter is that most experts in this subject area don't interpret the end of the 'long count' calendar of the Mayans to mean anything other than another 'harmonic convergence' (which didn't seem to matter much when it occurred in 1987).

Many more authors who have written on the Mayan Calendar and its meaning see hope in the spiritual and psychic changes to come – not destruction. Regardless of which way they fall on the issue of the apocalypse, I wouldn't take a big stake in their predictions.

DEEP DIVE NUMBER 13

Chapter 26: The Wrath of God

Apocalypse – The Dominant Image of Judgment and Wrath

When we discuss the subject of the *Apocalypse* and the study of eschatology, the most vivid imagery, which comes to mind, is 'fiery judgment and utter destruction' befalling the earth. Assuredly, we associate the fear of 'the world coming to an end' as our principal reaction to these pictures. In the Old Testament, the prophecies of virtually all the prophets bear witness to cataclysms that will transpire in the last days during the period known as *'the Day of the LORD.'* It may be of little comfort the world doesn't actually *end*—for the destruction is so great and so many appear to lose their lives during this horrific time.

In this lengthy section, we have three objectives:

1. Demonstrate the Old Testament prophets testify to severe judgments which transpire during the 'time of Jacob's trouble' or *Daniel's 70th Week*. The Old Testament provides a consistent message in broad-brush strokes.

2. Correct a perspective often asserted both casually and formally: The Old Testament portrays a wrathful, vengeful, and merciless God, while the New Testament pictures God through Jesus Christ as a compassionate, forgiving, and merciful deity. We will see that this *popular observation is actually inaccurate.*

3. Next, we will discuss whether the *Doctrine of the Wrath of God* is still relevant. Does it conflict with or inform our understanding the true nature of the Judeo-Christian God whom Jesus Christ portrays through His life and teaching?

The Old Testament and the Day of the LORD

First, let's recall a number of the classic Old Testament passages that provide this picture of impending judgment and doom. From Isaiah, we read once again of the heavens and earth trembling, and how they are shaken from their place by the wrath of the LORD:

> *9 See, the day of the LORD is coming*
> *—a cruel day, with wrath and fierce anger—*

> *to make the land desolate*
> *and destroy the sinners within it.*

> *10 The stars of heaven and their constellations*
> *will not show their light.*
> *The rising sun will be darkened*
> *and the moon will not give its light.*

> *11 I will punish the world for its evil,*
> *the wicked for their sins.*
> *I will put an end to the arrogance of the haughty*
> *and will humble the pride of the ruthless.*

> *12 I will make man scarcer than pure gold,*
> *more rare than the gold of Ophir.*

> *13 Therefore I will make the heavens tremble;*
> *and the earth will shake from its place*
> *at the wrath of the LORD Almighty,*
> *in the day of his burning anger.* (Isaiah 13:9-13)

The prophet Joel speaks of a mighty army that comes forth that has no equal in times past or ever again.[1] God will use this army in His judgment:

> *1 Blow the trumpet in Zion;*
> *sound the alarm on my holy hill.*
> *Let all who live in the land tremble,*
> *for the day of the LORD is coming.*
> *It is close at hand-*

> *2 a day of darkness and gloom,*
> *a day of clouds and blackness.*
> *Like dawn spreading across the mountains*
> *a large and mighty army comes,*
> *such as never was of old*
> *nor ever will be in ages to come.*

> *3 Before them fire devours,*
> *behind them a flame blazes.*
> *Before them the land is like the garden of Eden,*
> *behind them, a desert waste—*
> *nothing escapes them.*

> *4 They have the appearance of horses;*
> *they gallop along like cavalry.*

> *5 With a noise like that of chariots*
> *they leap over the mountaintops,*

like a crackling fire consuming stubble,
like a mighty army drawn up for battle.

6 At the sight of them, nations are in anguish;
every face turns pale...

10 Before them the earth shakes,
the sky trembles,
the sun and moon are darkened,
and the stars no longer shine.

11 The LORD thunders at the head of his army;
his forces are beyond number,
and mighty are those who obey his command.
The day of the LORD is great;
it is dreadful.
Who can endure it? (Joel 2:1-6, 10, 11)

Zechariah fills in more details about this 'day' and promises that the LORD will deliver Jerusalem although all the armies of the world surround it with the intent to wipe it off the map:

1 A day of the LORD is coming when your plunder will be divided among you.

2 I will gather all the nations to Jerusalem to fight against it; the city will be captured, the houses ransacked, and the women raped. Half of the city will go into exile, but the rest of the people will not be taken from the city.

3 Then the LORD will go out and fight against those nations, as he fights in the day of battle.

4 On that day his feet will stand on the Mount of Olives, east of Jerusalem, and the Mount of Olives will be split in two from east to west, forming a great valley, with half of the mountain moving north and half moving south.

5 You will flee by my mountain valley, for it will extend to Azel. You will flee as you fled from the earthquake in the days of Uzziah king of Judah. Then the LORD my God will come, and all the holy ones with him.

6 On that day there will be no light, no cold or frost.

7 It will be a unique day, without daytime or nighttime—a day known to the LORD. When evening comes, there will be light.

8 On that day living water will flow out from Jerusalem, half to the eastern sea and half to the western sea, in summer and in winter.

9 The LORD will be king over the whole earth. On that day there will be one LORD, and his name the only name.

10 The whole land, from Geba to Rimmon, south of Jerusalem, will become like the Arabah. But Jerusalem will be raised up and remain in its place, from the Benjamin Gate to the site of the First Gate, to the Corner Gate, and from the Tower of Hananel to the royal winepresses.

*11 It will be inhabited; never again will it be destroyed. **Jerusalem will be secure.***

12 This is the plague with which the LORD will strike all the nations that fought against Jerusalem: Their flesh will rot while they are still standing on their feet, their eyes will rot in their sockets, and their tongues will rot in their mouths.

13 On that day men will be stricken by the LORD with great panic. Each man will seize the hand of another, and they will attack each other.

14 Judah too will fight at Jerusalem. The wealth of all the surrounding nations will be collected—great quantities of gold and silver and clothing. (Zechariah 14:1-14)

Zechariah's description is vivid and frightening. Verse 12 appears to describe some manner of 'WMD' (weapon of mass destruction). He also indicates that the enemies of the LORD will turn against one another. Yet he declares that the returning Messiah, who 'touches down' on the Mount of Olives, will secure and protect Jerusalem, despite its being the target of the world's outrage.

It is clear from a survey of all the prophets of the Old Testament that 'apocalyptic literature' isn't just limited to the Book of Daniel. Almost all of the prophets touch on the images and visions of destruction in the final days. The 'Day of the LORD,' the 'Day of God's wrath,' and other similar names, is a frequent and common theme. Without any question, the warning *that in the last days a time of judgment is coming* remains as one of the universal proclamations throughout the Old Testament.

Jesus, Judgment and the Idea of Eternal Punishment

There is no doubt that the theme of judgment and the wrath of God is a common topic for Jesus too. While there has always been a

'Marcionite'[2] view prevalent in the Church – that the God of the Old Testament is harsh and vengeful and the God of the New Testament loves us and is merciful—the reality is that Jesus speaks more about the judgment of God with more detail than perhaps any Prophet in the Old Testament does! There is another equally mistaken view about the New Testament. Many suggest that Paul was the 'founding influence' that brought the concept of hell into Christianity – Jesus didn't teach about it. The reality is just the opposite. Jesus speaks of eternal punishment in a number of situations and uses the word 'hell' (*Gehenna*[i]) many times (11 to be exact)[3]—Paul talks about judgment but doesn't directly talk about the concept of a place of eternal punishment at all.

From Matthew we read the following sayings of Jesus:

*"You have heard that it was said to the people long ago, 'Do not murder, and anyone who murders will be subject to judgment.' But I tell you that anyone who is angry with his brother he will be subject to judgment. Again, anyone who says to his brother, 'Raca,' is answerable to the Sanhedrin. But anyone who says, 'You fool!' will be in danger of the **fire of hell**.* (Matthew 5:21, 22)

*"If your right eye causes you to sin, gouge it out and throw it away. It is better for you to lose one part of your body than for your whole body to be thrown into hell. And if your right hand causes you to sin, cut it off and throw it away. It is better for you to lose one part of your body than for your whole body to go into **hell**."* (Matthew 5:29, 30)

"Do not be afraid of those who kill the body but cannot kill the soul. Rather, be afraid of the One who can destroy both soul and body **in hell**." (Matthew 10:28)

Luke records Jesus' teaching as follows:

"I tell you, my friends, do not be afraid of those who kill the body and after that can do no more. But I will show you whom you should

---

[i] *Gehenna* may refer to the Valley of Hinnom, a waste dump southwest of Jerusalem. However, it came to be known as the 'gates of hell' by Jewish Apocalyptic writers between the Testaments. Hence, we see Jesus use the term too.

*fear: Fear him who, after the killing of the body, has power to throw you into **hell**. Yes, I tell you, fear him.* (Luke 12:4, 5)

*"There was a rich man who was dressed in purple and fine linen and lived in luxury every day. At his gate was laid a beggar named Lazarus, covered with sores and longing to eat what fell from the rich man's table. Even the dogs came and licked his sores. The time came when the beggar died and the angels carried him to Abraham's side. The rich man also died and was buried. In **hell, where he was in torment,** he looked up and saw Abraham far away, with Lazarus by his side. So he called to him, 'Father Abraham, have pity on me and send Lazarus to dip the tip of his finger in water and cool my tongue, because I am in **agony in this fire**.' But Abraham replied, 'Son, remember that in your lifetime you received your good things, while Lazarus received bad things, but now he is comforted here and you are in agony. And besides all this, between us and you a great chasm has been fixed, so that those who want to go from here to you cannot, nor can anyone cross over from there to us.'* (Luke 16:19-26).

Jesus also makes many references to the *'day of judgment.'* From the Gospel of Matthew (quotations also recorded in the Gospel of Luke), we read a number of these sayings:

*I tell you the truth, it will be more bearable for Sodom and Gomorrah on the Day of **Judgment** than for that town.* (Matthew 10:15)

*But I tell you, it will be more bearable for Tyre and Sidon on the Day of **Judgment** than for you.* (Matthew 11:22)

*But I tell you that men will have to give account on the Day of **Judgment** for every careless word they have spoken.* (Matthew 12:36)

*The men of Nineveh will stand up at the **judgment** with this generation and condemn it; for they repented at the preaching of Jonah, and now one greater than Jonah is here. The Queen of the South will rise at the judgment with this generation and condemn it; for she came from the ends of the earth to listen to Solomon's wisdom, and now one greater than Solomon is here.* (Matthew 12:41, 42)

Likewise, there are many quotations in the Gospel of John where Jesus speaks of judgment. Selecting just a few:

> *Moreover, the Father judges no one, but has entrusted all **judgment** to the Son, that all may honor the Son just as they honor the Father.* (John 5:22, 23)

> *Jesus said, "For **judgment** I have come into this world, so that the blind will see and those who see will become blind."* (John 9:39)

> *Now is the time for **judgment** on this world; now the prince of this world will be driven out.* (John 12:31)

From the many verses quoted here, it should be plain that no comfort comes from the words of Jesus to those who would soften or deny God's judgment and wrath. While the Gospel of Christ is clearly one that portrays a loving Father God who goes out of His way to reconcile us to Himself, the reality is that the God who Jesus presents in His teaching and for which He provides a living portrait is a *God who intends to mete out justice. He is longsuffering, but He will finally judge.* Those who do not repent according to Jesus will experience an existence in 'the life hereafter' apart from the love and presence of God. And that, as they say, is putting it mildly.

Is God's Wrath Legitimate?

The next topic in this section is the relevancy and indeed *the legitimacy of the idea of God's wrath.* We have just displayed the predictions of wrath in the Old Testament and the teachings of Jesus in the New that confirm this element of God's character. However, do we really believe that this language is appropriate? Isn't this picture of 'fire and brimstone' archaic?

There is little doubt that in our day we are careful not to upset others by challenging their beliefs. We seek to be 'politically correct'. We are reluctant to propose that any form of societal retribution is justified. There are many who, for strong reasons, oppose the death penalty. To the same end, excessive leniency has become more normal in our courts than stark punishment.

Likewise, in religion today, we are startled and dismayed when we hear of the incomprehensible behavior of Islamic fundamentalists. We cannot condone the atrocities of the extremists. Certainly, their concept of such a vengeful God is partially to blame for their reprehensible acts of terrorism.[i]   As Christians, we are always 'amazed by grace' and bear witness to a loving and merciful God. Because of this modern mindset, we are prone to raise questions like, "Do we believe that God is capable of wrath? Is the future wrath of God a legitimate Christian doctrine?" There can be no escaping the testimony of Scripture from both Old and New Testaments—from the prophets through to the Messiah Himself—all predict and warn that the wrath of God *may have been concealed* but one day it will *no longer be contained.* The 'Day of the Lord' is that day when finally, after thousands of years, the LORD judges those who have denied and despised Him, done injustice in the world, broken His laws, and failed to care for the unfortunate. Jesus said,

> *37 As it was in the days of Noah, so it will be at the coming of the Son of Man.*
>
> *38 For in the days before the flood, people were eating and drinking, marrying and giving in marriage, up to the day Noah entered the ark;*
>
> *39 and they knew nothing about what would happen until the flood came and took them all away. That is how it will be at the coming of the Son of Man.* (Matthew 24:37-39)

Jesus makes several points in this passage:

1. God's judgment has happened before—it will happen again.

2. However, God delayed His judgment for hundreds of years while Noah built the Ark and gathered animals into it.

3. Meanwhile, people everywhere around the world continued their lives the same way as before. They dismissed the possibility that the cataclysm Noah predicted could actually occur.

Everything was normal until in a matter of a few days the waters of the Great Flood inundated their entire world. This is what Jesus said it would be like in 'the last days.' Those alive in the last

---

i In contrast to the Christian and Jewish God, the Koran never refers to Allah as a God of love. There is no surety of salvation. Even living a good life is no guarantee. Allah is capricious, not longsuffering. The God of Islam has much less in common with the Judeo-Christian God than what most people think.

days will assume that the predictions of judgment are the ravings of fanatics or the discarded teachings of the Jewish or Christian fundamentalists. However, just when they believe there will be *"peace and safety"* (II Thessalonians 5:3), then the Apocalypse will appear. Jesus Himself sternly teaches us, "Make no mistake. As in the days of Noah, so shall it be in the Days of the Son of Man."

There is little space here to examine the issue of the holiness of God, the justice of God, and the wrath of God—and to reconcile these realities with the love of God, His Grace, and His patience and forbearance. Such an examination is a lengthy one and deserves its own study, which many theologians have accomplished throughout the ages. Here I can do little more than encourage the reader to consider the weight of evidence of the Bible and to form your own opinion. You may choose to believe that God is a loving God who is incapable of wrath. You may be convinced that the idea of divine punishment or retribution is an outdated perspective that modern man has overcome. There is no question that as an author of Christian persuasion, I am reluctant to champion any perspective of God that repudiates the intimate portrait of God Jesus provided us, both in His teachings and in His incarnation. Jesus called His Father, *"Abba"* (Daddy). Jesus taught us about 'unconditional love' (*agape* in the Greek). This was a much-needed correction for an overly abstract and distant deity that many Jews professed in Jesus' day.

Nevertheless, the problem is the weight of Scripture sides with those who believe *that the gates holding back God's wrath will finally break open*. The Apocalypse includes this dimension of divine vengeance. The passages adduced here demonstrate how this warning appears throughout the Bible. There simply is no escaping it.

Modern and Subjective Witnesses to God's Holiness

However, allow me press further, offering just a few words, which point out that God's legitimate actions against evil, confirm the "rightness" of this approach within our own character and conscience. The Bible's testimony does not stand alone.[4] Certainly, the holiness of God is not only abstract—it can also be an existential phenomenon. Many of us are moved when we contemplate the scene in Revelation Chapter 4 as the four living creatures and the 24 elders along with the multitude of angels cry out *"Holy, Holy, Holy"* before the throne of God. Many more of us sense the palpable ⁱ fear when the Voice of God causes the Hebrews before Mount Sinai to shake and tremble. Most of us can understand how in ancient times that those who 'saw God' felt their lives threatened. We can 'relate' because even today there is a consciousness among many that the experience of God is overwhelming. 'Otherness' or transcendence can be frightening. One philosopher has labeled this awareness 'the *mysterium tremendum'* (the 'indescribable awesomeness'),⁵ a feeling of dread that we encounter when we experience firsthand the 'holiness' of God. This inner sense is something that many have shared in those moments when we encounter the divine. Our experience is often difficult to articulate, but somehow we are compelled to express we have encountered *a God that is utterly pure*; that when we are in His presence, we are painfully aware that while He is Holy, we are not.

Peter said to Jesus after experiencing an astounding miracle at Jesus' dictate, "Depart from me for I am a sinful man." Likewise, when we feel this 'awesomeness,' we fall to our knees or we seek to hide. God is too virtuous for us. This awareness is dramatic and overpowering.

Nevertheless, not everyone has experienced this 'sense of the Holy.' Indeed, the common counterpoint is the undeniable fact that evil flourishes in the world. Such a presence of evil makes many wonder if we should summarily dismiss the subjective experience of the 'holy' as an emotional human eccentricity. Perhaps 'the holy' is just an ideal we hold to that has no concrete basis in reality. Some believe this. However, most don't. Many more believe in some higher power, they just question the nature of this power: If God can allow evil to exist, He must be an evil god, or He must not be all-powerful. This logic has led many to avoid believing in the God of the Bible and many others, when personally confronted with evil, to fall away from their faith.

ⁱ Word's dictionary defines *palpable* as "so intense as to be almost able to be felt physically."

However, there is an equally poignant rebut to this traditional argument which favors the justice of God and explains how this apparent contradiction can be. Let's think along these lines: What would we conclude about any form of government that never 'brought the guilty' to justice? Is it right that there be no consequences for the heinous acts of murder, rape, beatings, kidnappings, torture, even the theft of millions of dollars from charities and the retired? Should we overlook and forget all of these crimes against humanity? It's hard to answer *yes* to this hypothetical question if we know persons that have been victims of horrendous actions like these. When we personally encounter evil and see the harm that it does, we all cry out for justice to be done. We instinctively know that as far as human institutions go, a *government that has the power to bring the evil to justice but fails to do so is just as evil as those persons who deserve punishment.* In fact, it may be more culpable. This is the existential interplay between 'goodness' and 'justice.' You simply can't have one without the other. As thorny as this may seem, it is the reality of our experience. It is exactly what our 'conscience' communicates to us. It is what our humanity compels us to admit. The 'leap' is whether what we consider good and right regarding a human institution should also be true of God – whether real or supposed.

Let's look at another matter, *guilt*. While it is true that 'guilt' can be a destructive force in our lives, what do we think of those that 'have no guilt' or exhibit no conscience? Failure to demonstrate conscience and to acknowledge what is right is oftentimes what we mean when we say someone is *'inhumane.'* Our sense of being 'truly human' is to be 'good.' But most of us will go further than this: We often judge such inhumane persons *sociopathic*. To have no remorse after committing unconscionable acts is a sure sign of mental disorder. Some of us will go so far as to ascribe the word 'evil' to such a person. For the most part, this pronouncement will go unopposed because in extreme cases there is often consensus on what is right and wrong. Humans make moral judgments. Those that fail to make moral judgments we consider less than human.

So, if we project these moral principles onto the being we call God, what can we conclude about His nature? If God is a being who exhibits no sense of right or wrong, if God is a being who is indifferent about injustice, *God is not worthy of adoration or love*—for such a God is not good. For God to be good, He must also be just. For God to be just, He must also be good. *The two attributes are intertwined so tightly there is no separating them.* Without a doubt, when one considers the matter carefully, the attributes are almost one-and-the-same. Furthermore, if God is God, he must be more upright than we are, not less so. If humans are moral agents, God is much more so.

But the Christian God (and the Jewish God rightly understood through appreciating the 'whole' of the Old Testament), is not only moral, He is not only good and just, He is also a *God of love* who makes provision for those who acknowledge their failure to do what is right. The *mercy* of God is what mediates between the goodness of God and His justice. The Bible teaches God can forgive sin because He has taken on Himself the punishment, which He must dispense. Jesus Christ is God in human form willingly accepting our sin and our punishment so that God can be both *"just and the one who justifies"* those whom He forgives. We read about this in Romans, Chapter 3:

21 But now a righteousness from God, apart from law, has been made known, to which the Law and the Prophets testify.

22 This righteousness from God comes through faith in Jesus Christ to all who believe. There is no difference,

23 for all have sinned and fall short of the glory of God,

24 and are justified freely by his grace through the redemption that came by Christ Jesus.

25 God presented him as a sacrifice of atonement, through faith in his blood. He did this to demonstrate his justice, because in his forbearance he had left the sins committed beforehand unpunished—

26 he did it to demonstrate his justice at the present time, so as to be just and the one who justifies those who have faith in Jesus.

God's justice demands God's wrath—but God's love demands God's mercy. This is the God that Christians know and why they worship Him. This God requires both goodness and justice. But because of His love for us, He provides the means to satisfy His just demands. Does a God like this merit our reverence and adoration? Sometime during your life, you must answer this ultimate question.

Just remember: Failure to answer is also an answer. However, it may not be the answer to which you wish to be held accountable.

> ## Key Points Covered in This Chapter
>
> - The end of the world isn't what the Bible predicts – it predicts a future state of the world that is peaceful and free of fear and death.
> - The strongest and most memorable images in Revelation are those that forecast judgment and destruction on the earth.
> - The Old Testament records predictions of horrible events 'in the last days' – and refers to the final judgment as 'the Day of the LORD.'
> - Isaiah, Joel, and Zechariah, along with virtually all the prophets comment on the Day of the LORD – it is a universal prophecy of the Old Testament.
> - The common belief is that the God of the New Testament, which Jesus represents, is a very different God from the God of the Old Testament.
> - Surprisingly, Jesus talks more about judgment and hell than any other prophet in the Bible does.
> - Many liberal scholars accuse Paul of bringing the wrath of God into the New Testament; however, Paul actually never directly mentions hell.
> - The Marcionite heresy still lives in the Church today!
> - Is there room today for a God of Wrath?
> - Is there any argument to support the validity and relevance of a God like this in today's politically correct world?
> - A just God and a good God are "one and the same." You can't have one without the other.

Technical Notes

---

[1] The reader should compare Joel's passage with the description of the 'Kings of the East' in Revelation Chapter 9. They appear to have many common metaphors that cause me to believe that these descriptions relate specifically to that army. Joel appears to be describing an army of locusts that John later describes as locusts that have 'stingers' like scorpions. In both descriptions, this army wreaks havoc upon the world destroying in John's vision, 1/3rd of all humankind.

[2] Marcion was a proponent of an 'alternative Christianity' that held this view. He believed that the Old Testament God was a different deity than the deity that Jesus Christ represented. This heresy was defeated in the second century, but it has remained as a standard interpretation of the Bible and to this day, we still hear people voice this position. Some comedians have joked that Jesus is the *Happy God* (George Carlin's 'Buddy Jesus' in the movie, *Dogma*) and the God of the Old Testa-

ment, a miserable tyrant. While I would hardly suggest that Jesus fails to portray a God of Love (He certainly does present such a God), it is selective reading to overlook the fact that He is direct and stern with those who do not repent and especially harsh to those who are hypocrites. *"Woe unto you, Scribes and Pharisees, hypocrites that you are. After you make a convert* **you make him twice as fit for hell as you are your-self**" (paraphrasing, Matthew 23:15).

[3] Taken from the *The NIV Compact Dictionary of the Bible,* "GEHENNA (Gr. *geenna,* a transliteration of the Aramaic form of Heb. *Geben hinnom, valley of the son of Hinnom).* The Valley of Ben Hinnom (NIV) or the valley of the son of Hinnom (KJV, RSV, ASV). A valley west and SW of Jerusalem that formed part of the border between Judah and Benjamin (Josh 15:8; cf. 18:16; Nehemiah 11:30-31). Here Ahaz (2 Kings 16:3; 2 Chronicles 28:3) and Manasseh (2 Kings 21:6; 2 Chronicles 33:6) sacrificed their sons to Molech (Jeremiah 32:35; cf. 7:31-32; 19:1-13). For this reason Josiah defiled the place (2 Kings 23:10). After the OT period, Jewish apocalyptic writers began to call the Valley of Hinnom the entrance to hell, later hell itself. The NT distinguishes sharply between Hades, the intermediate, bodiless state, and Gehenna, the state of final punishment after the resurrection of the body. Gehenna existed before the judgment (Matt 25:41). The word is used 12 times in the NT (11 times by Jesus), always translated 'hell.' Terms parallel to Gehenna include 'fiery furnace' (Matthew 13:42, 50), 'fiery lake' (Revelation 19:20; 20:14-15), 'lake of burning sulfur' (20:10), 'eternal fire' (Jude 7), and 'hell'" (2 Peter 2:4)."

[4] Romans 1:18-20 provides the biblical basis for this position: *"For the wrath of God is revealed from heaven against all ungodliness and unrighteousness of men who suppress the truth in unrighteousness, because that which is known about God is evident within them; for God made it evident to them. For since the creation of the world His invisible attributes, His eternal power and divine nature, have been clearly seen, being understood through what has been made, so that they are without excuse"* (NASV).

[5] Rudolph Otto is the author who wrote about this phenomenon. Wikipedia provides a good synopsis of the issues inherit in Otto's view: "Otto's most famous work is *The Idea of the Holy,* published first in 1917 as *Das Heilige - Über das Irrationale in der Idee des Göttlichen und sein Verhältnis zum Rationalen (The Holy - On the Irrational in the Idea of the Divine and its Relation to the Rational).* It is one of the most successful German theological books of the 20th century, has never gone out of print, and is now available in about 20 languages. The book defines the concept of the holy as that which is numinous. Otto explained the numinous as a "non-rational, non-sensory experience or feeling whose primary and immediate object is outside the self". He coined this new term based on the Latin *numen* (deity). This expression is etymologically unrelated to Immanuel Kant's *noumenon,* a Greek term referring to an unknowable reality underlying all things. The numinous is a mystery (Latin: *mysterium*) that is both terrifying (*tremendum*) and fascinating (*fascinans*) at the same time.... This paradigm was under much attack between approximately 1950 and 1990 but has made a strong comeback since then, after its phenomenological aspects have become more apparent." See *en.wikipedia.org/wiki/Rudolph_Otto.*

Chapter 27: The Signs of His Soon Return

Signs of the Times

My Mom loved her family. The youngest of 11 children and raised by her sisters after her mother died when she was 9 years old, it seemed she committed the better part of her life to winning and keeping the affection of all her siblings. As her child, I often felt the emphasis she placed on family was more than a little abnormal. Nevertheless, she loved her family and taught us to as well. As a result, growing up I enjoyed many aunts and uncles; and today I am blessed with many wonderful cousins, most of whom stay in contact.

After the television sensation *Roots* (Alex Haley) appeared in 1977 and ancestry became a national obsession, it was inevitable that she too would look into the history of our family. At one point, she made a trip through the South to locate long lost cousins and discover our 'roots.' She found some surprising things – some of which were better not to have uncovered! However, one letter she unearthed stuck in my mind then and to this day.

I remember my Mom reading a letter from a great, great, great, grandfather (I think that many generations are about right!). He was a Tate – a famous family of the South[i] - many of whom lived in South Carolina before the Civil War. In his letter, he worried that war was approaching and he fretted that it might portend the end of the world. He wrote, "The love of many grows cold," one of the signs that Jesus predicts in the epoch after His death (Matthew 24:12). As far as the Old South was concerned, my ancestor was quite right. An apocalypse was coming.

Indeed, there are many pictures identified in the Scriptures of fateful events that speak of the future. However, the Bible does not connect all of these signs to the Apocalypse. Many are associated with the past 2,000 years leading up to the Great Tribulation. Fortunately, Jesus differentiates these two sets of signs. Let's look close-

---

[i] In fact, the British Art Museum (now four in number) is known as the Tate Museum in London. These Tate's are related directly to my ancestors. My Mom was very serious about tracing our roots. This was a good find!

ly at the whole passage to which my 'super-great grandfather' was referring.

In Matthew 24, Jesus predicts many specific events warning His disciples that calamities lie ahead. He talks of earthquakes, famines, wars, and rumors of wars, as well as many who will call themselves Christ. And yes, he indicates that 'the love of many will grow cold.' However, he indicates that while these things must happen, *the end is not yet*. Jesus distinguishes the specific indicators of His imminent return from the signs of those events that come before. We read of both in this lengthy chapter of the Bible known as the 'Olivet Discourse.'

Determining What Signs Are the Most Telling

Matthew provides the details of this dialogue between the disciples of Jesus and their Master:

3 Jesus was sitting on the Mount of Olives. There the disciples came to him in private. "Tell us," they said. "When will this happen? And what will be the sign of your coming? What will be the sign of the end?"

4 Jesus answered "Keep watch! Be careful that no one fools you.

5 Many will come in my name. They will claim, 'I am the Christ!' They will fool many people.

6 "You will hear about wars. You will also hear people talking about future wars. Don't be alarmed. Those things must happen. But the end still isn't here.

7 Nation will fight against nation. Kingdom will fight against kingdom. People will go hungry. There will be Earthquakes in many places.

8 All these are the beginning of birth pains.

9 "Then people will hand you over to be treated badly and killed. All nations will hate you because of me.

10 At that time, many will turn away from their faith. They will hate each other. They will hand each other over to their enemies.

11 Many false prophets will appear. They will fool many people.

12 Because evil will grow, most people's love will grow cold.

The age before them, Jesus warns His Disciples, portends eight distressing realities:

1. False Christs will appear and deceive many (verses 4, 5).

2. Wars and people talking about wars—nation against nation, kingdom against kingdom will be commonplace (verses 6, 7).

3. People will go hungry (verse 7).

4. There will be earthquakes in many places (verse 7).

5. Christians will be persecuted in every nation (verse 9).

6. Many who professed faith will fall away, hating and betraying one another (verse 10).

7. False prophets will appear and deceive many (verse 11).

8. Evil will grow and people will lose the ability to love (verse 12).

But as bad as these matters are, they are not the final signs that testify *to the Apocalypse.*[i]

The Key Signals of His Soon Return

Jesus speaks of several very specific prophecies that are the signal of the Apocalypse:

14 This good news of the kingdom will be preached in the whole world. It will be a witness to all nations. Then the end will come.

15 "The prophet Daniel spoke about 'the hated thing that destroys' (the Abomination of Desolation) — (Daniel 9:27; 11:31; 12:11). Someday you will see it standing in the holy place. The reader should understand this.

16 Then those who are in Judea should escape to the mountains...

23 "At that time someone may say to you, 'Look! Here is the Christ!' Or, 'There he is!' Do not believe it.

---

[i] Make note of how these signs compare to the Four Horsemen 'of the Apocalypse.' As we stated earlier, these signs will be constant during the 'Church Age.' As noted here, they do not signal the end.

24 False Christs and false prophets will appear. They will do great signs and miracles. They will try to fool God's chosen people if possible.

25 See, I have told you ahead of time.

26 "So if anyone tells you, 'He is far out in the desert,' do not go out there. Or if anyone says, 'He is deep inside the house,' do not believe it.

27 Lightning that comes from the east can be seen in the west. It will be the same when the Son of Man comes.

28 The vultures will gather wherever there is a dead body.

29 "Right after the terrible suffering of those days,
" 'The sun will be darkened.
The moon will not shine.
The stars will fall from the sky.
The heavenly bodies will be shaken.' — (Isaiah 13:10; 34:4)

30 "At that time the sign of the Son of Man will appear in the sky. All the nations on Earth will be sad. They will see the Son of Man coming on the clouds of the sky. He will come with power and great glory.

In this last passage, Jesus identifies six specific occurrences that *do signal His soon return*:

1. The *gospel must be preached throughout the entire world* (verse 14). Many scholars believe this has been accomplished before and with the advent of modern technology has been accomplished already in our generation.

2. The *abomination of desolation* must take place (verse 15). This is the most decisive and unmistakable sign. Clearly, this has not yet happened.

3. False Christs and false prophets *will appear that do great signs and miracles* (verse 24). Since Jesus had previously mentioned both false Christs and false prophets (verse 4, 5, and 11), we could surmise that this third mention underscores something vastly more alarming about these deceivers. Could this be a specific reference to the *Antichrist* and the *False Prophet*? Certainly the performance of *"great signs and miracles"* would be consistent with this conclusion. The comments about *"far out into the desert"* or *"deep inside the house"* infer that any 'Christ' that is isolated, far away, reluctant to appear, or hidden—is a dead giveaway that he isn't the true Christ. Many of the 'Mas-

ters' talked about by the New Age leaders are characterized by these words. Supposedly, they are high in the Himalayas or in hidden deep in deserted places. Benjamin Crème describes *Lord Maitreya,* the Buddhist-cum-New-Age Christ, in this way. In contrast, when Jesus returns it won't be a secret! Jesus won't be playing 'hide-and-seek.'

4. *Lightning that comes from the east can be seen in the west* (verse 27). Traditional commentators (such as Strong) regard this comment as little more than the mode of Christ's return: Sudden, brilliant light, public, and seen by all. In the context with the previous contrast between the 'hidden false Christ' and the real one, this would be a logical interpretation. On the other hand, it could be something else that is worrisome. Some scientists speculate, because the magnetic field surrounding our earth has weakened considerably, the earth could suffer a magnetic pole reversal in the very near future (the North and South poles could reverse—the compass would point South!). There is geological evidence to substantiate that this happens every few hundred thousand years. Others go further and suggest that the axis of the earth could reverse itself and the sun could rise in the West! Either of these events is possible and both would be horrendous for life on earth. Could Jesus be referring to the latter here? The Word for *lightning* in the Greek can be translated *lightning, light, or ray or light.* I can infer this 'about turn.' However, it is speculation on my part. Take another grain of salt with this one.

5. *Signs in the heavens that are unmistakable*—the sun is darkened, the moon turns to blood, stars fall from the sky and *"the heavenly bodies are shaken"* (verse 29). Mere astronomical events like eclipses would seem to be far too mundane to be the fulfillment of these signs. To continue with the axis reversal hypothesis, a reversal of rotation at night might make the stars appear to fall from heaven—particularly if it was sudden. The fact that heavenly bodies "are shaken" suggests that something significant will happen to the sun or moon beyond changing appearance. No doubt, such conjecture is inevitable; but once it happens *it will be unmistakable.*

6. The *"sign of the Son of Man will appear in the sky"* (verse 30). This could easily be interpreted as a spectral image of the cross appearing in the heaven. But how this will be accomplished or how it might actually appear if literally fulfilled we could only imagine. We can also conjecture that this may be only moments before He physically appears. When this sign occurs, for those who aren't ready and eager to see Him, it will be too late!

Preconditions and Their Probabilities

Assuming we will see **Daniels' 70ᵗʰ week** fulfilled in the future, when might this final seven years commence? Are there any preconditions, anything that has to happen first?

Perhaps there aren't any 'clear-cut' pre-conditions—only 'probabilities' (greater or lesser) that *certain events may happen first.* Three key events qualify for this evaluation: *(1) The Covenant between Antichrist and Israel for Seven years, (2)* The *Battle of Gog and Magog, and the (3) Rebuilding of the Temple in Jerusalem.*

The *seven year covenant* 'kicks off' the 70ᵗʰ week. We know that this agreement appears to be between Israel and a world leader who leads a group of ten nations (we can only describe this leader 'generically' because the Antichrist is not officially 'revealed' until three and one-half years later). Over the past four decades, the dominant 'precondition' that has been up for debate is *who these ten nations are.* Until very recently, scholars assumed it would be composed of ten nations from the European Union (EU). However, today we have come full circle. Some wonder whether the EU will continue to exist! Others, like Missler, point out that there could be a 'peace pact' between ten nations in the Middle East (Iran, Egypt, and Arab nations) and Israel. Three and one-half years into this agreement, the Antichrist emerges and breaks the covenant for peace. The probability of this 'Middle East Confederation' scenario is much higher today than in times past. It seems the whole world is concerned with bringing peace to the troubled Middle East.

If we believe that the *Battle of Gog and Magog* happens before the Tribulation, it also becomes an event to consider. What kind of answer would we get if we were to ask the political experts about a war between Israel and an alliance of Iran, Libya, and Russia? Would they suggest that it is probable, possible, or impossible? Most would likely suggest that it is certainly possible. Those that know more details of what is happening in Israel today, might say it is probable—and soon! Russia continues to threaten nations to its south like the Georgian Republic. It continues to arm Iran with anti-aircraft missiles and nuclear technology. It doesn't take much nerve

260

to predict that a conflict is coming that could become the Battle of Gog and Magog.

On the other hand, if we believe that the Temple must be re-built in Jerusalem before the Antichrist can appear (which seems likely), how far into the future might it be before this could occur? Without a 'world changing event' like the Battle of Gog and Magog, it *seems very unlikely*. The politics of the Arab-Israeli conflict just won't allow it. However, such a 'game changer' may be looming immediately ahead. When the Battle of Gog and Magog is a *'fait accompli,'* access to the Temple Mount will not be a problem. The rebuilding process might begin immediately—especially since the Bible says that the Jewish nation will recognize that God's hand was evident in their victory.

However, there is still the delay implied because of the *time it takes to build the Temple*. Rome wasn't built in a day and the 'Third Temple' won't be either. However, are we so sure that the *Tribulation Temple* will take *years to build?* Perhaps a house of worship we don't know

> **THE KEY POINT TO PONDER:**
>
> *There is no certainty that the best-researched scenario will happen as proposed. Nevertheless, Jesus commands us to 'watch.' Still, there should be no reason for Christians to be surprised at what comes to pass. The Bible supplies numerous indicators of what will happen.*

about will be utilized—maybe the ancient *Tabernacle of Moses,* which housed the Ark of the Covenant before Solomon's Temple, will be dis-covered and utilized during the Tribulation period. As noted before, David Flynn suggests that the location of the *Ark and the Tabernacle* is on *Mount Nebo*, where Jeremiah the Prophet buried it (as re-counted in the Book of Maccabees). If true, this circumstance could create such an eventuality. Or perhaps only the establishment of the sacrificial altar, without the Temple being fully erected, will suffice to commence Jewish sacrificial worship.

In the final analysis, we simply can't assert dogmatically how these events will transpire. Many voices speak together on probable trends and likely outcomes. Yet, there is no certainty that even the best-researched perspective, including mine, will play out as proposed. However, that doesn't mean we are foolish attempting to foresee what might transpire in the years ahead. Indeed, if there is one consistent teaching fostered by all of the writers of the New Testament, it is 'to watch.' Be alert! There is no reason we should be caught off guard. The Bible supplies numerous indicators of what will soon take place. While we may not know the exact day or hour of His coming, we are to be wise and aware. *The closer we come to time's conclusion, the clearer prophetic truth becomes.*

Speculating on What Comes Next

While almost all authorities in prophecy are guilty of too much speculation, sometimes wildly and irresponsibly, I believe we should analyze what is going on in the world and keep our eyes open. We can evaluate events for probable outcomes based upon the teachings of predictive prophecy and world developments. Therefore, I will make a number of suggestions regarding what we should be watching for in the months and years ahead.

1. *Watch for tensions to increase in the Middle East.* The terrorism we see today will likely grow worse—not better (although we should always hope and pray for peace). We may see incidents occur that precipitate the coming of the Battle of Gog and Magog. The war in Gaza, the fighting in the Golan Heights, and the continued struggle between the Palestinians and the Israelis is unlikely to slow down.

2. On the other hand, *watch for a treaty between a world leader from Europe, from the United States, or from the Middle East that will seek to protect Israel* or at minimum bring peace to the area. Obviously, if we see this treaty or covenant established for a seven-year period, we would be foolish to dismiss the possibility that the clock – known as Daniel's 70th Week – just clicked on.

3. We shouldn't be surprised if we continue to see a strengthening *of the relationship between Russia, Iran, and other radical Arab nations.* Russia has long sought a 'warm water port' for economic reasons. Having access to the oil reserves in the Middle East is yet another strong reason why they seek relationships with the Arab states. Finally, opposing Israel and the United States in this area has given Russia

advantage in other matters of international importance. Most experts see Russia continuing to walk a fine line between 'making friends in the West' and enabling the Iranians to make war on Israel.

4. *The tension on the issue of control of the Temple Mount is likely to increase.* While the Jordanian (and Muslim) Trust known as the *Waqf* controls the Mount today, there is continued pressure from orthodox Jews to reclaim the Mount to make way for the Messiah, who they believe will rebuild the Temple (for the Third and final[i] time). Assuming the *abomination of desolation* occurs as described by Daniel, John, and the Apostle Paul—the Temple or some sacred building of Worship must be in place before it can happen. Any move on the part of the orthodox Jews to open the Mount for construction would be another key confirming event that the Tribulation may soon commence.

5. *We should track the popularity and influence of particular leaders in Europe, the United States, or the Middle East,* to the outcome where a leader becomes the fulfillment of *Antichrist.* We know from the descriptions of his character in the Bible that he will be a charismatic leader—the entire world will find him attractive and will succumb to his leadership. He will likely be a leader who seeks world unity and many regard a peacemaker. He will also command respect from both the Arab and Israeli camps. While he is depicted as 'the man of sin,' 'the lawless one' and other no doubt disparaging but well-deserved appellations, these attributes may not be displayed (or in fact, even a part of his character), until AFTER he experiences a 'mortal wound to the head' (i.e., the fulfillment of Revelation 13—an event that could radically alter his persona). His miraculous 'return from the dead' could transform him into the dreaded Antichrist. Clearly, he will not first appear on the scene with a 666 on his hand or his forehead. Consequently, because this transformation might take place after the 'the mortal head wound' (possibly an assassination attempt?), it will be improbable that we will know beforehand with any conviction that this person is destined to be the *Beast.* This is yet another reason why I am reluctant to speculate on any particular world leader as the likely Antichrist.

---

[i] If the Ezekiel Temple is built as described in Chapters 40-48, there will actually be four Temples.

6. *Watch for the increase in popularity of the view that 'God' is nothing more than intelligent beings from another planet* or dimension, that aliens who have supposedly stimulated our growth and development into 'Homo Sapiens' will soon visit our world. This is one of the disturbing themes in our culture today. Fueled by popular movies from *2001: A Space Odyssey* in the 1960s to the latest edition of *Indiana Jones, (Indiana Jones, and the Kingdom of the Crystal Skull*, 2008), the religion of aliens-who-are-our-gods is becoming commonplace. Why is this happening? The widespread belief in UFOs and the probability of life on other worlds is the primary reason. 'Gods' who we can see (even if it is just their spaceships!) are easier to believe in than a God who we can't see at all. This theme will continue to grow in popularity and the belief will likely become more widespread and deep-seated.

There is no surety that the 'scenarios' discussed here will happen exactly as depicted. Hindsight is always 20/20. Nevertheless, Jesus and His Apostles command us to watch and be alert. We are not to hide our heads in the sand and avoid the subject because it is too controversial or too alarming. We should take comfort in knowing that God is in control and He can clearly see the end from the beginning. If we have professed faith in Jesus Christ and demonstrated a transformed life, we have assurance that we are in His loving hands. Even if the events unfold as described here, those who trust in Jesus Christ as their savior and Lord can look forward to the future. *We are not destined to experience the wrath of God.* Quite to the contrary, we are destined to experience wonderful things that we have never experienced nor even imagined when we finally join one another *"in the clouds."* The Apostle Paul in I Corinthians 2:9 quotes Isaiah the prophet when he says,

"It is written,
'No eye has seen, no ear has heard,
no mind has known what God has prepared
for those who love him'" (Isaiah 64:4).

Recapping the Key Points Covered in This Chapter

- Those that believe many Bible prophecies are yet to be fulfilled (futurists) have strong reasons to make note of what the Scripture predicts will happen 'in the last days.'
- Not all signs presented in the Scripture specifically relate to the Apocalypse.
- There are many signs predicting tribulation for believers in all ages – suffering isn't exclusive to the apocalypse! Jesus lists eight such examples.
- There are six very specific signs of the 'last days' that Jesus mentions. These do relate directly to the Apocalypse.
- Of particular interest is His warning of false Christs and Prophets that will work great signs and wonders. His specific words are intriguing.
- A curious sign is the phrase 'as lightning appears in the east but can be seen in the west' – it causes us to consider a variety of interpretations that might connect to some of the current day warnings from science and from the 2012 'Mayan' apocalyptic literature.
- Signs in the heavens also purport the same connection.
- What preconditions must be met before the Second Advent occurs?
- Three possible issues seem worthy of consideration: A peace treaty or covenant between Israel and its rivals; the Battle of Gog and Magog; finally, the rebuilding of the Jewish Temple in Jerusalem.
- Six specific issues to monitor are identified which include the topics that could be 'preconditions' plus keeping an eye on world leaders and their position on peace in Israel.
- Lastly, watch the continued emphasis on the new religion of 'God in an alien spacesuit.'

Chapter 28: Choosing Sides in the Conflict of the Ages

Choosing Who, Not What, to Believe In

Having covered so many topics together regarding the Second Coming of Christ, by now you've observed that my approach encourages the reader to consider alternative points of view and make a reasoned decision about what you believe. I also have tried to caution readers that just because there are strong disagreements on certain topics in prophecy, one camp of Christians shouldn't necessary conclude that the other group that disagrees with them does so because it is being dishonest or 'apostate'. There are too many crucial commonly held beliefs to let eschatology matters provoke conflict.

However, the decision I am most concerned about for all my readers isn't about what form of eschatology you choose to believe, but *who you choose to believe in*. The story of the Bible is the story of God's attempt to reconcile all of us to Him. God is our Father and He sent His Son Jesus Christ to make this reconciliation possible. *"God was in Christ reconciling the world to Himself, not counting (our) trespasses against (us)."* (II Corinthians 5:19) But whether or not reconciliation happens is now *up to us*. It takes two to be reconciled. We can participate in that reconciliation or we can reject it. In short, *we have to make the choice to be reconciled to God.*

We noted in the section on *The Wrath of God* that the apocalyptic message is a warning. God's mercy and grace are not limitless. The teaching of both the Old Testament and the New are alike: Frightening times may lie just ahead. How we respond to these warnings decides our fate. Still, the choice is yours.

We have heard the phrase, *"receive Christ"* almost to the point of 'wearing it out.' Yet, it is a biblical phrase – both a correct and appropriate concept. The language comes from the first chapter of John's gospel. *"But as many as **received Him** to them He gave the right to become children of God, (that is) to those who believe in His name."* (John 1:12). So what does it mean to *receive* Christ?

One way to understand it is to think of the opposite—*to reject Christ.* If we *reject or refuse* His offer of reconciliation, we settle the issue. We choose to live apart from God for time and eternity. If we chose to be 'receptive' to His invitation, to *accept or receive* the invitation, we become a true child of God. Moreover, we are transformed into a new creature. *"Therefore if anyone is in Christ, he is a new creature; the old things passed away; behold, new things have come."* (II Corinthians 5:17).

This new character or person that we have become is made possible because God did an exchange of sorts when Christ was on the cross. We read, *"He (God) made Him (Jesus) who knew no sin to be sin on our behalf, so that we might become the righteousness of God in Him."* (II Corinthians 5:21). We can be God's child because God 'imputed' the righteousness of Jesus Christ to us and Jesus took our sins upon Himself. In God's eyes, if we become a child of God, not only are we are now spotless, we are far more: *We are righteous in God's eyes to the very same degree that Jesus is righteous in God's eyes.*

It is hard to believe, particularly for those of us that have committed horrible sin in our lives, but it is what the Bible teaches.

Not that we are free from the effects of sin. We will see sin's effects upon our lives as long as we live in this present age. In addition, we will struggle every day with the power of sin to influence us. However, something crucial happened when Christ died on the cross. *Whatever power that sin had over us was broken.* The cross of Christ 'legally' terminated the power of sin. We are no longer *captive* to our old ways—we now have the presence of the indwelling Christ to enable us to live very different lives.

Our Certificate of Adoption Once We Become a Christian

In Romans Chapter 8, the Apostle Paul provides us with what amounts to our *Certificate of Adoption* as believers. He states the following giving us the details of what it means to become a child of God:

1 Therefore there is now no condemnation for those who are in Christ Jesus.

2 For the law of the Spirit of life in Christ Jesus has set you free from the law of sin and of death.

3 For what the Law could not do, weak as it was through the flesh, God did: sending His own Son in the likeness of sinful flesh and as an offering for sin, He condemned sin in the flesh,

4 so that the requirement of the Law might be fulfilled in us, who do not walk according to the flesh but according to the Spirit.

5 For those who are according to the flesh set their minds on the things of the flesh, but those who are according to the Spirit, the things of the Spirit.

6 For the mind set on the flesh is death, but the mind set on the Spirit is life and peace,

7 because the mind set on the flesh is hostile toward God; for it does not subject itself to the law of God, for it is not even able to do so,

8 and those who are in the flesh cannot please God.

9 However, you are not in the flesh but in the Spirit, if indeed the Spirit of God dwells in you. But if anyone does not have the Spirit of Christ, he does not belong to Him.

10 If Christ is in you, though the body is dead because of sin, yet the spirit is alive because of righteousness.

11 But if the Spirit of Him who raised Jesus from the dead dwells in you, He who raised Christ Jesus from the dead will also give life to your mortal bodies through His Spirit who dwells in you.

12 So then, brethren, we are under obligation, not to the flesh, to live according to the flesh—

13 for if you are living according to the flesh, you must die; but if by the Spirit you are putting to death the deeds of the body, you will live.

14 For all who are being led by the Spirit of God, these are sons of God.

15 For you have not received a spirit of slavery leading to fear again, but you have received a spirit of adoption as sons by which we cry out, "Abba! Father!"

16 The Spirit Himself testifies with our spirit that we are children of God,

17 and if children, heirs also, heirs of God and fellow heirs with Christ, if indeed we suffer with Him so that we may also be glorified with Him.

18 For I consider that the sufferings of this present time are not worthy to be compared with the glory that is to be revealed to us.

19 For the anxious longing of the creation waits eagerly for the revealing of the sons of God. (*NASV*)

Let's consider all the specific points and promises one by one:

- Paul assures us that all condemnation that we might have experienced (or might still feel in our spirits) is past, once we are *receptive* to the offer of reconciliation (verse 1).

- In fact, at that moment, we become new creatures and the Spirit of Christ comes to live within our spirits. The *"Spirit of Life"* has broken the power of sin and has freed us from the inevitability of death (verse 2).

- Paul reminds us that it wasn't God's law that made this happen or our ability to follow that law—with only ourselves and our own power to rely upon (our *'flesh' or our human nature),* we were too weak to achieve this (verse 3).

- However, Christ's coming into the world as a human being who died on the cross *somehow broke the hold of sin* and now we are able to live a life that can fulfill what God wants us to do (verse 4).

- To achieve this, we must set our minds on the power of Christ and His Spirit in us, not on our human capacities because they are limited and fatally flawed (verse 5).

- If we set our minds only on what we can do 'self-powered,' we will persist in living defeated lives that end in death. But if we set our minds to think in terms of God's Spirit living in us, relying upon His power, we will experience a renewed life and inner peace (verse 6).

- *We must plug into a new and stronger power source!* Indeed, to be a Christian, Paul states clearly that you *must have the Spirit of God living in you*—for if you don't have the Spirit in you—you are not a child of God (verse 9).

- Having the Spirit inside you is a *sine qua non* (an essential condition, without which you have none of the benefits). Because this Spirit that lives in us *is the same Spirit that raised Jesus from the dead,* this Spirit will give us new life and keep our new life thriving (verses 10 and 11).

- Does this mean that we are free to live in our old ways? Paul tells us that living the old way is not an option. We are now under *a different obligation*—not to attempt living the law of God in our own strength—but to *let the Spirit put our old activities and behaviors to death*. By doing this, we will experience the new Life of the Spirit (verses 12 and 13).

- To put it succinctly, if we are being led by the Spirit in this way, we are absolutely the sons (or daughters) of God (verse 14)!

Thinking About God in a Different Way

Paul continues to elaborate in order to transform our notions about the nature of our heavenly Father:

- We must change our way of thinking *about the nature of who God is*. He is not a heavy-handed tyrant or a Father who only knows how to scold us for failing to do what He wants. To the contrary, He is our 'Daddy' and the Spirit in us reminds us how much He loves us (verses 15 and 16).

- To prove the remarkable love He has for us, He has made us heirs of His inheritance, right alongside Christ—He will transform us into the same glory that Christ has in His resurrected body right now (verse 17).

- In addition, whatever trials or challenges we face, Paul tells us that the future holds such amazing things that we will wonder how we could have ever let the difficulties of our former lives matter so much to us (verse 18).

- We will be revealed to the creation that we are God's children with the same glory that Christ has in God's eyes. The creation itself longs for this day (verse 19).

Best of all, *our future is assured!* By receiving Christ and being reconciled to God, we will enjoy the amazing opportunity to participate with Christ in His coming Kingdom, whether it be here on earth (the Millennium) or in the New Heavens and New Earth. *Making it 'personal' is really what the most important element of eschatology is all about!*

Making Your Choice

If you want to make this choice, to be receptive to God's invitation to be reconciled to Him, you only have to tell Him that you are making this choice now. You can pray a simple prayer like this (aloud or not—no matter, He hears either way):

> *God, I would like to become one of your Children. I understand that through what Jesus Christ did, I can now be fully reconciled to You. I accept Your offer. I wish to be made new. I open my spirit to Your Spirit. Please come into my heart and into my life. Teach me how to walk daily in your Spirit's power. Help me to put my old life in the past. Show me each day what my new life is about. Teach me how to dwell on the Spirit so that I can please you and can experience a truly different way of living. Thank You for all that You have done for me in Christ. Amen.*

If you said this prayer *with sincerity*—congratulations! You have just been transferred from one Kingdom to another. You are now a part of the Kingdom of Christ! I encourage you to find someone you know that you trust is a good Christian and tell him (or her) what you have done. Ask them to help you find others that you can associate with that can help you learn more about living your new life in Christ. If you are not familiar with the New Testament already, please read the *Gospel of John*. It will be a great place to start!

Parting Thoughts

Think upon these amazing words of Paul at the 'other end' of Chapter 8 of his letter to the Romans:

> [38] *For I am convinced that neither death, nor life, nor angels, nor principalities, nor things present, nor things to come, nor powers,*
>
> [39] *nor height, nor depth, nor any other created thing, will be able to separate us from the love of God, which is in Christ Jesus our Lord. (NASV)*

Finally, I will close this chapter with Paul's prayer for those he persuaded to become followers of Jesus Christ:

> *I pray that he will use his glorious riches to make you strong. May his Holy Spirit give you his power deep down inside you. Then Christ will live in your hearts because you believe in him. And I pray that your love will have deep roots. I pray that it will have a strong foundation. May you have power with all God's people to understand Christ's love. May you know how wide and long and high and deep it is. And may you know his love, even though it can't be known completely. Then you will be filled with everything God has for you.* (Ephesians 3:16-19).

Recapping the Key Points Covered in This Chapter

- Interpreting prophecy can create divisions among evangelicals, but it shouldn't be such a divisive matter.
- The most important issue is 'who do you believe in' not 'what do you believe in regarding the Second Coming of Christ' – this choice is of pre-eminent import for what happens now and in the life to come.
- The warnings have been sounded – the apocalypse may come soon.
- What does it mean to receive Christ? Think of the opposite: rejecting Him. Receiving Him is 'welcoming Him' or 'inviting Him in.'
- The offer 'on the table' is *reconciliation*. God has done everything for you, but you must still decide you wish to be reconciled.
- The lessons in Paul's letter to the Romans, Chapter 8, are like a 'certificate of adoption' to believers.
- We consider here all of the promises and provisions made to enable us to live a very different life.
- Lastly, I make a final call for choosing sides and a prayer to enable it!

Chapter 29: Conclusion – Selecting a Method for Interpreting the Bible

The Importance of Hermeneutics

It's usually good to be conscious about how you do things. Sometimes we talk about a person who is 'methodical.' More often than not that attribute is a complement rather than a criticism. Furthermore, being mindful of how you approach a significant endeavor is usually worth the extra time it takes. Lewis Carroll (1832-1898), author of *Alice in Wonderland*, said, "If you don't know where you are going, any road will take you there."

So we must settle on our destination before we chart the best way there. If our goal is to read the Bible and understand it, then we must see if a map exists that helps show us the path forward. When it comes to interpreting the Bible, which is no easy matter, most would agree that an accurate 'map' is essential to make the journey. That map in biblical interpretation as noted before is *hermeneutics*. With it, we will likely get to our destination with far fewer missed turns along the way.

One of the first principles for 'reading the map' correctly – which is in our metaphor for interpreting the Bible – requires *keeping matters in context by appreciating the history of who wrote the passage in question and when they wrote it*. Generally, evangelicals from all camps follow tradition when they identify who wrote a particular book in the Bible; however, they often debate *the timing* as to when a particular book of the Bible was written. On the other hand, Liberalism not only questions timing, it also rejects the traditional authors. For instance, if Christian tradition holds that Matthew is the author of the first gospel of the New Testament, Liberalism disputes it. Evangelicals likely do not. On the other hand, if the conventional view believes that Luke, the companion of Paul, wrote the third gospel in 65 AD (just before Paul's beheading in Rome around that date), Liberalism may contend that the gospel was actually written much later (perhaps 20-25 years later), preferring to 'late date' most books of the New Testament (and Old for that matter), due to their assumptions. These assumptions being that (1) writing was not as important as oral tradition to the early church and that (2) the Apostles had little to no interest (*and perhaps no ability*) to record what Jesus said and did. Liberalism supposes this is so also because (3) the Apostles labored under the false assumption that Jesus would return within their lifetime.[i]

A second principle that is even more important: Our *approach to interpreting the Bible must become conscious and well articulated.* Without a *conscious* hermeneutic, biblical interpretation is open to blatant mistakes, missed inconsistencies, bad doctrine, and harmful conjecture. We need to put our method into words. Hence, the intent of this chapter is to help you accomplish this important goal.

Now, it is not my intent to provide a *scholarly* argument for the correct interpretive methodology—which is what hermeneutics is— it would become too detailed and complex for the average reader. However, the important objective of *finding a consistent approach to interpret the Bible* is paramount for everyone. Indeed, we can't correctly interpret the subjects of predictive prophecy, the Apocalypse, and the Second Coming, if we have the wrong method for understanding the Bible. We could look at it this way: We have explored over 25 topics together. Each topic has more than one opinion. Some of them have many points of view. The only way to sort out what to believe is by deciding what our hermeneutic is. *With it clarified, we can select what we believe and why we believe it.* Without such clarity, we will likely adopt a position fundamentally indefensible.

How can you determine which hermeneutic to adopt? Together, we will analyze the different ways Protestants interpret the Bible, and then decide which method makes the most sense. We can make this decision ultimately based upon (1) our reason, or (2) what we believe is the most biblical approach, or (3) based upon we have learned and what we have relied upon to get us to this point in our lives, or (4) a combination of all of the above. So what's our map to be?

---

[i] As we discussed at the outset, they may have had a very legitimate reason for believing this.

The Three Alternative Hermeneutics

I have argued that there are three primary ways that Protestants interpret the Bible. Here I will endeavor to simply articulate the *hermeneutic alternatives, each in one page or less.* After we have provided this one page summary of each position, we will 'drill down' into much more analytical detail for each of the three views. First, our summary statements for each:

- *The Liberal method of interpretation,* based primarily on detecting the religious or spiritual value in the Bible that helps us live ethical, moral, and fulfilled lives. Its key assumptions would include:

  1) The *Bible is a collection of literature that teaches us about God and who we are.* We are to live in right relationships with God, with our fellow humans, and with ourselves. The liberal Christian perspective may also assert that the Bible is perhaps the greatest book ever written to instruct us on these topics.

  2) However, *we should feel free to discard any miraculous element that we find unbelievable* from our modern perspective. Any biblical passage which relies upon miracles or supernatural gifts (such as telling the future) must be interpreted in light of the fact that such things do not occur (this infers that we embrace the notion of *naturalism*—all effects have natural causes). There is no need to reach for fantastic explanations that are outside our ability to prove or disprove.

  3) To learn the value or truth behind a passage's meaning, *we must assess its value to teach us spiritual lessons that can be applied to our living today.* Whether or not the reported facts are accurate is of no concern. There are valuable lessons in parables, myths, and fables. Historical validity is not the issue. Once we get past the fact that (according to Liberalism), the Bible is a book written by humans of limited understanding in pre-scientific times, it liberates us to concentrate on *meaning* instead of whether such-and-such a person really lived as the Bible says he did as well as whether or not the event described happened in a particular way.

4) In this methodology, biblical inspiration has nothing to do with ensuring the Scripture is free from error; *it has to do with God inspiring the Bible's authors* to tell stories that teach us about who God is, who we are, and how we should live. *"For whatever was written in earlier times was written for our instruction, so that through perseverance and the encouragement of the Scriptures we might have hope."* (Romans 15:4, NASV). Apocalyptic literature, like any other form of biblical material, must be evaluated in light of these principles.

- *The Key Doctrine method of interpretation,* (used by many evangelicals), based primarily upon decisions about the core truths of Christian doctrine, which once agreed upon, guide our interpretation. These doctrines affect other aspects of the Bible's story to ensure that we rigorously uphold these *core doctrines. Covenantal Theology,* historically closely aligned with the Reformation, emphasizes several key doctrines that become the tests for how we must understand Scripture (those sections not directly teaching key doctrines). These essential doctrines are the following:

1) *The primacy of Christ's death on the cross* and His fulfillment of the Jewish sacrificial system (He is *"the Lamb of God that takes away the sin of the world"*—the Old Testament sacrificial system was a picture of the redemptive work of Christ—Hebrews 7:27).

2) *The integration of Gentiles and Jews into a single fellowship of believers* (The Body of Christ, the Church) which, according to this view, spans both Old and New Testament (Galatians 3:28).

3) *The culmination of our history and the fabric of space-time into Christ's Kingdom* which today is heavenly (with brief 'glimmers' of His Kingdom in our world now), while tomorrow it requires a recreation of the heavens and earth (Revelation 21:1).

4) The infallibility (or inerrancy) of the Bible which tells us that the Bible cannot err, *"All Scripture is inspired by God and profitable for teaching, for reproof, for correction, for training in righteousness..."* (II Timothy 3:16), so we must always find ways to understand all passages in the Bible that can be reconciled to these key doctrines—even if it

means we must 'spiritualize' what the Scripture says in any given instance. To interpret the Bible correctly, we must understand that these greater truths guide us.[i]

5) Of lesser value, but still important is the history of what the Church has traditionally taught and believed. This teaching can also be an important element in helping us to interpret the Bible correctly. The underlying assumption is that the more recent an interpretive method is, the more likely it is to be inconsistent with orthodox thinking.[ii]

- *The Plain Meaning method of interpretation,* (espoused by Dispensationalists). This approach tries to:

1) *Understand what the language is expressing in normal grammatical rules and historical context.* It recognizes that some language means to be figurative, symbolic, or allegorical. However, if it is clear that the author's intent was to have his words taken 'at face value'—then this perspective should be the basis for interpretation. We could also call this methodology 'literalism' although this term has many ambiguous connotations as I noted at the outset.[iii]

2) *Base belief upon the Bible as God's infallible and inerrant revelation to us.* All doctrines should be established upon the plain meaning of the Bible's authors. All doctrine is subject to revision if the language of God's revelation (through Scripture) corrects our current doctrinal creedal assertions.

3) *Reexamine our understanding of doctrine as we learn more about what the Bible teaches.* As such, Christian doctrine can be more fluid as we progress in our understanding of God and His saving work in our lives.

---

[i] This should not be taken to mean that some Scripture is inspired and some is not. Conservatives in all camps are steadfast in the assertion that all Scripture is inspired by God. Conservatives would nonetheless agree that not all Scripture is of equal importance to determine the most essential doctrines of Christianity.

[ii] We all know that 'recency' is not a good thing for fine wine. Apparently, it is not good for a biblical interpretation either! Later, we will see that in eschatology this guideline is actually incorrect.

[iii] See Deep Dive #1: *When Literalism is Harmful to Biblical Interpretation.*

4) *Evaluate each concept on its merits.* The 'recency' of an idea, in and of itself, does not make the idea right or wrong. Its veracity relates to whether or not it is what the Bible teaches to be true. Our interpretation of any Scripture and doctrine is open to change if when we read the Scripture we become convinced that its meaning is different from what we previously thought. *"For the word of God is living and active. Sharper than any double-edged sword, it penetrates even to dividing soul and spirit, joints and marrow; it judges the thoughts and attitudes of the heart."* (Hebrews 4:12, NASV). God's Word is alive and continues to teach us. This does not mean that our understanding of doctrine is likely to experience frequent change however. This is so because we...

5) *Assume that there is one right interpretation.* *"But know this first of all, that no prophecy of Scripture is a matter of one's own interpretation, for no prophecy was ever made by an act of human will, but men moved by the Holy Spirit spoke from God."* (II Peter 1:20, 21, NASV). God spoke and God knows what He meant to say. Nevertheless, we cannot be sure that now we fully appreciate what God has been trying to teach us. Our understanding can grow— wisdom comes with age! We must have conviction about what we believe but always be open to the possibility that our interpretation is wrong. We can think of Martin Luther's words when he was on trial for heresy:

> *"Unless I am convinced by proofs from Scriptures or by plain and clear reasons and arguments, I can and will not retract, for it is neither safe nor wise to do anything against conscience. Here I stand. I can do no other. God help me. Amen".*[i]

One of my primary assumptions is that we benefit by understanding the various positions that serious Christians take on the subject of prophecy. However, I now am also ready to insist it's important *to come to a definite conviction about what we believe!* [ii] Therefore, I hope the outcome of your study with me is precisely that!

---

[i] This is Martin Luther's response to the *Inquisition at the Diet of Worms (1521).*

[ii] Which is to say, 'Don't be so open minded that your brains fall out!"

Clearly, there is not a unified voice in Protestant Christianity when it comes to eschatology. As just defined, there are three principal positions and *they are distinct because of how they interpret the Bible.* In this section, we will summarize the case for each of these perspectives.[i] As we discuss these viewpoints, I will push my 'neutrality' aside and provide my perspective on the most compelling position. (For your convenience, I have included **Figure 15** below to recap once again these three protestant eschatology viewpoints).

A reminder: Christians from all persuasions agree that the primary messages of the *Apocalypse* and the prophecies of the Bible are these (1) *Good* will defeat *Evil* and that (2) Jesus Christ will be crowned 'King of Kings and Lord of Lords.' These will happen either *figuratively*, through a victorious Church influencing the world toward good, or *literally*, upon a physical and visible appearing. After that generalization, as we have seen, pathways sharply diverge.

The Case for Liberalism

Liberalism tends to distance itself from almost all the subjects associated with eschatology. Liberalism professes very little about the Apocalypse because it is 'preterist,' believing that most prophecy, including Revelation, has already been 'fulfilled.' They contend, the nature of apocalyptic literature isn't to predict the future. Instead, it's only a mode of literature to assert optimistically that Good will defeat Evil. Furthermore, the author of the Book of Revelation wrote for his 'contemporary' audience – helping many who suffered persecution overcome their ordeal. *Certainly, we should not interpret it as a playbook for the end times.* Because almost all aspects of eschatology imply a supernatural intervention of the divine, Liberalism disregards centuries old orthodox teaching. Since divine intervention is deemed outside the realm of possibility, most eschatology to the Liberal is a study of apocalyptic 'pep talks,' imagery and fanciful stories. There may be value, but only through interpreting these aspects of Scripture as 'myth' (see ***Deep Dive #14*** below).

---

[i] Admittedly, this summary is high level, to fit the confines of the study.

The liberal position is comfortable with the separation of reason and faith as far as biblical interpretation is concerned. Liberalism chooses not to challenge scientific theories that may discredit what the Bible teaches. Liberalism is ready to admit that the Bible does not report history accurately either. It is willing to accept historical discrepancies and accommodate scientific findings through separating religious meaning into a different realm of human knowledge. If this intellectual sleight of hand can silence the critic, then there is no real need to defend the Bible. It is purely a source book for matters of faith and practice only. Once we affirm these truths, Liberalism asserts the Bible can speak for itself!

However, Liberalism doesn't stop there. It is also willing to agree that the Bible may be wrong about religious teachings too. It can be mistaken when it offers direct guidance on what to believe (doctrine) and on how the church should 'run its business' (polity). Old doctrines may be out of line with current thinking. Old creeds may need new interpretations. To make Christianity relevant in today's world, Liberalism believes we should be willing to forfeit most of the trappings of our historic doctrines and focus on just the most irreducible essentials – namely, *how do we bring meaning and fulfillment into the lives of Christ's followers?* If we can still do that through the powerful stories and symbols of our religion, we still have something worth promoting. Consequently, we can readily conclude that to Liberalism, the meaning of the Bible's message is quite different from what the Bible presumes to say. In addition, as to the matter of biblical inspiration, it certainly is not in line with historic Protestant positions on the nature of Holy Scripture (see **Deep Dive #15** below).

However, the Liberal hermeneutic is not without appeal. There are several strong reasons to consider it carefully. Liberalism promises an approach to Christian belief that frees faith from 'fussing over the details.' This methodology can be a powerful rubric[i] for a Liberal 'apologetic.' They draw "the line in the sand" around *the subject of value to human fulfillment* – the historical details of Bible sto-

---

[i] A *rubric* governs or guides how to accomplish a matter, often intellectual in nature – as in 'rules and instructions.'

ries don't matter. The proponents of this perspective argue that it avoids forfeiting faith altogether by losing debates due to picayune matters like 'was there enough space on the Ark to house all the animals?' 'How could Methuselah really live to be almost 1,000 years old?' 'Did Jesus really walk on water?'

However, the ultimate question you the reader must answer to be comfortable in this camp is this: Are there enough reasons to believe in spite of all the reasons to doubt? If we admit that so many errors are "part-and-parcel" of the Bible, can we still argue that there is reason to regard its 'spiritual value?'

Furthermore, there is mounting evidence that the Liberal position has proven to be wrong. Originally, the denial of the supernatural motivated this school or thought. That assumption is no longer so sacred. Many believe the so-called supernatural is part of the world in which we live too. Additionally, the 'signs of the end' continue to mount up the way that evangelicals have preached for many decades. C.S. Lewis posed to *pantheists* the story of the kids 'playing burglar in the darkened main hall.' "What happens if you really do hear footsteps? What if there really is a burglar in the hall?" His point being: What happens if you find out that God really is a Being that intervenes in history and His Son really is going to come back to earth? Like the old good news/ bad news joke about Jesus returning: Merely 'looking busy when He comes' may not be enough!

At the end of the day, if your assumption is that naturalism and modernism should ground your worldview — yet you are still predisposed to take the Bible seriously believing it offers valuable spiritual truth — the *Liberal interpretive method* is clearly for you (see **Deep Dive # 16** below for further discussion on this approach). You won't be alone if you choose this approach. Millions do.

So where do I stand on Liberalism? I grew up and served in a number of 'liberal' churches during my ministerial tour of duty; I served both in Presbyterian and Methodist churches. However, I remained firmly convinced then and remain so now that the essential meaning of Christianity is best represented by *the most biblical approach.*

Protestant Christianity	**Evangelical or Fundamentalist**	**Amillennialist** Post-Tribulation Rapture **Key Doctrine** Hermeneutic **Covenants** Adamic Covenant Noahic Covenant Abrahamic Covenant Mosaic Covenant Davidic Covenant New Covenant *Preterist*—Except for the Physical Return of Christ	**Covenantal Theologians** B.B. Warfield (1851-1921) Charles Hodge (1797-1878) J. Gresham Machen (1881-1937) Cornelius Van Til (1895-1997) J.I. Packer (1926-) R.C. Sproul (1939-) **Seminaries** Westminster Theological. (PA) Covenant Theological Sm. (MO) Greenville Presbyterian (SC) Knox Theological Seminary (FL) Reformed Theological Sm. (MS)
		Millennialist Pre-Tribulation Rapture **Plain Meaning** Hermeneutic **Dispensations** Innocence (pre-Adamic Fall) Conscience (Adam to Noah) Government (Noah to Abraham) Patriarchal (Abraham to Moses) Mosaic Law (Moses to Christ) Grace (Christ to Today) Millennial (Future, 1,000 Yrs.) *Futurist*—For all eschatological events	**Dispensational Theologians** C. I. Schofield (1843-1921) Lewis Sperry Chafer (1871-1952) Dwight L. Moody (1837-1899) John F. Walvoord (1910-2002) Charles C. Ryrie (1925-) J. Dwight Pentecost (1915-) **Dispensational Schools** Dallas Theological Seminary (TX) Moody Bible Institute (IL) Biola University (CA) Baptist Bible Seminary (PA) Philadelphia Biblical Univ. (PA)
	Modernist	**Post-Millennialist** No Tribulation or Rapture **Liberal** Hermeneutic **Theologies** "Social Gospel " (A. V. Harnack) "Synthesis with Existentialism" (P. Tillich) "Process Theology" (A.N. Whitehead) "Neo-orthodoxy" (Barth, Bultmann) "Liberation Theology" (R. M. Brown plus) "Theology of Hope" (Multmann) *'Historicist' or Preterist*	**Liberal Theologians** F. Schleiermacher (1768-1834) Harry E. Fosdick (1878-1969) Alfred Whitehead (1861-1947) Paul Tillich (1886-1965) Karl Barth (1886-1968) Rudolf Bultmann (1884-1976) **Seminaries** Princeton Theological Sm. (NJ) Chicago Theological Sm. (IL) Perkins School of Theology (TX) Harvard Divinity School (MA) Trinity Lutheran Seminary (OH) Berkeley Divinity (Yale) (CN)

FIGURE 15 – PROTESTANT ESCHATOLOGY OVERVIEW

From my point of view, Liberalism fails to win my favor for essentially one reason: *It superimposes a concept of faith and truth that is inconsistent with the Bible's teaching.* This failure to accept the core teaching of the Bible about what faith and truth means puts Liberalism on a course more in line with eastern religion and less so with the Judeo-Christian tradition. Clearly, I believe *the concept of truth is vital.* Making distinctions between true and false is just as important in spiritual matters as it is in human affairs. Therefore, I can't support the *hermeneutic of Liberalism* and its underlying concept of spiritual truth. The Bible challenges us to believe on its terms – not on ours. Fundamentally, as Francis Schaeffer exposed almost forty years ago, Liberalism seeks to 'escape from reason.' Based upon its theological presuppositions, it ultimately asserts that living a life of faith is an irrational 'leap into the dark.'

Despite the widespread conventional wisdom to the contrary, among the many liberally minded, I argue that the evangelical stance is a defensible position. It is supported by evidence. Indeed, the notion of faith is not that of 'blind faith.' In other words, it begins with the contention that faith must have a rational basis in order to allow us to make affirmative statements about what we believe and to understand God's revelation of Himself to us in a way that corresponds to the way we understand truth about our other relationships. *Propositional truth undergirds personal faith.* Whether mirrored in the relationship between parent and child or between husband and wife, we must base relationships on communication. We must be able to say effectively what we think and how we feel. Our ability to communicate through language is crucial if we are to relate successfully to one another.

Our relationship with God is no different in this regard. As humans, we can love one another and express this love propositionally. Our wedding vows are a perfect example. Certainly, no one would want our love to end there – especially a young couple looking forward to their wedding night! However, we must base 'true love' – a responsible relationship – on truth, not fuzzy feelings, not lust. Rather, it must be based upon a conviction about what we are willing to do – committing ourselves to the other's betterment – for in making this commitment we achieve substantial fulfillment for our partner as well as ourselves. Despite all the complaints we hear about marriage (mostly sarcastic statements seeking a laugh), history has proven that societies that revere marriage prosper and those that deride its commitments perish. Is it accidental that historically the leader of the religious community in most cultures normally performs marriages? Hardly. The sanctity of marriage is a reflection on the sacredness of the relationship between God and potentially each member of the human race.

Recall that the Bible compares the relationship between the divine and human, in both Old Testament and New, to the relationship between a husband and wife. We see lessons for marriage applied to all relationships – especially our relationship with God.

Indeed, God has chosen to communicate with us and extend Himself to us in a meaningful committed way (to save us from our sins, to transform our lives, and to interact with us experientially through prayer and other means). So why would we accept information from Him that is irrational or beyond reason? If God calls us to live in meaningful relationships with one another (and He does), it is unexpected and in fact, to be so bold, unacceptable that He would express this commandment to us in a manner inconsistent with how He has created us to interact with one another.

Do I hear a word of concern or doubt? If you object to this line of reasoning, may I suggest that it is because your concept of God is different from mine? It would be truly outrageous for me to carry on about love and relationships in this way if God is in fact incapable of demonstrating personality and linguistic communication. But you say, "Surely you are constructing a God in man's image. You are giving God human qualities. You are guilty of anthropomorphism." Now, if that is your complaint, then it has become clear that we are not talking about the same God. Once again, I am talking about the God of the Bible who has chosen to communicate to us through His prophets and through His incarnation in Jesus Christ. This God created us in His image. And guess what? Language is certainly one of the most divine features we possess. What other creature on the earth uses their tongue quite as we do? On the other hand, if you insist that your God is the same concept of God that I've just expressed, then I stand by my all of my remarks!

To Liberalism, I say "No thank you." Liberalism may proudly boast that it has made religious truth claims immune from disproof, but in declaring itself victorious in battle, it accidentally lost the war. As I just hinted at above, it is truly in danger of not knowing the same God who has communicated to us through the Bible and Jesus Christ. That is rather frightening outcome to contemplate. Therefore, I must reject Liberalism's interpretive methodology.

Now, what is our choice when it comes to evangelical positions on interpretive methods? As we have discussed in many places there are two essential choices: *Covenantalism* and *Dispensationalism*.

Summarizing the Evangelical Position

As shown on **Figure 15** (page 284), there are two groups of Protestant Christianity which represent *evangelicalism*. They share all the principal doctrines of historic Christianity. These are: (1) regard for Jesus Christ as fully human and fully divine; (2) His death on the cross is fully sufficient for our salvation from sin and death; (3) salvation is by 'grace through faith' and not as a result of 'works' (i.e., doing good deeds); (4) The Bible is our only source of faith and practice; it is fully reliable and communicates infallibly to us about our condition and what God has done to remedy it; and finally, (5) the view that salvation means redemption from an eternity separated from God and experiencing eternal life in fellowship with God and others who believe in Him.

Furthermore, they share a common understanding of the relationship between 'faith and reason' that differs radically from Liberalism. They not only believe that the Bible is the Word of God, infallible for faith and practice—but that it also speaks truth when it touches history or matters related to science. They distinguish between faith and reason but they don't separate them as different ways of 'knowing' – one rational and the other not. Both share the conviction that historical analysis, archeological evidence, and fulfilled prophecy support the Bible's claim to be the Word of God. Consequently, there is willingness to debate such things as whether the

Bible makes mistakes and how convincing the historical evidence is for the resurrection of Christ. Evangelicals in both camps will allow their faith assertions to be 'disqualified' in order to prove that their beliefs do 'hold water.' Did the whale swallow Jonah? Evangelicals wouldn't reject this 'out of hand.' Instead, they might say, "Let's sit down and discuss why this may not be a myth." One of us actually could change his mind.

However, in regards to *interpreting biblical prophecies and the value of the Old Testament* there is a big distinction. Evangelicals are broken down into two groups that have strongly divergent positions:

1. There are those that believe most prophecy regarding the Second Advent is *future*. This group believes that Israel is still very much crucial to God's plan. It also believes that interpretation of the Bible must take into account the meaning of all of Scripture as it was meant to be understood *by the authors*. They are reluctant to 'spiritualize' any Scripture unless from the context of the passage, it is the plain meaning of the Bible to do so. The Bible is best understood by identifying the 'dispensations' of how God and humankind relate. This is the *Dispensational* position.

2. Then there are those that believe most Biblical prophecies are already *past*. Israel has been replaced by the Church in God's plan. Scripture's interpretation hangs foremost upon understanding the vital doctrines of the Bible. When passages are considered that appear to challenge the essential doctrines held dear by this group, the meaning of Scripture must not be 'literal'—it may be seen as metaphor, imagery, typology, or allegory. Lastly, the Bible is best interpreted by keeping the covenants of the Bible firmly in mind. This is the *Covenantalist* position.

The Case for Covenant Theology

Covenantal Theology believes that certain teachings in Dispensationalism *conflict with the essential doctrines* they place at the top of the list. What are those doctrines?

- First, there is strong biblical support *to see the Church as the spiritual children of Abraham* and that it came into being because the Jewish nation (and many individual Jews) rejected Jesus Christ as the Messiah (Romans Chapters 4, 9, 10, and

11). The arguments of Paul are many and compelling as to why Gentiles are now full heirs to the promises God has made to the Jews in times past.[i]

- Second, *there is no distinction between Jew and Gentile* in the Church (Galatians 3:28). These differences have been eliminated. The Church is composed of all races. No race or lineage has any advantage over another. We are all 'one in Christ.' Furthermore, Covenantal theologians teach (perhaps not quite so compellingly), that believers of all times and periods should be understood to be a part of the Body of Christ, the Church. Some covenantal scholars will talk in terms of the *Old Testament Church*.

- Third, as Christians, they believe that *without the death of Christ on the cross, there would be no forgiveness of sins.* Christ's death saves all believers from before the time of Christ to today and to the very end of the world. Adam, Abraham, Moses, as well as believers from New Testament times to now must rely upon the *Blood of the Lamb* for their salvation. *One cannot be born a believer.*

- Fourth, individuals must make commitments from their 'heart' and must receive Christ. Salvation is a *personal*, not *national* matter. John states at the outset of his gospel, *"He came to His own, and those who were His own did not receive Him. But as many as received Him, to them He gave the right to become children of God, even to those who believe in His name, who were born, not of blood nor of the will of the flesh nor of the will of man, but of God"* (John 1:11-13, *NASV*).

- Fifth and finally, Jesus Christ fulfilled the prophecies of the Old Testament regarding 'the suffering servant' (Isaiah 53). He was the true savior foreshadowed in the Passover. His work is final and conclusive. Having completed this work, He has sat down at the right hand of God (Hebrews 10:12). He is worthy and therefore able to 'break the seals' of the Seven Scrolls because He withstood temptation and purchased our redemption (Revelation 5:9).

However, the essential point is this: Can these key doctrines *only be true if* the Church has, 'for time and eternity,' replaced Israel

---

[i] This would be so at least in terms of salvation and eternal life—not in terms of a physical, earthly Kingdom.

as God's Bride? That is the position of the Covenantal theologian. My considered opinion is 'no.'

The Case for Dispensationalism

The Dispensational viewpoint *to a major extent concurs with all the points that Covenantal Theology emphasizes as laid out in the previous summary.* However, there is more to the story. Dispensationists can still support all these statements but do so without forfeiting their view on God's continued plan to redeem Israel during 'the last days' and to establish an earthly Kingdom.

First, in regards to being the children of Abraham, Dispensationalists agree that true children of Abraham are those that have the faith that Abraham had. Israel as a nation and Jews as individuals must embrace this faith, otherwise they will not inherit the promises that God has made to all His children.

However, this does not invalidate the possibility that God still 'has promises to keep' that include the blessings of an earthly kingdom that may center on the nation of Israel, but will nonetheless bless the entire world.

> *For I do not want you, brethren, to be uninformed of this mystery--so that you will not be wise in your own estimation--that a partial hardening has happened to Israel until the fullness of the Gentiles has come in; and so all Israel will be saved; just as it is written,*
>
> *"THE DELIVERER WILL COME FROM ZION;*
> *HE WILL REMOVE UNGODLINESS FROM JACOB."*
> *"THIS IS MY COVENANT WITH THEM,*
> *WHEN I TAKE AWAY THEIR SINS..."*
>
> *For the gifts and the calling of God are irrevocable.* (Romans 11: 25-27, 29, NASV).

There is a limited time-period where this partial hardening occurs. It is 'until the fullness of the Gentiles has come in'—until Gentiles are made joint heirs during this present age of the Church—then all Israel will be saved. For God has not given his gifts conditioning, basing them upon what the Jews may do. Ultimately, God's calling will prevail.

Second, regarding the unity in the Body of Christ, all believers that come to faith in Christ are joined into the Body of Christ. However, the Body of Christ is the fellowship of believers that began with Pentecost and will end with the Rapture. Dispensationalists believe it is an unnecessary and unwarranted stretch of biblical language to talk of the Body of Christ in the Old Testament. Believers of all time receive their salvation through the sacrificial death of the Messiah, Jesus Christ (Romans 3:29, 30). Nevertheless, it is somewhat arrogant and unnecessary for Christians to suppose that New Testament language, in this case the word *ekklesia* (translated, *church*), conveys the 'association for all who believe'—a unified body that the Old Testament never mentions. This seems implausible if we hold in high regard God's revelation through the Hebrew writers and prophets. We must be cautious that we don't go overboard in attempting to see the Jewish religion through Christian eyeglasses. If anything, once we come to appreciate more about Jewish customs, laws, and traditions, it makes Christianity much more meaningful and the salvation provided through Christ all the more powerful.

This is not to say that Christians should embrace the law as the means to salvation or that the law from the time of Moses to Christ was truly the means whereby the Jews were saved.[i] The *law leads us to Christ* for we learn we cannot follow the law without the Spirit of Christ (Romans 8). Nevertheless, it does say that God's revelation to the Jews was part of the process of salvation history and is best understood in the context in which it was given. 'Retrofitting' Christian language onto Judaism is actually one of many examples in Covenantal theology where once the doctrines are settled the Bible's language has to be interpreted symbolically or figuratively to make the Bible consistent with their position.

Of course, this is to get the cart before the horse. From a philosophical standpoint, this is *circular reasoning*—starting out to prove what you have already assumed to be true—which is both unscientif-

---

[i] Dispensationalism is sometimes accused of allowing for 'two paths to salvation.' This accusation can be inferred incorrectly from the assertion that 'all Israel will be saved.' However, clear and absolute denials to this charge should be considered when the dispensational position is finally judged.

291

ic and illogical. It is the same as saying that we are making the facts
fit our theory rather than letting the facts speak for themselves. We
must consider the entire Bible to build sound doctrine. We can't
carve out and discard what doesn't fit into our framework. Our doctrines must be further refined as we understand the Bible better—
otherwise our *systematic theology* becomes authoritative rather than
the words of Scripture. It may seem a subtle difference, but this is
where the '*key doctrine interpretive method*' falls short in my opinion.

Accountable Only For What We Know

Next, *salvation is only through personal choice.* This is certainly true for individuals and is a teaching that we can find in both Testaments. However, we must remember that humankind is responsible and accountable to God for *the truth that God has revealed to us*—
not for truth He has *not* yet revealed. Abraham was not responsible
to keep the Mosaic Law. Moses was not required to 'receive Christ.'
We are only accountable for *the revelation that God has given us at
the moment in history in which we are.* How we articulate that 'personal faith' may be said differently at different times—that doesn't
make it any less valid, nor does it make one person any less 'saved'
than another. Salvation is always through grace and received
through faith. We read:

> ⁶ Consider Abraham: "He believed God, and it was credited to
> him as righteousness."
>
> ⁷Understand, then, that those who believe are children of Abra-
> ham.
>
> ⁸ The Scripture foresaw that God would justify the Gentiles by
> faith, and announced the gospel in advance to Abraham: "All nations
> will be blessed through you."
>
> ⁹ So those who have faith are blessed along with Abraham, the
> man of faith. (Galatians 3:6-9)

God did not ask Abraham to 'receive Christ'—He asked Abraham to trust in Him and that His word was true. Abraham did. His
faith in God saved him. Does this mean that Christ did not have to
die to save us from our sins? Certainly not—Jesus Christ did have to
die so that the salvation for Abraham and those who pre-dated Jesus'

death could receive salvation just the same as those who believe to-day are saved because of His atoning work. It points out however, that God's grace and our faith are the key factors in individual choice and that without faith we cannot lay hold of that salvation which was procured for us by Christ Jesus (Romans 3:24).

National as well as Personal Salvation

Finally, *salvation can be both individual and societal.* Nations are subject to destruction and judgment. Nations are also subject to redemption and deliverance from their enemies. When Christ returns He will defeat the enemies of Israel—for their enemies will be the enemies of Christ and His Saints too. Christ can redeem Israel as a nation; he can redeem individual members of that nation at the same time. The Prophet says, *"I will pour out on the house of David and on the inhabitants of Jerusalem, the Spirit of grace and of supplication, so that they will look on Me whom they have pierced; and they will mourn for Him, as one mourns for an only son, and they will weep bitterly over Him like the bitter weeping over a firstborn."* (Zechariah 12:10, NASV). Both individual salvation and national salvation can be true—and true simultaneously. Therefore, if one begins with a method of interpreting Scripture that attempts to let the *plain meaning* of the Scripture speak for itself, it will lead one to draw a larger circle and take other Scripture into account that a narrower view would cause one to miss entirely. This method is the essential *reformed* principle: Scripture interprets Scripture. A good way to remember how to utilize this principle is to use an aphorism[i] I coined just for this purpose:

> *We understand what any one Scripture teaches by applying what the entire Bible preaches.*

Inconsistency in Approach—Spiritualizing Key Passages

As should be evident to the reader, we have looked at various topics in eschatology, many of which were not just irrelevant to Libe-

---

[i] An *aphorism* is defined by Microsoft Word as "a succinct statement expressing an opinion or a general truth."

ralism—they were irrelevant to Covenantalism too. When topics are covered that don't fit into the assumptions of Covenantal theology, particularly those discussed in the final three chapters of Revelation, the Scripture has to be 'spiritualized' in such a way to make the Scripture fit into their creedal framework.

Nevertheless, there is a difference between Liberalism and Covenantalism. Liberalism can just dismiss the scriptural witness 'out of hand' because it doesn't regard the Bible as infallible. Not so, with Covenantalists. They believe the Bible is free from error. Therefore, if the Scripture says something that appears to be doctrinally inconsistent, the Covenantalist must reconcile it to his core beliefs. The tried and true way to do this is to 'spiritualize' the passage in question. Numerous apocalyptic topics become symbols of something else.

The Top Ten Most Significant Spiritualizations

Let me summarize the *Top Ten Most Significant Spiritualizations* in the following list:

1. The *salvation of the nation of Israel*—becomes the salvation of the Church. The Church replaces Israel. The nation of Israel can no longer legitimately expect God to step in to save it from its enemies.

2. The *Millennial Reign*—becomes the 'Church Age' lasting an indefinite period.

3. The *Kingdom of God and the Reign of Christ* on the earth— becomes the Reign of Christ in the New Heavens and New Earth.

4. The *Rapture* is subsumed into the one event of Christ's return and is made much less than 'the blessed hope.' The meaning and intent of the Rapture is discounted.

5. The *Church* is 'spiritualized' to mean all believers from both the Old and the New Testament. Moses was a church member and so was Abraham—according to Covenantal terminology. This goes so far afield from proper biblical language and context that it evokes the question, "You got to be kidding, right?"

6. *Watchfulness* for the return of the King— is made insignificant. Instead, we can wait until the appearance of the Antichrist because He must come before Christ can return. *Jesus' instruction*

must be spiritualized—the Doctrine of Imminence is down-played.

7. Escaping the 'wrath to come'—means being protected *through the wrath.* The Covenantalist plans to be present when the judgment of God bursts forth. However, like Noah in the Ark, those who remain hope to be comfortable and dry within, keep-ing their heads 'above water.'

8. The *rebuilding of the Temple,* promised throughout Scripture in reference to the Coming of the Messiah, is reinterpreted to be the resurrection of Christ and the transformation of His mortal body to an immortal one.

9. As it relates to the many kingdom prophecies of the Old Testa-ment, these prophecies have to be dismissed almost altogether because the Covenantal view simply doesn't believe that *this Kingdom will come.* The Kingdom of God is the *Kingdom of Hea-ven*, exclusively.

10. The *Old Testament also becomes diminished* to the point where it becomes almost irrelevant. If Israel is forsaken, the covenant and the promises are only distant memories and only a meta-phor of God's plan for the Church. If so much of the intent of God's old covenant was thwarted, why does it merit our atten-tion today?

Dispensationalism as a means to provide an interpretive framework to understand the Bible still may have flaws to resolve, but to an increasing number of evangelicals it seems to offer the most honest and most consistent approach to understand the plain mean-ing of the language of the Bible. That is why over the past 30 years, Dispensationalism has become the majority view of the evangelical world. In contrast, Covenantal Theology makes interpreting the Bi-ble far more 'free form' and subjective. As such, *in regards to escha-tology, it often finds itself sitting in the same group as Liberalism.* This accusation may be hurtful, but the next one will likely be worse: *Covenantalism tends to have the same indifference to eschatology as Gnosticism did.* To expand on upon this point:

- Gnostics had little purpose for eschatology due to their insis-tence that salvation was not about the return of Christ but about *being freed from the body.*

- Like the Gnostics, *there is no plan for a physical kingdom on this earth.* Furthermore, Gnosticism could not 'catch hold' until such time as the 'catching up of believers' was no longer believed imminent.

- The bodily resurrection has a diminished purpose—it is not intended to allow us to reign upon this earth *but to reign in 'another world.'* Gnostics had no desire whatsoever for a bodily resurrection.

- Gnostics *spiritualized the meaning of Scripture* to appropriate the vocabulary of Christians and imbue it with the meaning they wanted. Of course, Gnosticism goes much further—it *twists* the Scriptures to say things expressly foreign to the orthodox doctrines of Christ and redemption from sin.

- Gnostics *had no connection and no use for to the Jewish religion.* This is fundamentally, why a 'Gnostic Christianity' could not have directly sprung from the Jewish faith. It requires several intermediary steps before Gnosticism could 'infuse' itself into Christian theology. My contention is this: If Christianity had begun with the Gnostic notions of the 'lost Christianities' that Bart Ehrman seems to champion, it would never have crossed the Jordan!

- Marcion believed the God the Old Testament was not the same God represented by Jesus Christ. Therefore, the Old Testament was rejected. While Covenantalism stops far short of 'throwing the baby out with the bath water,' so much of the Old Testament is disavowed that it has much less relevance today.

To be clear, this 'Gnostic-like approach' is limited to eschatology. It is not true in *Soteriology* (salvation), *Christology* (the doctrine of Christ), *biblical infallibility*, and many other important doctrines where Covenantal theology and Dispensationalism agree. Neither should we miss how many comparisons we can make. My point: *If there is that much similarity to Gnosticism, something is amiss with the hermeneutic.*

Another point that I feel compelled to make, but do so reluctantly, is how for centuries Christianity, *dominated by concept of replacement theology*, often led the pogroms against the Jewish community. Christians didn't just regard Judaism poorly – they often considered it their enemy! It is not a coincidence that Dispensationalism and Judaism have an affinity for one another while Covenantalism clearly does not.

It is most unfair to charge the Covenantalist believers today with any form of anti-Semitism. However, the same philosophy regarding the relationship of Israel and the Church often in times past tainted Christianity with intolerance and sometimes, merciless inquisition. Because of their respective tenets, Dispensationalism is almost immune to this problem; but one could see intellectually how Covenantalism could slip back into this way of thinking. Not that I am predicting it will.

Finally, there is little question that those who are most zealous about promoting the Gospel of Christ through the emphasis on eschatology be it in books, seminars, television, or the Internet, are almost all dispensational in their orientation. The most fervent evangelistic activities reside with Dispensationalism.[i] As a result, Dispensationalism continues to outgrow Covenantalism in influence in Christianity today.

For all these many reasons, *I embrace the Dispensational approach to interpretation.*

Not a Point of Division

Having been so critical above, I would be remiss if I did not quickly point out that although there is strong disagreement on matters of eschatology, evangelicals who embrace the reformed theology of Luther and Calvin, are 'on the same page' theologically in virtually all other matters.

I do believe *this is a family squabble* and it is best not to accuse one another of dishonesty and certainly not heresy (although some do). So if my polemics are too fiery, please overlook my exuberance! We are all striving to do the best we can to understand God's word and to apply it to our lives. As Christians our *priority charge* is to love God and one another—being consistent in our theology is good too, but not at the expense of the other. We must always *maintain a*

---

[i] This last point is not conclusive. However, if the reverse was true, (as it is with Covenantalism), it would certainly infer that Dispensationalism might have the story wrong.

humility that allows for the possibility we could be mistaken. We must also maintain a respect for another believer who sees things differently than do we. Being right in eschatology is not as crucial as being Christ-like in what we say and do.

I would propose that the verdict of time and history (as it happens) determines who is right. We may remember *Gamaliel* (the Pharisaic teacher who tradition says taught the Apostle Paul when he was still Saul the Pharisee—and regarded as one of the Greatest Judaic teachers of all time), who warned the other members of the Sanhedrin to be cautious about persecuting the Christians lest they find themselves fighting against God (Acts 5:39). "Give it time..." he would have said in the vernacular of today. "We will see whether these believers in Jesus amount to anything that God highly regards. If they do we won't be able to stop them."

We should say the same about Dispensational eschatology. There are many points where it verified and validated as the months and years go forward. We can watch for a number of prominent events in the years ahead that will 'tell the tale' as outlined in a previous chapter.

> **THE KEY POINT TO PONDER:**
>
> *"The words of prophecy are sealed until the end of time... but those who have insight will understand" (Daniel 12:9-10). The closer we come to the conclusion of time, the clearer prophetic truth becomes.*

These events will inform us which approach is right and which isn't. The words of God to Daniel are perhaps the final and *most strategic interpretive principle* to keep in mind:

> *"Go your way, Daniel, for these words are concealed and sealed up until the end time. Many will be purged, purified, and refined, but the wicked will act wickedly; and none of the wicked will understand, but those who have insight will understand"* (Daniel 12:9, 10, NASV).

The words of prophecy are concealed until the end times. Then those who have insight will understand. This is a strong rebuttal to the argument that 'recency' is a shortcoming of the Dispensational interpretive method. Biblically, *recency may in fact be the most biblical of all methods for interpreting prophecy.* Based upon the words in the Book of Daniel above, old ways of seeing things are less likely to be right than are new ways. God will grant new vistas and reveal fresh insights as time marches forward.

This doesn't mean we should discard the old. Nevertheless, it means we are more likely to interpret the Bible accurately as time moves closer to the 'last trump.' Another way to express this approach is with yet another aphorism coined for this moment. I will close this chapter with this thought:

The closer we come to time's conclusion,
the clearer prophetic truth becomes.

Recapping the Key Points Covered in This Chapter

- Protestants are not in one voice regarding the apocalypse and the Second Advent - all agree that good will defeat evil and that Jesus Christ will be demonstrated to be King of creation. However, after this affirmation, paths diverge dramatically.
- *Liberalism* tends to be 'preterist' and devalues prophecy altogether; it tends to separate religious truth from other spheres of truth; lastly, in most respects Liberalism does not uphold the orthodox doctrine regarding the authority of Scripture.
- *Evangelicalism* emphasizes the dual nature of Jesus Christ (human and divine), His death, as the way to salvation, salvation through faith not works, and redemption from eternal separation from God.
- Both *Dispensationalism* and *Covenantalism* share in these 'creedal affirmations' and both denounce the Liberal's 'escape from reason,' regarding the Liberal's position on how spiritual truth differs from other forms of human knowledge.
- Evangelicals differ with one another on a number of matters in eschatology: Dispensationalism emphasizes future fulfillment of most prophecies related to the 2nd Advent, 'dispensations' as the proper way to distinguish how God has related to humankind through the ages, and supports Israel's future salvation (a national salvation exclusively for Israel that fulfills the prophecy of the Old Testament).
- Covenantalism sees most prophecies 'in the past tense,' 'covenants' as the manner of differentiation rather than dispensations, and believes that the Church has replaced Israel in God's Kingdom plans.
- Ten examples of 'spiritualizing scripture' are identified that challenge the Covenantal position – along with six similarities to Gnosticism, which call into question the Covenantal hermeneutic.
- At the end of the day, eschatological differences aren't sufficient for generating and maintaining hostility between the two camps!
- The closer we come to time's conclusion, the clearer prophetic truth becomes.

DD #14 Liberalism, Miracles and Mythology

If we rule out miracles *a priori*, it can be more difficult to substantiate why the Bible's teachings matter. The Bible asserts it is God's revelation to man, a presupposition that is by definition *supernatural* (beyond nature). If the reader rejects miracles, the verdict on predictive prophecy is negative. Critics would assume that the Bible is rightly relegated to fanciful literature and no more than a history of religious assertions. It fails to be relevant because modern assumptions about what comprises reality (i.e., a reality *where only 'natural' events transpire)* disqualify its claim to be true.

To the evangelical, if the passages of prophecy are demonstrated to accurately predict future events, it not only allows us to consider the Bible's prophecies seriously, but virtually everything else the Bible teaches too. Biblical inspiration is supported by prophecy and prophecy by biblical inspiration. Hence, the study of prophecy, for the evangelical, is a foundational matter to rightly understand the meaning of the Bible and thus provide a foundation for spiritual belief.

While we don't take up the subject of the many prophecies fulfilled by Jesus in his 'first coming,' the Gospel of Matthew specifically is built around this phenomenon with its attempt to prove that Jesus was the fulfillment of the Messiah, the 'prophet' spoken of by Moses, and the coming King of Judah. Traditional Christianity asserts that fulfilled prophecy is a strong confirmation of Jesus' claim to be the Son of God. Critics contend that this fulfillment was coincidental or contrived. Yet, even most Liberals assert that Jesus fulfilled the prophecy of the 'anointed one.' 50 years ago, this would not have been the case. Today, there is a small dose of 'mysticism' included in Liberalism, which opened the door just a crack for the *supernatural*. We can thank the seepage of eastern spiritualist traditions into our western religions for this change (Indeed, *Kipling was wrong:* East and West can meet in the middle!)

As to the meaning of 'myth,' Liberalism generally would attempt to convey that there are 'deeper meanings' than the literal story itself, just as in Greek or Roman mythology, the story of the particular gods and their interactions with humans are telling us as much about the nature of humanity as about the gods. Certainly modern psychology has also contributed to this new openness in Liberalism to the '*super-nature*.' C.G. Jung (1875-1961), in particular looked to ancient myths to illustrate subconscious elements of the human psyche. The 'meaning of myth' suggests we can draw out valuable lessons from the Scripture even if the details of the story are not historically accurate. However, this causes other problems.

DEEP DIVE NUMBER 14

DD#15 Are there Errors in the Bible?
The Position of Liberalism and Neo-orthodoxy

Liberalism is a multi-faceted creature. Given our primary subject matter is eschatology, I won't take the space necessary to differentiate between the Liberalism that evolved from Friedrich Schleiermacher (1768-1834) in the early 1800's and the reaction to it, Neo-orthodoxy, which began with Karl Barth (1886-1968) in the early 1900's and continued through the time of World War II.

What is relevant to the issue of hermeneutics is that both of these camps dismiss the Reformed position of Biblical infallibility. Both are heavily influenced by Kantian philosophy and the influence of scientific findings that in the 20th century appeared to contradict the Bible. Liberalism is more inclined to admit 'errors' in the biblical text but minimize their relevance to the issue of religious meaning. Neo-orthodoxy is more likely to sidestep or ignore the issue of whether there are 'errors' in the biblical text. Karl Barth would admit that the Scripture might have the capacity to include error but he refused to point out any errors that he might have thought existed. For both Liberalism and Neo-orthodoxy, when science and the Bible conflict, these positions uphold science as true and reinterpret the meaning of the Bible in a symbolic or psychological way thus denying a 'unified field of knowledge' (as Francis Schaeffer, an evangelical philosopher, points out). They share the position that a story with errors can still provide religious truth—no matter that the Bible's historical validity is seriously compromised. That isn't the issue.

One could conclude that what both schools have attempted to do is to make their beliefs immune to *disproof*. In other words, by arguing that religious meaning isn't linked to historical or scientific facts, you protect it from being discredited. However, this gives the person oriented to 'reason' serious heartburn. Historians and scientists aren't easily convinced this is playing fair with the concept of truth! We can almost hear one of them begin the questioning as follows:

"So I can be wrong about all the facts: When something happened, who was there, what they did, even what they said. But if I can tell a good story that makes you feel good or helps you become a better person, then my story can be given weight. Is that what you mean when you say 'the Bible tells religious truth?' Excuse me if I have my misgivings! If I'm wrong about matters you can verify, why believe me on matters you can't?"

There is no free lunch. This challenge is the principal issue that those that adopt the Liberal approach at some point must address.

DEEP DIVE NUMBER 15

DD# 16   Existential Truth versus Propositional Truth

Existentialism is for the most part, a 20th Century philosophy, associated with authors like Jean Paul Sartre (1905-1980) and Martin Heidegger (1889-1976). Existentialism conveys that important truths flow from our existence and that apart from our experience as humans, 'objective truth' is at best useless and at worst unknowable. The short definition that is often cited is, "*existence precedes essence.*" The philosophy of *Existentialism* has two schools of thought: One, which is secular, and another, which is religious. Religious existentialism found its genesis with the Danish philosopher Soren Kierkegaard (1813-1855) in the 19th Century. Kierkegaard is famous for originating the phrase, "leap of faith." He is often criticized in certain evangelical books (particularly by Francis Schaeffer) for taking us down the path of 'irrationality.' But when one studies SK, as he is often called for short, there is a great deal to be said on his behalf in representing a genuine Christian position (at least in some regards). One such surprising example includes a 'reformed' position on election, which can be detected within his book, *Concluding Unscientific Postscript to Philosophical Fragments*. It is rather unexpected that 'the father of personal choice'—the founder of existentialism—actually held a view of predestination in the tradition of Calvin.

In contrast to existential truth, propositional truth stands as a way to assert 'objective truth.' 'Propositional truth' simply refers to making a rational assertion that can either be proved or disproved by reason or empirical evidence. Propositional truth also conveys in part that truth can *cohere* to, or *reflect* reality. Likewise, historical evidence can be seen as both empirical and rational. Additionally, science has an underlying reliance upon propositional truth—if we can't state something propositionally, we can neither prove nor disprove it. Moreover, if we can't disprove it, it can't be science. It's counter-intuitive: *we can only prove something true if we can gather evidence to prove it false.*

Richard Dawkins in his recent book, *The God Delusion*, takes all religion to task for its unwillingness to allow *evidence to falsify its claim to be true.* He asserts, which is often true, that no amount of contrary evidence will cause a 'true believer' to change his or her mind. This is not Dawkins' only criticism, but it is a particularly important one. I would submit that this is not universally true for all 'the faithful.' Perhaps surprisingly, it is true for Liberalism. Technically, there is no means to disqualify it! However, this statement is NOT true for Christians *who have been schooled on the principles taught by Schaeffer.* True, this group is hardly the majority of evangelicals today—but those who are students of 'modern apologetics' are inclined to believe, not based on the old proofs for the existence of God, but in light of evidence they consider compelling for the resurrection, fulfilled prophecy, and no doubt, personal experiences which have become robust 'reasons to believe.'

So is there really a great chasm between science and religion? Are reason and faith irreconcilable? For SK, faith involved *believing even when the evidence tells you otherwise*—this is the 'leap of faith.' Liberalism and Neo-orthodoxy in part built their schools of thought upon this proposition. However, evangelicals in most cases strongly disagree. *They believe that the two 'types of faith' can be reconciled.* First, it is worthwhile to distinguish between the (1) 'act of trusting' and the (2) conviction or commitment that specific 'religious' assertions are true. We should, with Kierkegaard, stress that the *act of trusting* extends beyond 'knowledge.' Trusting includes risk and reliance upon a third party (namely, God) to keep His promises. Secondly, professing faith in the creeds of the Church has a much different quality. One can assert that certain things are true and can stand up for those assertions based upon his or her conviction that such assertions represent *reality*—as did Martin Luther and many martyrs of the faith. Faith as a statement of belief is one thing—being willing to die for one's beliefs in quite another. *The first is propositional and the second is existential.* The point is that (1) these 'acts of faith' are different kinds of human 'acts' and (2) one can logically lead to the other. However, one doesn't invalidate the value of the other. That is where SK goes too far in his insistence that faith is intimate or *intensely personal* to the detriment of a creed, a statement of faith, or a 'system of belief' (SK hated *systems*, particularly *the Hegelian system* that was infecting the study of history and religion in his time). Therefore, Christian belief is not necessarily the opposite of science as many suppose. Indeed, faith must have some propositional foundation or it becomes inconsistent with human knowledge and how we live the rest of our lives. On the other hand, *faith isn't only propositional.* As pointed out earlier, it encompasses all of what it means to be a human being and the various ways of 'knowing' (consciousness)—including having visions and appreciating the value of symbol and imagery—that however 'irrational' they may seem, can still be articulated and recorded just as the Prophets of the Bible did. It is noteworthy that even no less a thinker than Descartes, the father of Rationalism developed the famous phrase, COGITO ERGO SUM ("I think therefore I am") after reflecting upon a *dream*. See Rene Descartes, *Discourse on the Method*, 1637.

There is a place for *mysticism* (defined as *"the belief that personal communication or union with the divine is achieved through intuition, faith, ecstasy, or sudden insight rather than through rational thought"*)—but it isn't' by creating a dichotomy of 'faith' and 'fact' or 'religion' opposed to 'reason.' The knowledge of God can transcend reason and rely upon other human faculties (such as dreams, visions, prayer)—but this knowledge doesn't have to contradict reason and propositional truth. If it does, evangelicals believe that the 'encounter' must be questioned, not reason itself. As John, the Apostle reminds us: *"Not every spirit is from God... but test the spirits... for many false prophets have gone out into the Word."* (I John 4:1).

DEEP DIVE NUMBER 16

For Further Reading

Rather than provide a bibliography to document the research done to prepare this book, I feel it would be more useful for the reader for me to recap those books that I recommend for further study. I hope you find my brief synopses useful in making your determination as to whether you wish to spend additional time delving into the subject of eschatology.

Catherwood, Christopher, *Churchill's Folly: How Winston Churchill Created Modern Iraq,* **Barnes and Noble, Inc., (New York), 2007, 268 pages.**

Catherwood provides the historical background for how the nations of the Middle East were structured at the beginning of the 20th century by Churchill and other Western leaders immediately following World War I. It also explains why different Arab kings took control in different areas based upon policy decisions by these Western leaders. After having read this book, it is much easier to understand the conflicts in the Middle East. The problems aren't just with the creation of Israel. Looking at the three key groups smashed together in Iraq should make that plain enough. The conclusion: The mistakes made in the past unfortunately continue to haunt us today.

Church, J.R., *Hidden Prophecies in the Song of Moses,* **Prophecy Publications, (Oklahoma City, Oklahoma), 1991, 363 pages.**

Since the 1980's, J.R. Church has promoted the concept that the Psalms provide many prophecies of the end times. His research is always fascinating. In 'The Song of Moses,' J.R. helps us understand of the meaning of the Hebrew holidays. Church and his colleague Gary Stearman are the most capable commentators today that make extensive use of Jewish sources to amplify their perspectives.

Cornuke, Robert, *Relic Quest,* **Tyndale House Publishers (Wheaton Illinois), 2005.**

Bob Cornuke is a real Indiana Jones, minus the degrees in archeology. However, his investigative skills (a former detective) and his daring are put to good use to follow the pilgrimage of the Ark of the Covenant from Israel circa 600 BC, to its possible location today in Ethiopia. Relic Quest is well worth reading as are all of Bob Cornuke's books.

Flynn, David, *Temple at the Center of Time: Newton's Bible Codex Deciphered and the Year 2012,* Official Disclosure, A Division of Anomalos Publishing House, (Crane, Mo.), 2008, 296 pages.

David Flynn has written perhaps the most fascinating book I have read in the past three decades. Flynn has done extensive research on the topic of 'ancient or pristine knowledge' (prisca sapientia) that was the obsession of many scholars in the 16th and 17th centuries. Newton in particular believed that ancient humankind had certain knowledge of the earth and the heavens that had been lost. He believed that the Bible held the key to identifying 'the code' to unlock this knowledge. Newton's key achievements in Natural Philosophy—physics, mathematics, and optics—were arguably reliant upon what he learned from the Bible about this 'ancient wisdom.' In the book, you learn how the Bible has linked vital information about prophecy to time and space. I encourage you to read this book if you can read no other. The discoveries here are truly amazing.

Horn, Thomas R., *Nephilim Stargates: The Year 2012 and the Return of the Watchers*, Anomalos Publishing House, (Crane, MO.), 2007, 232 pages.

Horn puts forward the hypothesis that the Mayans may have been onto something hidden in times past regarding the ending of the world. In their mythology they believe that their God, Quetzalcoatl, will return to the earth in 2012. Quetzalcoatl represents a Lucifer-like figure. He suggests that this may coincide with events in the Bible predicting the coming of the Antichrist. He spends considerable time analyzing Greek and Roman mythology to make his key point that history is laden with evidence that 'fallen angels' have attempted many times to contaminate the human race's God-created DNA (and links this with the Giants of Genesis, Chapter 6). While this study is speculative, the arguments are well articulated and in fact, the notion is gaining support in many circles. At the very least, it offers substantial and fascinating evidence that the future Antichrist may not be 'from this world.'

Jeffrey, Grant R., *Countdown to the Apocalypse*, WaterBrook Press (Colorado Springs, Co.), 2008, 227 pages.

In this work, Jeffrey does a particularly good job of interleaving historical context and recent information to give us an up-to-date commentary on the Book of Daniel. Jeffrey's writing style is very easy to follow and a pleasure to read. This history of Daniel is itself a grand story and deserving of the time it takes to read this book (perhaps more than once!) Jeffrey's perspective is strongly dispensational and his contention is that Christ's soon return is indeed imminent. His attention to detail and research, his trademark, is evident as he provides commentary on the essential passages of Daniel.

Jeffrey, Grant R., *The New Temple and the Second Coming*, WaterBrook Press, Colorado Springs, 2007, 204 pages.

Jeffrey provides very recent information on the possible rebuilding of the Third Temple in Jerusalem. Jeffrey, along with his wife Kaye, has explored the tunnels under the Temple Mount extensively and has outstanding insights into the relevant historical geography of Jerusalem. Additionally, because he has made so many friends in Israel, Jeffrey is able to supply a great deal of 'insider information' on what is really going on and what might soon come to pass there.

LaHaye, Tim, *The Rapture: Who Will Face the Tribulation?* Harvest House Publishers, (Eugene, OR), 2002, 255 pages.

Over the years there have been many books written about the Rapture. LaHaye does an outstanding job of summarizing the findings of other scholars and adding his own research into this book. As I pointed out in my writing, the Rapture is a controversial subject with many viewpoints. LaHaye is of course perhaps the most noteworthy 'pre-tribulation' 'pre-millennial' evangelical today having published so many books and sold so many copies of his "Left Behind" series. Of particular import is his in depth discussion of Dave MacPherson who wrote several books in the 1970's, all of which were scathing attacks on the 'pre-trib' Rapture. MacPherson's books indicate that J.N. Darby actually received his thinking about the pre-trib Rapture from an ecstatic vision of Margaret McDonald in an 1830's meeting; then he further claims that there has been a cover-up as to the origin of the pre-trib Rapture 'theory.' LaHaye puts this matter to bed with solid scholarship around correspondences that confirm Darby's viewpoint three years before this event in 1827. Additionally, LaHaye provides new insights into a

number of early 'pre-trib' writers in the history of the church show-
ing that the pre-trib Rapture by no means originated with Darby—
he was merely the 'popularizer' of the view in the 19th century because of his energy, hard work, and sometimes excessive zeal on the
topic. Finally, LaHaye covers a detailed discussion on the 'pre-
wrath' theory (a mid-tribulation Rapture variant) first proclaimed
with the published work in 1990 by Marvin Rosenthal. When one
digs into the conjecture about the pre-wrath view, it appears to readily fall apart. Like MacPherson, Rosenthal's arguments appear
motivated by personal vendettas against others who support the
pre-tribulation Rapture view. If you have questions about the timing of the Rapture, LaHaye's book is an excellent and relatively recent recap of the issues.

Lawrence, Joseph E., *Apocalypse 2012: An Investigation into Civilization's End*, Broadway Books (New York), 2007, 2008, 262 pages.

It is no overstatement to say that there are scores of books on the
subject of the coming end of the world in 2012. Lawrence believes
that there are many evidences to suggest that there is reason to be
scared. He has done extensive first hand interviews with Mayan
shamans, climate and solar scientists, and with astrophysicists.
His perspectives are compelling and the quality of the writing is
outstanding. Of the books I have looked at on the subject, his is
perhaps the most reasoned approach and best written. Plus, he has
strong credentials as both a scientist and writer. Though not an
evangelical, Lawrence professes his faith in Christ in the book although he does call into question the prophecy viewpoints of Evangelicalism (and thus, this author). Still, I recommend this book.

Lowe, David W., *Then His Voice Shook the Earth: Mount Sinai, the Trumpet of God, and the Resurrection of the Dead in Christ*, Seimos Publishing, 2006, 167 pages.

David Lowe has provided some very fresh and unique perspectives into the manner of the resurrection and rapture of the Saints
and the potential physical consequences of this event on the land-
scape of the earth. He ties his understanding to an alternative
'model' for the Seven Seals of Revelation 4 through 8, indicating
that the great earthquake of Revelation 6:12 may relate to this
worldwide resurrection and rapture. He also drills down into the
nature of the Trumpet of God, and the "last trump" to which the
Rapture of the Church is tied. His book is not a long one. It is a

summary version of his detailed study Earthquake Resurrection. I highly recommend it!

Marzulli, L.A., *Politics, Prophecy, and the Supernatural: The Coming Great Deception and the Luciferian Endgame,* Anomalous Publishing (Crane, Mo.), 2007, 248 pages.

Marzulli follows up his fictional trilogy on the Nephilim with a non-fiction book on what might be the 'final great deception' spoken of in the Bible. Marzulli touches on the current political issues in the Middle East, but moves quickly to the ancient history of the Nephilim mentioned in Genesis 6:1-4, and links them to the 'alien encounters' in our day, supposing that the aliens may be linked to the fallen angels and the Nephilim (who some believe are the 'demons' or evil spirits that are infrequently encountered and the subject of numerous books and movies in our times). The possibility that the final deception will involve aliens who claim to be our progenitors appears to be a real one. Furthermore, the Antichrist appearance may in fact include such alien references. Marzulli's book is of course speculative, but well reasoned and easy to read. This book is something of an update of I.D.E. Thomas' classic (among prophecy buffs), *The Omega Conspiracy,* which also is a good read.

Missler, Chuck, *The Magog Invasion,* Western Front Publishing, Coeur d'Alene, Idaho, (date not disclosed), 311 pages.

Missler's work on identity of Gog and Magog is a solid work citing numerous historical authorities. He provides a strong case that the identity of today's Russians and the other peoples who surround them are indeed descendants from the ancient Scythians and furthermore, the legacy of Magog. I have read a number of analyses on this subject, Missler's is the most comprehensive and compelling.

Missler, Chuck, *Prophecy 20/20: Profiling the Future through the Lens of Scripture,* Thomas Nelson Publishers, Nashville, Tn.), 2006, 280 pages.

Missler provides an excellent overview of the key prophecy topics (similar in some ways to my book), emphasizing the centrality of the nation of Israel, the Book of Daniel, and the Life of Christ. He also points out the importance of Hermeneutics to help identify the most scriptural way to interpret prophecy. Missler goes beyond topics I discuss in providing perspective on current events and how they impact the 'classic prophecy scenarios.' It was interesting to me to see the many areas of agreement and in some cases the similar arguments he advances (similar to my own). Reading Missler's book will make you think I read his book before I wrote mine. Not true. I read this book when I was finalizing *Are We Living in the Last Days?'* Consequently, I was not able to borrow from it as liberally as I might have preferred!

Ryrie, Charles C., *Dispensationalism, Revised and Expanded,* Moody Bible Institute, 2007, 265 pages.

Ryrie, a well-respected Professor Emeritus from Dallas Theological Seminary, voices an authentic and current view of Dispensationalism. This volume has been recently updated which is also very helpful. To understand prophecy, we must understand our assumptions and guiding principles of interpretation. Therefore, this book is indispensable to understand the framework upon which most of today's evangelical prophecy proponents base their work.

Price, Randall, *The Ark of the Covenant: Latest Discoveries and Research,* Harvest House Publishers, Eugene, Oregon, 227 pages.

Price is a prolific author on many subjects about eschatology, biblical inspiration, and archeology. He is a graduate of Dallas Theological Seminary and Hebrew University. His credentials are impeccable. He has done a sound bit of research of the whereabouts of the Ark of the Covenant including recent discussions with those (like Chuck Missler), where he may disagree. Like Missler and Jeffrey, Price is friends with many in Jerusalem and is plugged into what is happening in the holy lands today. Price's treatment of the Ark is factual and avoids sensationalism and speculation, which while interesting, is often misleading. I encourage you to pick up this book if you want to study the issue of the location of the Ark of the Covenant in a serious manner.

About the Author

S. Douglas Woodward ("Doug") is a management consultant working with dozens of start-up and emerging companies in the Pacific Northwest. Over the past twelve years, Doug has served as CEO, COO, and CFO of numerous software and Internet companies. Prior to his tenure in entrepreneurial efforts, he worked as an executive for Honeywell, Oracle, Microsoft, and as a Partner at Ernst & Young LLP. His technical background is in software development and most recently in venture financing and business strategy.

Doug grew up in Oklahoma City, going to high school and college nearby (Norman). At 15, Doug was struck with a serious form of adolescent cancer, *Rhabdomyosarcoma*, which forced him to lose his left leg as a means to treat the disease. At the time of his illness (1969), recovery was likely in only 10% of the cases diagnosed. The experience had a dramatic impact upon Doug's spiritual life, linking him with dozens of family members, friends, ministers, nurses and doctors who showed great compassion and provided him with remarkable support. Doug cheated death however, through the great efforts of many doctors and the prayers of parents, brothers, family, and friends. However, as so many others who have a true near-death experience, it led Doug to the conviction that God had a special plan for his life.

Doug attended the University of Oklahoma where he received an Honors Degree in *Letters* (Bachelor of Arts), graduating Cum Laude. His studies focused principally on religious philosophy and theology as well as European history and Latin. In particular, Doug studied under Dr. Tom W. Boyd, a renowned professor, teacher, and speaker there. Doug actively participated in *Young Life* and *Campus Crusade for Christ* throughout his college experience.

Upon graduation, Doug served as a Youth Minister and Associate Pastor in the Methodist and Reformed Churches for three years before experimenting with the computer industry as another possible career choice. He grew to love it and has spent thirty-four years in various capacities there. He has written various articles and spoken at many conferences and seminars throughout his career on the topics of Advanced Office Systems, database technology, and more recently, on financing and growing start-ups. During his experience at Oracle and Microsoft, much of Doug's efforts were devoted to education and introducing new approaches making use of distanced learning technologies. Through the years, Doug has served in various capacities in Methodist, Presbyterian, and Reformed Churches. Most recently, Doug served as Elder in the Presbyterian Church.

Doug is married to Donna Wilson Woodward and together they are celebrating thirty-four years of marriage. The Woodward's lived in Oklahoma City until 1987 then moved east. For six years, they lived in New England and then have spent the last seventeen years in Woodinville, Washington, a suburb of Seattle. They have two children, Corinne, 30, and Nicholas, 25, and four dogs treated far too well.

Made in the USA
Charleston, SC
16 May 2010